For information about permission to reproduce
sections of this book, please write to:
Permissions
Total Sports Publishing
100 Enterprise Drive
Kingston, New York 12401
www.totalsportspublishing.com

ISBN 1-892129-88-4

THE LIFE OF REILLY was prepared by
Bishop Books, Inc.
611 Broadway
New York, New York 10012

Printed in Canada

CONTENTS

Chapter 4: Roots

Chapter 5: Rough

Chapter 6: Wrecks

Chapter 7: Royalty

FOREWORD

Me and Rick Reilly are old school.

We can remember a time in the NBA when you had to be good to make the monster money. When not every player had an entourage and seven cars in the garage, all of them $100,000 each, and six of which they never drive.

We can also remember when sportswriters weren't so bitter toward the players. We can remember when they wanted to really get to the truth about a guy.

Lately, most sportswriters resent any strong athlete who speaks the truth and doesn't care what gets written about him. That's why my dealings with the press have been bittersweet. In Philadelphia, mostly bitter.

But, for some reason, Rick never seemed like that. I have very few personal relationships with writers, but for reasons I'm still trying to figure out, I have one with Rick.

He never seems bitter. The more you talk about the truth—even if it's about society, racism, politics—the more his eyes kind of lock in on you. He seems like he's actually interested with what you're trying to say, instead of just filling his little notebook up. When you've answered thousands and thousands of questions night after night, you notice when somebody's taking you down a road you've never been before.

I remember once, after another one of my few hundred mini-controversies, Rick came up to me, shaking his head, and said, "A lot of athletes are jerks who want us to think they're great guys.

You're a great guy who wants us to think he's a jerk."

(Hey, keep it down.)

I always came away from a piece he'd written about me think-ing, "Yeah, that *is* how I feel." And if I feel he got me right, then I can read what he writes about other athletes and be pretty sure he's getting *them* right. Shaq. Elway. Tiger.

Yeah, I read his columns. Sometimes I agree with them and sometimes I don't, but they're always insightful. Sometimes they're funny and sometimes they're angry and sometimes they make you cry, but they're always trying to get at the truth.

I know this is crazy, but he's one of the few sportswriters I would actually classify as human. Half the time I see him, he's got one of his three kids with him. Or he wishes he did. I remember once, I invited him to play golf with Michael Jordan and me and he said no, he had to get back for his eight-year-old son's birthday party. Passing up golf with MJ for a birthday party? The guy's either a really good dad or on crack, one of the two.

I guess the best compliment I can pay Rick Reilly is this: Of all the people I'd like to throw through a plate-glass window, Rick wouldn't be one of them.

Too bad, too. Skinny white boy looks *real* aerodynamic.

—Charles Barkley

INTRODUCTION

I get letters from people who hate me, people who love me and people who think I can get Tiger Woods to come to their prison poetry readings.

I get letters from people who think I should run for Senate and people who think I should run for cover. I get idle threats, veiled threats and death threats. I get letters in pen, pencil, Magic Marker, calligraphy, crayon, blood, and magazine cut outs.

But the letter I get the most is this one:

Dear Mr. Riley,

Are journalism teacher, Mrs. Finsterknocker, said we had to write to a well-known journlist but I do not know any at this time so that is why I am righting to you.

Then they want me to answer a few questions, and they're always the same:

1. Is writing for Sport Illustrated *a rewarding career path for a young person such as someone like myself?*

I always give the same answer, which is . . .

Depends.

For every unforgettable Fijian poolside lunch I've eaten with swimsuit supermodels wearing only paint, there have been 10 New Year's Eves at the Cleveland Stalag-by-Marriott, toasting midnight with 320-pound sportswriters with much of last Thursday's free buffet on their tie.

For every two days spent with Jack Nicholson ("Come by the house about two tomorrow afternoon," he'd say. "I should be up by then."), there was a week spent with Cincinnati Reds owner Marge Schott. (You do not know the meaning of despair until you've seen Marge in a fuchsia teddy.)

For every stomach-flipping, jaw-dropping Joe Montana comeback I've gotten to write, there's been a half-dozen Penn State 41, Iowa 6s, in which the best quote was from an Appalachian running back with the look in his eye of a comatose chicken, who said, "Uh, I'd say we've got our backs to the driver's seat."

2. What's it like going to so many grate sporting events?
Depends.

You go to so many, you sometimes forget to tingle. You forget that another week on the job for you at, say, the U.S. Open or the Super Bowl, is the biggest week in a lot of people's entire lives. You take it for granted. I can't tell you how many days I've found my way to my day's work by following the blimp. I've checked maps by the light of burning police cars. I always try to get a room on the top floor of hotels so I can sleep through the morning parade.

Still, it's steady work and there's no heavy lifting.

3. Do you ever get recognized?
Sometimes. I was in an airport when a guy came up to me and said, "Are you the guy on the back page of *Sports Illustrated*?"

"Why, yes," I said, feeling famous.

"Hey! I go to sleep every week reading your column!"

4. What is the greatest moment in sports that you, personaly, were able to wittness, first hand?
Hmmm. Let's see. I was there when 46-year-old Jack Nicklaus came from five down in the last nine holes to win the 1986 Masters. I saw Mike Tyson try to bite a man's ear off—twice. I saw Jim Valvano's collection of midgets, walk-ons and stiffs win an NCAA championship on an airball.

I was standing 10 feet away when Mary Lou Retton landed two perfect 10s on the vault to win the gold in Los Angeles and Bela Karolyi, desperately seeking someone to hug, nearly collapsed my esophagus with one. I was there when Magic Johnson won an All-Star game MVP trophy two months *after* retiring. I saw Michael Jordan win his first title and his last. I saw Shaq win his first. I saw Dr. J win his last. I saw Big Mac's 62nd. I saw a Tiger destroy Augusta and Augusta destroy a Shark.

I beat Arnie out of $5 on the 18th hole at his own course. Did three innings of play-by-play. Drove a NASCAR stock car 142 m.p.h. per lap. Teed it up with a president, and a vice president and O.J. Simpson. Was the only man fool enough to try out for the WNBA. Threw up in an F-14. Threw down a few with Barkley. Dined with Gretzky. Bet with Rose. Went around the world trying to find the best golf holes. Went around America trying to find the worst.

5. Why did you choose sportswriting as your chosen vacation?

Mostly because I was fired at everything else. Pumped gas—until I left an oil cap off a guy's engine and it fell down in there and ruined it. Worked at an equipment rental shop—until I got fired for putting 15 parts oil and 1 part gas into the jackhammers. (Turned out it was the other way around.) Tellered at a bank—until I got fired for losing $500 in $20 bills. They just disappeared. (No, *seriously*.)

The only thing I could do is write. I won a first-grade writing contest and they put my story up in the bank window downtown. I won the sixth-grade spelling bee and the nuns gave me a plaque. I won a state high-school journalism contest and, years later, got a job from the judge of it.

Of course, if there's ever a nuclear war, I'll be about as useful as a chia pet. There's not gonna be a big call for emergency metaphors.

6. What advise would you give to someone who would have no career choice other than to be a sportswriter?

1. Never write a sentence you've already read (Oscar Wilde). Why say, "He beat the hell out him," when you can say, "He turned the guy into six feet of lumps"? Much more fun.

2. Lighten up a little. This ain't cancer research. As the late Jim Murray—the greatest sportswriter there ever was—used to say,

"There's no city ordinance says they gotta read you." Make them *want* to.

3. Be tough, but don't be afraid to write something nice once in awhile, either. Or make people care. Or cry. God knows we could use the moisture.

    7. *Are you ever going to do a book of your favorite pieces?*
Nah. Who'd read it?

        Best,
        Rick Reilly
        August 2000

P.S. Please cut this page out and give it to a high-school student who doesn't know me either.

CHAPTER ONE: RANTS

CHAPTER ONE: RANTS

The Swooshification of the World

FEBRUARY 24, 1997—I must get more Swoosh in my life. More, more, more. It's not enough to have the Swoosh on every jersey and scoreboard and dugout roof. It's not enough that the Swoosh is on basketballs, footballs, soccer balls and volleyballs. It's not enough that the Swoosh is slapped all over more than 40 universities, eight NFL teams, six NHL teams (two more next season) and five Major League Soccer teams.

I want the eye black under baseball and football players' eyes to take the form of a Swoosh. I want hockey sticks, nine-irons and yardage markers to be made in the shape of a Swoosh. I want to know who's in the on-deck Swoosh. I want to watch the Swoosh Channel. I want Swoosh condoms (Just Do It).

It's not enough that the Swoosh is on Michael Jordan's beret and Mary Pierce's headband and Gabrielle Reece's beach volleyball top. It's not enough that the center on the Hawaii basketball team had his sideburns shaped into Swooshes. I want a Swoosh tattoo. I want a Swoosh lasered onto my retinas. I want to name my son Swoosh. (If it's a girl, Swooshie.)

I want these things because the Swoosh is the most ubiquitous symbol in sports history. The Swoosh is so huge that the name of the company that goes with the Swoosh doesn't even appear anymore. In the ads, on the shoes, even on the company letterhead, all you get is the Swoosh, and you just *know*. Try that with Keds, pal.

Happiness is a warm Swoosh. Do you see the way it *swooshes* upward, a snappy little check mark, letting you know that everything in your life is A-O.K.? It's airy, windswept, uplifting. It's the delighted little final stroke your pen makes when endorsing the biggest check of your life.

But there is not enough of it in our lives yet. From here on in, instead of H-O-R-S-E, I want kids to play S-W-O-O-S-H. I want skis to go *Swoosh!* I want to get the autograph of Sheryl Swoosh.

Woe to you who underestimate the Swoosh. Tiger Woods, the coolest athlete on Planet Swoosh, has the Swoosh on the front of his hat and the side of his hat and the back of his hat and on his turtleneck and on his shirt and on his sweater and on his vest and on his pants and on his socks and on his shoes. But when Woods arrived in Thailand two weeks ago, he found that his luggage had been misplaced, and he had to play a pro-am without his usual complement of Swooshes. He lasted just 13 holes before heat and exhaustion got to him. Don't you see? The Swoosh is the source of all his powers!

I wasn't always like this. I used to rage against the Swoosh. "Why?" I yelped at strangers. "Why must the Swoosh run the world?" Why, I asked, after almost 30 years, did the Denver Broncos let the Swoosh people redesign the team's uniforms and logo so that they were suddenly uglier than the jerseys of a meat-market softball team. I cried out against the subliminal Swooshing all over the new Denver uniform. "Don't you see it?" I railed, pointing to the Broncos' new logo. "The horse's nostril! It's a Swoosh!"

In protest I determined to go an entire day without getting Swooshed. I made it 14 minutes, just past my Eggo, when my wife came down in her Swoosh sports bra. Something snapped in me that morning. I gave in. You cannot fight the Swoosh.

I want my kids to attend the University of California at Swoosh. I want to get up in the morning and eat a big bowlful of chocolate Swooshios as part of a nutritionally balanced breakfast. I want to meet Carolyn Davidson. She's the graphic designer who, after graduating from Portland State in 1972, came up with the Swoosh for Phil Knight, Zeus of Swoosh, for $35. Thirty-five dollars! When she handed it to Knight, she remembers, he said, "I don't love it, but maybe it'll grow on me." Twenty-five years and a zillion dollars later, you think it's all right now, Phil? (Davidson, who in 1983 was given some Nike stock by Knight and who recently retired, says her second most famous work is the wallpaper she designed for a motel in Yakima, Wash.) Carolyn Davidson, stand up and take your place in world history!

Some experts believe the Swoosh is better known than the McDonald's golden arches. Nine national soccer teams, including Brazil's, wear the Swoosh. The Tour de France leader wears the Swoosh. When the U.S. played Russia in hockey's recent World Cup, both teams were wearing the Swoosh.

The Swoosh is like Jell-O: There's always room for the Swoosh. I want Swoosh on the periodic table of the elements, right next to boron. I want Swoosh to be the 27th letter of the alphabet. I want to order raw eel at a Swooshi bar.

Do not fight it, brothers and sisters. Trust in the Swoosh. The Swoosh is good and powerful. If our government leaders would only let it, the Swoosh could bail us out of this deficit thing like *that*. Of course, we would have to make a few small concessions.

Al, does the presidential seal look different to you?

POSTSCRIPT: *Somebody told me that Nike chairman Phil Knight had this column framed and put up on the wall behind his desk. Maybe* that's *how you become a billionaire in America today. Take every rip as a compliment.*

Sis! Boom! Bah! Humbug!

OCTOBER 18, 1999—Every Friday night on America's high school football fields, it's the same old story. Broken bones. Senseless violence. Clashing egos.

Not the players. The cheerleaders.

According to a report by *The Physician and Sportsmedicine* cheerleaders lose more time from their activity because of injury—28.8 days per injury—than any other group of athletes at the high school level. The University of North Carolina found that cheerleading is responsible for nearly half the high school and college injuries that lead to paralysis or death.

It's crazy, isn't it? We have girls building three-story human pyramids, flipping one another 30 feet in the air, and we give the *boys* helmets.

A buddy of mine has twin daughters, both cheerleaders. At the end of last school year one needed plastic surgery on her cheek after another girl's teeth went through it during a pyramid collapse; the other broke her hand and finger. They're not cheering anymore.

I don't hate cheerleading just because it's about as safe as porcupine juggling. I also hate it because it's dumb. The Velcroed-on smiles. The bizarre arm movements stolen from the Navy signalmen's handbook. The same cheers done by every troupe in every state.

What's even dumber is that cheerleaders have no more impact on the game than the night janitorial staff. They don't even face the game. They face the crowd, lost in their bizarre MuffyWorld. They cheer, they rah, they smile, they kiss, they hug. Meanwhile, Milford High just scored three touchdowns against their guys. A UFO could land at the 30-yard line, disgorging a chorus line of tiny, purple Ethel Mermans, and most cheerleaders would still be facing the other way yelling, "We got the fever!"

Exactly what does a girl get out of cheerleading, anyway, besides a circle skirt and a tight sweater? Why do we encourage girls to cheer the boys, to idolize the boys? Why do we want them on the sideline when most of them could be *between* the sidelines?

Studies show that by the time otherwise smart girls hit high school, they start to raise their hands less in class, let the boys take the lead. Isn't cheerleading the same thing, only outdoors?

Look, I married a cheerleader. My sisters were cheerleaders. I could see it then: Cheerleading was just about the only way a girl could be a part of sports. Not now. Not in the age of Mia Hamm and Marion Jones and the Williams sisters. Not when most high schools offer as many girls' sports as boys'.

Oh, right, nowadays cheerleading is classified as a sport. There are now "cheer gyms," where kids go to learn to throw each other around like Frisbees. You can even watch the National High School Cheerleading Championships on ESPN, just after the Harley-Davidson Olympics. This is the event in which 408 girls named Amber attempt to create a human Eiffel Tower, screaming, "Two! Four! Six! Eight!" while displaying all their gums at once. I'm not saying it's not hard. I'm just saying it's pointless.

Do you realize colleges are even giving cheerleading scholarships? Can you believe that? *Sorry, Mrs. Roosevelt, we just gave away your daughter's chemistry scholarship. But you should have seen Amber here do "We've got spirit!"*

If cheerleading is a sport, Richard Simmons is a ballerina. It's athletic, but it's not a sport. In fact, what's sad is that most cheerleaders would make fine athletes. Watch for five minutes and you'll see. But these girls won't be on anybody's gymnastics or diving or basketball team because every season is cheerleading season.

Cheerleaders don't just shake their pom-poms at football games; they're also at baseball games and wrestling matches and girls' soccer games and most everything else short of chess-club tournaments. No matter how many hours they've already put in, no matter how freezing it is, no matter how few fans are at the jayvee badminton match, the cheerleaders are out there in their short skirts.

What's that spell? Frostbite!

If they're lucky, they might grow up to become Dallas Cowboys

Cheerleaders. In the book *Deep in the Heart of Texas*, three former Cowboys Cheerleaders wrote that they snorted coke, gobbled diet pills and vomited to lose weight.

Rah!

I guess this is like coming out against fudge and kittens and Abe Lincoln, but it needs to be said. In four years my little girl hits high school. It's up to her, of course, but if my wife and I could choose her after-school activities, cheerleading would be next to last.

Just ahead of Piercing Club.

POSTSCRIPT: *My wife, Linda, gave me the idea for this column. We were talking about our little girl, Rae, when she said, "I know one thing. I hope she doesn't want to be a cheerleader." And my wife was head cheerleader at Boulder (Colo.) High School! Cheerleaders from all over tried to write me hate mail, but cheerleader hate mail is not terribly scary. They'd write, "I hope you die!" and put a little heart over the "i."*

That Signature Moment in Sports

APRIL 5, 1999—O.K., so it's Opening Day! What say we all go out to the ballpark and get nobody's autograph!

In fact, why don't we make autograph seeking punishable by one hour's worth of foul tips to the groin?

Is there anything more stupid and dehumanizing for everybody involved than asking for an autograph? What exactly is the thrill in making Ken Griffey Jr. put down his calzone, have to ignore his wife and kids, wipe the sauce off his face and hands, just so he can sign a napkin that will spend eternity in your junk drawer?

"What's wrong with a handshake?" says George Brett. "What's wrong with a 'Hey, really enjoyed watching you play!'"

Just once I'd like to see somebody go up to Mark McGwire,

interrupt him in mid-sirloin and say, "Sign this 'To Bruce,' will ya, Big Mac?" And McGwire would write:

To Bruce,
Do you mind? I'm trying to eat here, buddy!
—*Mark McGwire*

If fans feel abused by athletes, athletes feel abused by autograph hunters. It's a never-ending pain. "I'd give $100,000 to go a whole day in Denver and not have anybody know who I am," John Elway says. "Just one day."

Says Allen Iverson, "I sign all the time. I sign and sign. But I don't want to sign all day long. So the first person I finally say no to, it's 'Man, you can't do this for a kid? Aw, you ain't s---!' And I'm like, Damn!"

The basic autograph request has become more soulless and life-sucking than Tuna Helper. "The spirit of the whole thing has been lost," Drew Bledsoe says. People bring up boxes of baseballs for stars to sign and say, "It's for my collection." Really? You have six of every signature in your collection? Scumbag collectible dealers hire kids to get signatures and then sell them. Parents push their kid forward to get the autographs of people the kid has never heard of.

One time, former ABA and NBA star Dan Issel came out of practice in a hurry and signed as many autographs as he could until he finally had to stop. "Gotta go!" he said as politely as he could to the half dozen people left. Two days later he was ripped by a woman in a letter to the editor for being "exactly what's wrong with sports today." The reason Issel had to leave? His wife had gone into labor.

I understand the salary cap. I fathom the physics of the screwball. But I don't get the autograph. What do you get out of an autograph? Proof that you met an athlete? What kind of friends do you have that they don't believe you met somebody? O.K., you got Mo Vaughn's autograph, but did you speak with him? Did you tell Mo how you felt about him? Did you even make eye contact?

Nolan Ryan has a strict policy of one autograph per person, but since he has to look down in order to sign his name, there's only one way he has of telling if somebody is getting in line twice. He memorizes shoes. Is that something you're proud of? Your shoes were seen by Nolan Ryan?

Go to the Masters next week. Autographs are allowed only in a small restricted area near the clubhouse. You can't ask for them anywhere else at Augusta. So fans, unable to stop golfers and ask them to scrawl their names mindlessly on visors they'll lose by May, have to resort to new and bizarre methods of interaction, like shaking hands, taking pictures, talking to them about their rounds or their swings or their kids. And the golfers call it the best week of the year partly for that reason.

Unfortunately, the pros eventually have to leave the grounds, and it's back to the same old crap. One time Lee Trevino was in a bar when a woman came up and shrieked, "You're my favorite golfer of all time! Please give me your autograph!" Problem was, she had nothing to write on. Trembling, she dug a five-dollar bill out of her purse and handed it to him. Trevino signed it, "Best wishes, Lee Trevino." The women yowled, "Thank you soooo much! I'll frame this! I'll treasure it forever!" and rushed off to show her friends.

An hour later Trevino was buying a beer at the same bar and got a five-dollar bill back in change. It read, "Best wishes, Lee Trevino."

POSTSCRIPT: *The hilarious thing about this column was that it ran directly across from an ad exhorting people to join a* Sports Illustrated *cruise, which read, in part, "Get autographs from your favorite sports stars!"*

Glory to the Gridiron

AUGUST 29, 1988—Let's play the *$25,000 Pyramid.* Here are the clues: Watching hairlines recede . . . Reading the dictionary . . . Waiting for Godot . . . Cross-stitching . . . Alphabetizing your canned goods

...Attending a workshop somewhere on sorghum. . . .

You holler: "Things More Exciting Than Watching Baseball!"

Ding, ding, ding! You win! You also get the complete audio library of Jim Palmer explaining why Sid Fernandez sometimes throws screwballs on 2-and-1 counts to hitters missing one or more fingers.

Admit it: Baseball is to thrills what beets are to taste buds. If baseball is so exciting, why is there the seventh-inning stretch? You ever heard of the third-quarter stretch in football? Forget it. Nobody gets drowsy watching football.

In this country you're not supposed to say the D word about baseball: dull. Or dumb. Or dreary. If you tell people you would rather be stripped naked, covered in tuna oil and lowered into a tank full of barracuda than watch an entire baseball game on TV, they give you the standard, "Well, you're not *sophisticated* enough to appreciate the *subtleties* of the game."

From what I can tell, "sophisticated" means you don't mind watching a game in which out of 80 at bats—about 400 pitches— you might see five hits. "Subtleties" means you don't mind paying $12.50 to watch it in person. If baseball is so subtle and graceful, how come the guys in the bullpen never watch it? They're either trying to spit tobacco juice on each other's socks (very subtle) or figuring out how they can get Chinese food delivered.

Football is much too quick-fix for baseball fans. After all, who can find sports sophistication in a 60-yard diving-catch touchdown bomb? And it's true, there's no subtlety in a guy's getting hit so hard that the first thing he says when he comes to is, "Mom, let me sleep 10 more minutes."

Football is so terribly unsubtle that if you're at a game, you're afraid to leave your seat because you think you'll miss something. Baseball is so wonderfully sophisticated that you leave your seat in *hopes* of missing something.

How was the game, Fred?

"Terrific. Had a corn dog in the second, some Jujubees in the fifth and a twist cone in the seventh."

Yeah, but who won?

"It depends on how well you know the balk rule."

The best player in football history was Jim Brown, a granite statue of a man. The best player in baseball history was Babe Ruth, a Jell-O parfait of a man. The best arm in football is John Elway's. The best arm in baseball is John Elway's.

Football has cheerleaders. Baseball has batboys. Football has Joe Montana. Baseball has Bob Knepper. Football has instant replay. Baseball has Don Denkinger. Football has Dan Reeves nattily turned out in a $500 suit. Baseball has Don Zimmer spilling out of an ill-fitting uniform.

In football, an upset means something. The worst team beats the best team maybe one time in 25. In baseball, the worst team beats the best team two out of five times. What's to celebrate?

If you're at a football game, there are 11 different matchups you can watch on every play. Set your binoculars on the wide receiver trying to outjuke the cornerback or the center trying to bull the noseguard. In baseball, try setting your binoculars on anybody other than the pitcher or the batter.

What did the rightfielder do that time?

"Well, first he put his glove on his knee, then he bent over, then he stood up straight again. Just like last time."

Baseball lovers say that their game is timeless, that it has kept the traditions that link it to the past. Right. Let's go to the Seattle Kingdome and watch designated hitter Steve Balboni—here's a real athlete—get an AstroTurf double that the outfielder loses in the roof.

Which game is more athletic? Football players come off the practice field looking as if somebody had used their helmets to boil lobsters. Baseball players come off the practice field wearing their hats backward after a grueling game of pepper. Baseball is so taxing that sometimes guys can get in only 18 holes before a game. Put it this way: Nobody's surprised that guys like Charlie Kerfeld, Mickey Lolich and Terry Forster have played baseball. What's surprising is that Dom DeLuise never did.

So let's call baseball what it is—a nap aid. And the next time somebody tries to make you feel guilty about hating baseball, remind him of what ESPN college football commentator Beano Cook said in 1981 when commissioner Bowie Kuhn announced that the U.S hostages recently released by Iran would all receive free lifetime baseball passes:

"Haven't they suffered enough?"

POSTSCRIPT: *What that column did for me with baseball fans, the next one did for me with Detroit Red Wing fans . . .*

———•••———

This One's From the ~~Gutter~~ Heart

MAY 17, 1999—I never allow my personal feelings to affect what I write. That's why, even though I live in Denver, home of the Colorado Avalanche, I'd never speak unfairly about the ~~motherless~~ Detroit Red Wings.

When it comes to class, integrity and fair play, the ~~goon-laced~~ Red Wings rank with any team in ~~Roller Derby~~ the NHL.

It's true that at times in the past the ~~store-bought~~ Red Wings have exhibited some ~~criminal~~ aggressive behavior against the Avalanche, but what else would you expect out of ~~freaking animals~~ the best rivalry in all of sport?

Just because ~~referee-paying~~ Detroit jumped to a 2–0 advantage on Sunday in its second-round playoff series with Colorado, and just because on March 14 the Red Wings' Kirk Maltby ~~willfully~~ accidentally broke Avalanche star Valeri Kamensky's arm (Kamensky hasn't played since), and just because nine days later Detroit ~~stole~~ acquired one of the ~~dirtiest~~ most penalized players in NHL history, Ulf Samuelsson, just to intimidate the Avalanche, I don't necessarily think the Wings are anything less than ~~hitmen~~ gentlemen.

There is nobody Colorado fans ~~detest~~ respect more than Detroit's fine coach, ~~Elmer Fudd~~ Scotty Bowman. True, Bowman has done some ~~unspeakable~~ controversial things over the years in this rivalry, such as screaming profanities in the parking lot at the

Avalanche's Claude Lemieux, who was walking with his wife and child at the time. But this was only because Bowman ~~was receiving signals from hell on the steel plate in his brain~~ cares so much.

There are also a few isolated fans in Colorado who don't like Red Wings ~~wussy-boy~~ star Sergei Fedorov. I, for one, think his unusual white skates recall ~~Dick Button in *Cabaret on Ice*~~ a simpler time. And, true, critics poke fun at his alleged intimate relationship with teen tennis sensation Anna Kournikova, but can he help it if ~~Woody Allen keeps stealing all his dates?~~ unfounded rumors start going around?

And just because Fedorov is one of many Russians on the Red Wings, that doesn't mean Detroit fans ~~are rooting for godless Commies~~ can't relate to their players. In fact, I think if the average Red Wings fan could actually meet one of his hockey heroes, he would do what most fans do, which is buy him a cold ~~bowl of borscht~~ beer.

Also, unlike many Coloradans, I think Detroit is a wonderful place to ~~whack~~ meet somebody and, in fact, bring ~~charges~~ up a family. The citizens should be ~~under house arrest~~ proud. I once became lost in Detroit, and one ~~lit~~ local citizen was more than happy to help. ~~He said, "Go right at the second burning car and left at the corpse, and park. You can try and buy your car back later."~~

Some folks in Colorado poke fun at the fact that Detroit calls itself Hockeytown, even though the ~~butt-lucky~~ Red Wings have won only two ~~fluke~~ Cups in the last 44 years, whereas Montreal has won 17 in that time. But what people don't realize is that Red Wings fans eat, drink and sleep ~~in cardboard boxes~~ hockey.

In fact, Detroit fans, taken as a whole, ~~might have an entire set of teeth among them~~ are delightful zealots for their team. True, they kept pulling the fire alarm in the middle of the night at the Avalanche's hotel in 1997. Also true, one of them smeared dog feces on the door handle of Lemieux's car, but I'm sure that fan probably ~~had some spare in her purse~~ meant it only in good fun.

The Detroit media have pulled ~~grade-school~~ zany stunts in this rivalry, too. For instance, one of the city's papers ran a picture of bleeding Colorado goalie Patrick Roy under the huge headline, BLOODY GOOD. The same paper printed WANTED posters with Lemieux's face in the middle. That's just ~~so bush-league~~ friendly competition. I'm sure a number of Red Wings fans had a great time taping the posters to the walls of their ~~prison cells~~ dens.

All in all, the Colorado-Detroit rivalry is about mutual ~~loathing~~ respect. I can honestly say that if the Red Wings were to play, say, Iraq, I'd be there ~~holding up a picture of Saddam Hussein~~ supporting them. To me, the Red Wings represent everything that is ~~fully prosecutable~~ good in hockey.

In summary, even though it looks like the ~~puppy-kicking, handicap-space-parking, Michael Bolton-listening~~ Red Wings will eliminate Colorado, all of us in Denver hope they ~~grow goiters on every square inch of their faces~~ go as far as they can go.

~~And take the Lions with them.~~

POSTSCRIPT: *I always answered hate mail on this one with: "You mean they ran the* rough *draft?" Of course, I had the last laugh. Colorado came from 3–1 down to win this series and hasn't lost a playoff to them since.*

———•—•———

Too Many Spoilsports

JANUARY 11, 1993—So, who killed sportsmanship in this Country?

Was it the Atlanta Falcons' Deion Sanders, who thinks it's great fun to high-step the final 20 yards of a touchdown run just to embarrass the poor players chasing him? Or was it his teammate Andre Rison, who loves to perform his Highlight Zone strut after every touchdown, no matter what the score?

Was it the Kansas City Chiefs' Neil Smith, who after nearly every sack, springs to his feet and takes a baseball swing as if he had just hit a grand slam? Or was it the Pittsburgh Steelers' Greg Lloyd, who upon seeing that New York Jet wide receiver Al Toon had been knocked cold in a game three years ago, rolled on top of Toon and counted him out like a wrestling referee?

Was it the things Oklahoma basketball coach Billy Tubbs did? Like taking the courtside microphone to quell uproarious Sooner fans and saying, "Regardless of how terrible the officiating is, please don't throw things on the floor." Or was it just the things Tubbs said? Like the time he was asked about running up the score against a weaker opponent and replied, "Humiliating somebody—I guess when you get down to it, that's your job."

Was it furniture-heaving coaches like Indiana's Bob Knight, who says you have to "work the referees"? Or was it coaches like Miami's Dennis Erickson, who insisted that his team captains shake hands with Florida A&M's captains before a 38–0 rout this season and then didn't punish the Hurricanes when they didn't obey him. "We didn't mean any disrespect for Coach Erickson," said Miami defensive end Darren Krein, "but the bond of the team is stronger."

Was it that there were too few coaches like Rockdale County (Ga.) High's Cleveland Stroud, who gave up his team's 1987 state title on a technicality and then said, "You've got to do what's honest and right. People forget the scores of basketball games; they don't ever forget what you're made of." Or was it that there were too many like Colorado's Bill McCartney, who refused to forfeit his team's ill-gotten, fifth-down win against Missouri two seasons ago?

Was it too many athletes like San Diego Charger tailback Eric Bieniemy who think there's nothing to be gained in a loss? Bieniemy tells reporters, "You know me. I don't talk after losses." Or was it too few like runner Andy Herr of Bloomington, Ind., who chose to hold up and finish second in a 10K race in Toledo recently because the leader had accidentally taken a wrong turn?

Was it superstars like Michael Jordan who talked more trash on the court than prison hard-timers? Or was it pro sports front offices that marketed their teams as Bad Boys (Detroit Pistons) and Nasty Boys (Cincinnati Reds), and put slogans on billboards like WE'LL BE ON OUR WORST SUNDAY BEHAVIOR (the Falcons)?

Was it college football players like Nebraska tailback Calvin Jones, who after scoring a touchdown this season ripped off his helmet, held his arms up and out like Jackie Gleason after a big show, and ran from one side of the end zone to the other—obviously, a man in love with his mirror? Or was it greedheads like cornerback Albert Lewis of the Chiefs, who said, "The days of scoring a touchdown and throwing the ball to the official are over. When a guy scores now, he is promoting something for TV, a new dance. It's marketing."

Was it schools like Miami, birthplace of the finger in your face, the coin-toss brawl and the rain dance over a two-yard sack? Or was it just Miami alumni like the Dallas Cowboys' Michael Irvin, who announced before a recent game that he was going to try to reinjure Washington Redskin cornerback Darrell Green's broken right forearm?

Was it too many tennis players like Jimmy Connors and John McEnroe, who always seemed to time their temper tantrums to the moments their opponents began to gain some momentum? Or was it too few golfers like Greg Norman, who disqualified himself for a minuscule rule violation while leading the 1990 Palm Meadows Cup in Brisbane?

Was it fans like Nebraska's, who chanted "Where's Sal?" during a basketball game with Colorado in 1990, six months after the death of Buffalo quarterback Sal Aunese? Or was it fans like Arizona State's, who in 1988 taunted Arizona's Steve Kerr with chants of "P-L-O!" after Kerr's father had been assassinated by terrorists in Beirut?

Was it too many fathers who held their kids back a year in junior high school so that they would be bigger and meaner than their classmates in high school? Or was it too few fathers like the one who saw his 14-year-old son sniping and arguing in a big tennis tournament, walked on the court, took the racket out of the boy's hand and told him to go home? "Dad, I can *win* this match," the boy pleaded. To which his father replied, "I don't see how. You don't have a racket."

Was it too many mothers like the one in Texas, who put out a contract on the mother of her daughter's rival for the cheerleading squad? Or was it too many high school football coaches who taught their boys that picking up their opponents, dusting them off and saying "Good play" was the equivalent of wearing heels and a skirt?

Was it too many of us just in it for ourselves? Or was it too few of us remembering why we loved sports in the first place?

Yes.

———◆———

Look Out for the Bull!

MARCH 14, 1994—Caller? Caller? Can you turn down your radio?

Good. Now, can you hang up that phone?

Good. Now, *I've* got something to say. I quit. I can't go on. I've had to fill four hours of airtime a day, five days a week, talking about sports. This station fills 24 hours a day, seven days a week, talking about sports. We have beaten every issue into hotel-ash-tray sand, yet we will talk about this stuff again next week. If one more person asks me if I think Tonya Harding did it, I am going to get his address, drive calmly to his house and remove his larynx with a ball retriever.

Don't you see? It is all bullspit. I don't know any more than you. I have the newspaper in front of me, same as you. A lot of the people in my line of work were second-string punt-cover-age guys and country and western disc jockeys. Most of us can't get credentialed to the International Darts Festival. You ask me, "Do you think Tonya Harding did it?" And, just once, I would like to say, "I don't have a clue. I'm not within a toll call of a clue on that. I've never spoken to Tonya Harding or even over-hauled a transmission with her. You might as well ask me if I know any really great lunch spots in Gdansk." But just the same, I give you 13 minutes of prattle. Hey, I've got four hours to fill here.

The truth is, America is getting a B.S. degree in sports, and the b.s. part is spilling in through your car radio and out from under your big-screen TV. A nation that was once full of doers is now a nation full of dialers.

Three years ago there were a fistful of all-sports radio stations in the U.S. Now there are 78. There were only a few sports-round-table TV shows. Now nearly every big city has one. ESPN has, what, 17? It has gotten this sick: You can even participate in a live call-in sports show while you are on an airplane.

And passengers on the left side of the cabin will notice the Grand Can—I'm on the air? The Phillies suck!

"We have become a land of b.s. and sound bites," says CBS basketball analyst Billy Packer. "It's all diarrhea of the mouth."

This sports talk is doing bad things. Take three sportswriter friends of mine. Ordinarily you could spray WD-40 on their appetizers and they wouldn't arch an eyebrow. Yet whenever they appeared on a roundtable segment of ESPN's *NFL Prime Monday* last fall, they all became Morton Downey Jr., yelling, sneering and calling people names. What matters is not the most-considered opinion. What matters is the loudest opinion. Or, better yet, the last opinion before the beer ad.

On the Information Superhighway the only sure way to keep from winding up as roadkill is to be the loudest, the dirtiest or the meanest. It's the New McCarthyism. The Everybody Here in the Studio Is Cool and Everybody Else Is a Jerk school of broadcasting.

"It has distorted all of the things that we should be getting out of sports," says Penn State football coach Joe Paterno. "Nobody ever wins a game anymore; somebody else blew it."

And it doesn't matter who gets ripped, as long as *somebody* gets ripped. A talk-show host friend of mine calls me up every once in a while and says, "Give me something to rip him with today."

"Something to rip *who* with?"

"Whoever."

Do you really think you're getting inside stuff from guys like us? Four years ago in Tuscaloosa, Ala., some radio talk-show hosts crawled all over Alabama football coach Bill Curry, insisting that Auburn had whipped his butt in recruiting. Before long, discontented Alabama alumni, further incensed by what they were hearing on the radio, finally got Curry fired. Three years later those players recruited by Curry helped win the national championship.

In many cases the stations with sports talk shows also own the rights to broadcast the games of local teams, which means the stations could lose big bucks if Joe Talkshowhost makes Charlie Generalmanager angry. At one Los Angeles radio station this memo was distributed to on-air talent: "A reminder to be 'friendly' to our local teams, especially our flagships. There should be no bad-mouthing of these teams and if a caller or guest instigates such talk . . . our talk-show hosts . . . should carefully change the subject or move on to something else."

But forget the hosts for a minute. Have you ever met any of the callers? Most of these guys spend their days holding down couch springs. Kentucky basketball coach Rick Pitino says they're "basically frustrated at home, can't get a date, don't do well at their jobs and are basically at the nadir of their lives." In other words, if things got any worse for them, they would host their own shows.

"I've got a new policy," Packer says. "When I'm on a show and I get asked about a player I haven't seen yet, I just say, 'Sorry, I really don't have the background to answer that question.'"

Sounds like a movement. Now I have to get all the other hosts and all their guests and all the callers to agree. Then I would really be doing something to clean up the air.

POSTSCRIPT: *Still, even now, talk-radio hosts remember this column. And yet they still call! They still call and nearly every one of them says, "You didn't mean us, right?"*

———•———

Need an Excuse? Take It from the Pros

MARCH 16, 1998—Hey, kids! Next time you're in serious doo-doo, do what big leaguers do: Deny, alibi and justify! It's easy with this handy annotated excuse card! Just cut it out, keep it in your pocket and use it the next time the heat's on *you*!

I didn't do anything wrong.[1] I was taking allergy medication.[2] I don't think I was inflicting any danger on myself or others on the road. I was feeling fine.... I don't think I failed the tests.[3]

Don't forget, I'm 60 years old.[4] I was sleepy, very sleepy. Plus, I was very dazed by the accident.[5] Besides, how am I supposed to walk a straight line with my recurrent knee injury?[6]

I was harassed by the police, the whole nine yards.[7] The police arrested me to cover up their own negligence.[8] The officer disrespected me in front of my peers.[9]

I didn't do any. It was just the significant amount of time that I spend (around) marijuana users.[10] I did send him information.... That's all I sent....But there was no drugs in it.[11]

It's all lies....There was some high jinks going on. Partying.[12] I was told it was a good place to get a deep-tissue massage.[13] Actually, I'm shocked and amazed to be arrested at all in this matter.[14] And these handcuffs are scratching my Rolex.[15]

They were flimsy, anyway. All you had to do was sit on them, and they'd break.[16] Plus, I'm overweight. I put on a lot of weight in the off-season, and it makes me unstable.[17]

This is character assassination . . . false assumptions, misrepresentations and innuendos.[18] This is the greatest travesty I've ever seen.[19] I've been verbally abused.[20] Even if I did do this, it would have to have been because I loved her very much, right?[21]

Well, that's my story, and I'm stickin' to it.[22]

[1]Anaheim Mighty Ducks defenseman Dmitri Mironov after swearing at a referee, smashing his stick, nearly hitting an official and getting a game misconduct penalty.
[2]Boston Red Sox outfielder Mo Vaughn's reason, stated by his lawyer, for failing eight sobriety tests (when asked to recite the alphabet, he couldn't get past P) and refusing to take a Breathalyzer during an arrest for drunken driving.
[3]New York Mets outfielder Bernard Gilkey, when asked about a police report on his DWI arrest. According to the report, he swayed from side to side during sobriety tests and, when told to close his eyes and bring his outstretched finger to his nose, hit his mouth.
[4]Dallas Cowboys coach Barry Switzer on how he could've forgotten he was carrying a loaded revolver when he passed through an airport security check.

31

[5]More reasons given by Vaughn's lawyer for the failed sobriety tests.

[6]Another reason Vaughn's lawyer gave for the failed sobriety tests.

[7]Cincinnati Bengals running back Corey Dillon after being arrested for DUI, driving with a suspended license, running over a curb, refusing to take a field sobriety test and refusing to take a blood-alcohol test.

[8]Vaughn's lawyer's charge that the blame for Vaughn's crashing his pickup truck into an abandoned car should be laid on the Massachusetts state police for not having removed the car, which had broken down and been left on the highway shoulder for 13 hours. During that time thousands of other motorists had driven by it without incident.

[9]Philadelphia 76ers forward Derrick Coleman on his arrest for disorderly conduct at a Detroit nightclub. (Coleman's case ended in a mistrial.).

[10]Canadian Olympic officials' explanation for why snowboarding gold medalist Ross Rebagliati failed a test for marijuana in Nagano. Rebagliati said he hadn't smoked the weed in 10 months but probably tested positive because of inhaling second-hand smoke at a snowboarders' party.

[11]Jerry Poe, a high school teammate of former Red Sox manager Butch Hobson, after Hobson was arrested with an overnight package from Poe containing two grams of cocaine.

[12]Agent for Charlotte Hornets power forward Anthony Mason, maintaining his client's innocence on statutory rape charges after an alleged night of sex with two teenage girls, one 14 and the other 15. Mason denies that the encounter took place.

[13]San Francisco 49ers wide receiver Jerry Rice after police found him in a massage parlor they suspect was used for prostitution.

[14]New England Patriots running back Dave Meggett's reaction, according to his lawyer, after being arrested on charges of sexual assault and robbery of a 33-year-old Toronto woman, who said Meggett continued to have sex with her after his condom broke and then "took back" some cash he had given her "as a gift."

[15]Meggett at the time of his arrest. He denies the assault and robbery charges.

[16]U.S. Olympic hockey player Jeremy Roenick, on the chairs that were damaged as part of the ransacking of three rooms by U.S. players at the Olympic Village in Nagano.

[17]More reasons Vaughn failed the sobriety tests, according to his lawyer. (Vaughn was acquitted of the drunken driving charge.)

[18]John Spano, prospective New York Islanders buyer, reacting to charges from team owners that he did not have sufficient capital to acquire the team. Spano would later plead guilty in federal court to four counts of fraud for using phony documents to inflate his net worth.

[19]Indiana basketball coach Bob Knight, after engaging in a long shouting match with and then being ejected by Big Ten referee Ted Valentine, who has worked three of the last four Final Fours.

[20]Golden State Warriors guard Latrell Sprewell after choking his coach, P.J. Carlesimo, leaving the gym and then returning 20 minutes later and threatening to kill him.

[21]Hall of Fame running back O.J. Simpson on suspicions that he murdered his wife.

[22]Former NFL receiver Alex Hawkins, who arrived home at 6 a.m. after a night of carousing but claimed that he had fallen asleep at midnight on the porch hammock, upon being told by his wife that she had removed the hammock two weeks earlier.

———•———

Class Struggle at Ohio State

AUGUST 31, 1998—How are you with condoms?

Anything you might know about them could help No. 1–ranked Ohio State win college football's national championship.

If Buckeyes junior All-America linebacker Andy (the Big Kat) Katzenmoyer does a lousy job on his summer-school paper about condoms, he might not pass his AIDS awareness course. If he flunks AIDS awareness, he can't play. And if he can't play, Ohio State's entire season could go *splat*.

Also, do you know anything about golf? That's another course Katzenmoyer has to pass. Also, music. *Golf, music and condoms.* Sounds like a weekend with the President.

"It's my fault," says Katzenmoyer "I know if I don't play, it'll be all my fault."

It's funny about Katzenmoyer. He can fend off three linemen the size of small duplexes and grab a 230-pound running back by the bottom lip and plant him like a rhododendron, but he can't seem to get his butt out of bed for class. That's why he had to go to summer school in June and July (he passed tennis, communications and Arabic culture) and why he's there again this month.

August is the Big Kat's last chance. If the grades for his three intellectually daunting courses (Golf 1, Music 140, AIDS: What Every College Student Should Know), which are due on Sept. 4, don't raise his cumulative GPA to at least 2.0, then the man who may be the best player in the nation will be academically ineligible from Sept. 5, when Ohio State opens its season at West Virginia, until mid-December.

(Aside to Andy: *Academically ineligible* is French for *world's largest clipboard boy*.)

Which is why, if I were an Ohio State fan, I would have stood outside his apartment window every morning at 6:30 with a brick, hot coffee and, if necessary, Metallica.

"My only concern," says Ohio State coach John Cooper, "is that if they're in [summer-school] classes, they're not on the practice fields, and that affects us, because they're behind."

Then again, maybe if Cooper had made sure more players had done well in classes during the school year, he wouldn't have three starters on the academic ledge now.

Andy, these teachers, they're not kidding around. "If he deserved it, yeah, I wouldn't hesitate to flunk him," says the golf instructor, Clive Pope. "No hesitation whatsoever. I'm from New Zealand, so football doesn't mean all that much to me. Now, rugby might be another matter."

Andy! How tough can it be? The only thing you have to read in golf are the greens!

"If I had to, yes, I'd flunk him," says the AIDS awareness professor, Dr. Randi Love. (Seriously, that's her name.) Not that Love would want to. "I didn't know who he was," she says, "but my husband did. If I don't pass him, it threatens our married life."

AIDS awareness is dangerous because it meets at 7:30 a.m. on Mondays and Wednesdays. Most mornings at 7:30, Katzenmoyer is dreaming of reaching into a maize-and-blue helmet and pulling out a Michigan player's skull. To pass AIDS awareness, Katzenmoyer will have to write two papers, take two exams and complete two "reaction" projects, one of which is to go out and research condoms, meticulously recording their variety, size, color and cost and the reaction of the 16-year-old Rite Aid clerk when the Big Kat says, "Uh, do you have a fitting room?"

(Aside to Andy: Looking into your sock drawer doesn't count as condom field research.)

But the biggest roadblock to Ohio State's national championship hopes this season is the music class. Hey, it ain't Principles of Lunch. This one must be a bear. It's worth five credits, and the teacher wouldn't return any of our 10 messages. Not a good sign. Katzenmoyer is probably studying everything from baroque to disco.

(Aside to Andy: I'll use baroque in a sentence. If you don't get your butt to Music 140, a whole lot of guys who bet on Ohio State are going to go baroque.)

Forget November. Forget the bowls. This is pressure. This is when it counts. Katzenmoyer's teammates, his fans and the whole college football-loving nation are counting on him.

"I'm not worried," says the Big Kat, bored.

Uh-oh. Is it too late to change the cover?

POSTSCRIPT: *About the time this came out, Andy Katzenmoyer's mom said she thought schools should offer a pro-sports major for athletes who are really only in college to prepare for the pros, which gave me an easy column the very next week. (Lord, I love the Katzenmoyer family.)*

School Of Professional Athletics

AUGUST 30, 1999—Dear Student:

Lately critics of college sports have suggested that schools face facts about the modern Division I athlete and provide a major in pro sports. We at Colossus State University heard them. That's why we've inaugurated the nation's first School of Professional Athletics (SPA).

To enroll in the SPA, please fill out this application using the crayon provided. Then return the form as soon as possible, as we have an unusually high number of football players to sneak through the admissions office this year.

Thank you,
DEAN TARKANIAN
Colossus State University

APPLICATION FORM

(Please mark boxes with an **X**)
Choose your freshman housing:
❑ Barry Switzer Athletic Hall and Firing Range
❑ Delta Gramma Blow fraternity house
❑ Hotel Nikko at Beverly Hills

You would like to be awakened for your noon classes by:
❑ Cell phone
❑ Room service
❑ A gentle nudge from a recruiting hostess

For purposes of on-campus parking, your current handicap is:
❑ Attention deficit disorder
❑ Fumblitis
❑ Advanced narcissism

Which would you like attached to your illicitly obtained handicapped parking pass:
❑ Lincoln Navigator
❑ Lexus 400
❑ Cameron Diaz

Choose one of the following electives (this means you don't have to attend the class):
❑ Women's Studies: Women are studied—and may be tipped.
❑ Accounting for Your Whereabouts (formerly History of the Alibi): Students learn that they can be sleeping, packing their bags and/or chipping in the backyard all at the *same* time! Prerequisite: Heisman Trophy.
❑ The Poetry of Moses Malone: Students study the rhyme scheme and complex cadence of Malone's brilliant *Fo' fo' fo'*. This class also fulfills all math requirements.
❑ Know Your Squad Car: Students learn how to keep from bumping their heads getting in and out of a black-and-white, plus what the most fashionable pro athletes are wearing over their heads.

❏ Thermodynamics: The amazing Thermos™ keeps hot things hot, cold things cold. How does it know? (May be combined with The Meadowlands: Not Really a Good Picnic Area.)

Choose one core requirement (this means a tutor will attend the class for you):

❏ Pro Athlete as Rebellious Slave: Knicks forward Larry Johnson teaches students how to cope with the humiliation of living on $10 million a year.

❏ All That Glitters Is Probably Around Your Neck: Students learn to wear enough jewelry to sink an oil derrick. Prerequi site: Chiropractic 600.

❏ Human Anatomy: The physiques of Nate Newton, Gilbert Brown and Cecil Fielder are systematically studied. Bring lunch.

❏ Great Fiction: Students learn to write their own official statements, including . . .

"I know it's my autobiography, but I'm telling you, I never read it!"

"Well, what was his face doing there in the first place?"

"I sincerely apologize for dragging Ms. [woman's name] down the stairs. I didn't realize there was an elevator."

❏ Economics: How the gross national products of all developing nations compare to that of the Dodgers' Kevin Brown.

Each SPA student must take a hands-on science lab. Choose one:

❏ Nebraska chemistry

❏ Ben Johnson's refrigerator

❏ Laundry day at Michael Irvin's

Care to try one of our one-week SPA workshops?

❏ Balance Your Checkbook: Students enjoy a very "profitable" learning experience in which superagent Tank Black writes athletes "practice" checks, which they deposit into their "personal" accounts.

❏ The Suzuki Method: Students discover how to win the Heisman Trophy now that Suzuki customers can vote on it. Students learn essential phrases such as, "Whoa, nice Suzuki! How would you like to earn 50 bucks?"

❏ Modern Photography. Former members of the Miami Dolphins teach you how to get your photo taken from the front and the side.

Incoming basketball freshman: When do you anticipate leaving school?
❏ After freshman year is completed
❏ After freshman season is completed
❏ Thursday

Signature:_____
(Make another **X**)

The Buck Stops Here

OCTOBER 25, 1999—America's deer came up losers again this year on opening day of hunting season, getting trounced 11,476 to 1. The lone victory for the deer came outside Stump, Ohio, when a 33-year-old accountant was accidentally shot 17 times by his friends despite wearing an orange hat, vest, pants and boots plus a sandwich board that read, IT'S ME, STAN.

Joining us now to discuss the defeat, general manager and coach of the deer, John Doe. Coach, welcome.

Good to be here. Hell, it's good to be anywhere. I could be sitting on a plate next to a vegetable medley.

What frustrates you the most about your squad's performance in the season opener?

Well, we can't keep losing at home like this. Something's gotta change. To tell you the truth, I'm not sure we're competing on a level playing field anymore. We're gonna bring it up at the league meetings in Palm Springs this winter.

What will you ask for?

We've gotta have some help from the competition committee. I mean, we've got some good speed, but we don't have anybody that can outrun an Ultra Light Arms rifle with a 20X scope and 24-inch stainless-steel barrel, you know what I'm sayin'? Plus these hunters keep coming at us with more and more stuff. They've got solunar tables and laser sights and night goggles. We don't even have decent teeth! Put it this way: My grandpa didn't have to dodge a bunch of yahoos riding a damn six-passenger ATV and using a Global Positioning Satellite.

But this was such a lopsided loss, Coach. Is it purely a question of technology?

Well, they're fightin' dirty now. Used to be, we could sniff 'em out before they could get close enough to sever our family ties. But now hunters are taking chlorophyll pills that mask the human scent. They're using spray scent shields. Some guys are bathing with baking soda. Others are burying their clothes for a month in the backyard before they go hunting. I mean, get a life, huh? Hell, I read about hunters who douse themselves with powerful "deer attractant." You know what that is? Deer urine! Now what are we supposed to wear on dates?

Cruel.

Tell me about it. You know, I hear all these guys talking about the "sport" of hunting. I heard a guy say he never apologizes after he fills one of my guys with a bucketful of lead, but he always remembers to "thank the deer for the contest." Wait a minute. What contest? This ain't a contest anymore than the Exxon Valdez versus shrimp was a contest. Hey, you hunters want a contest? Hunt us with spears or knives. Hell, we'll give you rocks, too! I'd love to see one of these Stay Puft marshmallow men comin' at me with a Ginsu in each hand. My old lady would be cookin' humanburgers for a month!

Coach, there have been rumblings in your locker room about needing a change of leadership. What's your reaction to that?

Look, I'm not trying to pass the buck, but I can't think for our guys. Hunters are out there trying to pattern us—you know, keeping notes on where we hang out, where we eat, where we like to rub the old forehead now and again—and our guys are lettin' 'em do it! A lot of our guys are in a rut. What we need to do is pattern them. You know, follow a guy around. Where does he play golf? Where does he work out? Where does he stop off on the way home from work? Surprise one of these sonsabitches outside the old corner tavern with a 12-pointer right in the keister, the rest of 'em will think twice about coming into our backyard, I'll guarantee you that!

Any chance for a comeback?

We're not totally out of it yet. It's a long season. I'll tell you something, though. It would help our morale a damn sight if you guys would cut us a break once in a while.

Who?

The media. Do you know how depressing it is to pick up Field & Stream *and read about hunting "success rates"? I mean, success is kind of a sticky word, ain't it? And talking about the deer "harvest"? Harvest? Hey, I know lots of farmers, and I ain't seen one of 'em yet use a gross of .280 shells to bring in the corn, you with me?*

All right then, we'll close on a high note. How about that lone opening day win? Is there at least some satisfaction in that?

Well, it was kinda lucky. But ol' Stan'll look good over the fireplace at the union hall, won't he?

The Team I Love to Hate

NOVEMBER 1, 1999—Heard somebody grumble the other day that this year's New York Yankees are hard to hate. That statement is just so ignorant. Always remember this: *No* Yankees team is hard to hate, even these small-ball, Ken-doll Bronx Bunters.

That's why I'm coming out with my three-volume series, *The 4,008 Best Reasons to Hate the New York Yankees,* among them . . .

1. They fired Red Barber.

2. They hired Steve Howe. A seven-time drug offender.

364. Rooting for the Yankees takes all the courage, imagination, conviction and baseball intelligence of Spam. It's like rooting for Brad Pitt to get the girl or for Bill Gates to hit Scratch 'n' Win. (This is why I'm proposing legislation that would allow only those born in one of the five New York boroughs to be Yankees fans. All others who root for the team will be considered overdog-loving,

Eveready-chucking, bandwagon-hopping, fair-weather, brown-nose, pucker-lipped human goiters and be required to turn in their pinstriped underwear or be tossed into the East River with only Chuck Knoblauch to throw them a life preserver.)

1,011. The Yankees are the only team that doesn't sew its players' names onto any of its unis. Like kids are supposed to memorize the roster after their bedtime prayers. *Let's see, 3 is Ruth, 4 is Gehrig . . . and 55 is Ramiro Mendoza.*

1,312. Everybody is so charmed by Yankee Stadium public address announcer Bob Sheppard, with his teeth-clenched, perfect-diction English. He sounds British. Is he British? No, he's from Long Island! Why, then, does he speak like Thurston Howell III? Bunch of Yankees fans drunk on lighter fluid in the stands, screaming, "I paid a buck to see ya mutha naked, Rocker!" and the club has some guy on the P.A. making like Alistair Cooke. *Fuhgeddaboutit!*

1,500 through 1,850. Convicted felon and Lucky Sperm Club member George Steinbrenner III, the despotic Yankees owner, fills half of one volume by himself. For example, Georgie Porgie, as Boston Red Sox manager Jimy Williams calls him, just elevated his vice president of player development and scouting, Mark Newman, over his general manager, two-time American League pennant winner Brian Cashman, because Cashman lost two arbitration cases last winter. And forgot to salute.

1,855. After every nauseating, soul-sucking Yankees victory, radio play-by-play man John Sterling bellows, "Yankees win! Tha-a-a-a-a-a Yankees win!" like a goat stuck on an electric fence. Hey, John, give it a-a-a-a-a-a rest.

1,856. After every nauseating, soul-sucking victory at Yankee Stadium, tens of thousands of tin-eared fans hang around and sing the Frank Sinatra standard *New York, New York* over and over, until you pray the ghost of Sinatra himself will appear on the Diamond-Vision, screaming, "Stop!"

2,651. The Yankees' payroll this year was the largest in baseball, by the GNP of Guam. If YANKEES WIN WORLD SERIES is worth a headline, so is BULLDOZER DEFEATS TULIP.

2,651. According to *The Barnhart Dictionary of Etymology,* the word *yankee* was originally a "term of contempt." Isn't that great? The Yankees named themselves after an insult! It's like calling a team the Atlanta Rednecks or the Los Angeles Cokeheads. Iron that on your wife-beater.

3,199. In the spring after their 1996 championship the Yankees charged fans to have their pictures taken with the World Series trophy.

3,200. After they lost the 1976 World Series, the Yankees voted their batboys $100 shares. Their opponents that year, the Cincinnati Reds, gave theirs $6,591 each.

3,911. For decades Yankocentric Eastern seaboard media—like this magazine—have overhyped Yankees players to exhaustion, so much so that six of baseball's 30 All-Century team members were Yankees, including righthander Roger Clemens, who currently is New York's fourth starter and can't get a Bic lighter out. Do you realize the Yankees have retired the jerseys of a .273 lifetime hitter (Phil Rizzuto) and a .257 lifetime hitter (Billy Martin)? What, no Bucky Dent (.247)?

3,989. Lovable Yankees coach Don Zimmer, who has had more hard objects bounce off his skull than Gilligan, was on the bench for the perfect games by Don Larsen (1956) and David Cone ('99) and never got off in between.

4,008. Hating the Yankees is an American tradition that has been honored throughout this century. Remember, nobody ever wrote a play called *Damn Diamondbacks!*

POSTSCRIPT: *Turns out, somebody wrote an entire book about hating the Yankees. Can't wait for the movie.*

National Bunco Association

NOVEMBER 22, 1999—It was reported last week that the cost for a family of four to go to an average NBA game has risen 11% from last season, to $266.61. Wait, wait, wait! Can that be true—$266 to see an *average* NBA game? Like, say, the New Jersey Nets versus the L.A. Clippers? Two *hundred* sixty-six zops? For a family of four? Which family, the Rockefellers?

Do you have any idea what you could do with $266? You could buy 8,866 quarter-inch hex nuts (three cents apiece). You could ride a penny pony 26,600 times. You and your kid could go to a matinee of *Pokémon* ($4 a ticket) 30 times and still have enough left over for six bottles of Excedrin ($4 each).

For $266 you could rent a car from Alamo for two days ($30 a day), have it painted at Earl Scheib's ($199), return it and see if anybody notices. You could spend eight minutes in a room alone with naked former Playboy Bunny Teri Weigel ($2,000 an hour) at the Moonlight Bunny Ranch near Carson City, Nev. Or buy 26 bunnies from Critters Corner in Louisville, Colo.

Are they buggin'? Two hundred sixty-six dollars? An 11% hike in ticket prices for a league in which scoring *dropped* eight points a game last season? Since when did the price of sucking go up?

For $266 you could sponsor a kid through Save the Children (79 cents per day) for nearly a year. You could buy 169 homeless people Thanksgiving dinner at the downtown soup kitchen ($1.57 each). You could slip a quarter to a panhandler every day for almost three years.

You could buy a 10-by-12 storage shed ($250) and fill it with 120 cubic feet of feathers. Swallow 967 hot dogs (package of 80 for $10.99) slathered with 2,580 ounces of French's mustard ($2.68 per 52-ounce bottle). If the idea of spending $266 on an NBA game makes you want to york, think about this: You could buy 450 York Peppermint Pattys (59 cents apiece) for that.

Instead of watching some of the ball hogs in the NBA, you could enroll in the Swine Production and Management class at Des Moines Community College ($190.20) *and* buy eight doses of swine semen ($64) from Premier Swine in Michigantown, Ind. You talk about family fun!

This is just an *average* cost. To see the New York Knicks play at Madison Square Garden, it's $455.26! Four *hundred* fifty-five dollars? You could fly round-trip from Minneapolis to Mazatlán and get four nights' lodging ($396.90, MLT Vacations), bring your sunburn home and lie in a bathtub full of Miracle Whip ($5.99 a gallon) for that!

A puny lobster-salad sandwich at Boston's FleetCenter costs $10! Ten dollars? For $10 I want my lobster to do a reverse 2½ into a pot of boiling water while whistling the theme from *The Little Mermaid*.

The NBA needs to take a long look at what's going on here. I know a guy who became an NBA fan as a kid by watching Bill Russell on Sundays at Boston Garden from a $2 balcony seat. You don't see kids at NBA games now. All you see now are guys in Zegna suits and women in Donna Karan, drinking highballs, talking to one another on their cells and leaving early on a river of corporate ooze.

Two *hundred* sixty-six dollars? For $266 you could watch every NBA game for an entire season ($169 on DirecTV's NBA League Pass subscription) and buy a divorce packet from your county clerk ($20), which you'll most definitely need because your wife will have left with the tennis pro by December.

Do you know what $266 could become? On Opening Day of the NBA season a year ago, if you'd bought eight shares of Qualcomm ($32 per share), they'd be worth $6,048 today. For $266 you could cover 2,700 feet of your ex-husband's house an inch deep in sheep manure ($1.47 a bag). For $266 you could call Dick Vitale for 5,320 minutes (five cents per minute). Or hire a personal-services assistant ($65 an hour) to throw fresh rose petals ($25 a bag) in your path for two hours.

I mean, for $266 you could undergo three weeks of psychiatric counseling from Martin Mueller ($85 an hour) of Los Angeles. If you're thinking of spending $266 to see an NBA game, you really should see Dr. Mueller.

You're certifiable.

He Needs a Dream

JANUARY 24, 2000—I admire the Reverend Jesse Jackson. I think he's one of America's heroes. The man goes behind enemy lines to negotiate the release of captured U.S. servicemen, gets millions of minorities to register to vote and works the pulpit for equality the way Stradivarius worked spruce and maple.

That's why I say to him, respectfully and sincerely, Shut up, already! It's one thing to be wrong; it's another to be loud wrong. Seems just about every time Jackson has opened his mouth lately, he has been 140-decibel-Limp-Bizkit wrong.

Exhibit A: Jackson yelped that the Packers' recent firing of coach Ray Rhodes, after one 8–8 season, may have been racist. I love it. Former Green Bay star Reggie White reads from the Book of Rocker and Jackson yawns, but Jackson makes a football coach seem like Rosa Parks? Lord!

Did it ever occur to Jackson that Rhodes was fired on Jan. 2 not because he was black but because he was wack? Because under Rhodes the team with the best quarterback in the league won three *fewer* games than it had in 1998 and missed the playoffs for the first time in seven years? Because Rhodes lost to every Central Division opponent, botched managing the clock in a ridiculous loss to the Panthers and presided over the NFL's equivalent of Animal House?

A representative of the Coalition to Promote Respect, a Green Bay–area race-issues watchdog, didn't see any racism in the firing. Rhodes didn't see any, either. "Business is business," Rhodes said after he was fired. "We didn't get it done."

Didn't matter to Jackson. "Was Ray Rhodes, an African-American, held to a different standard?" he asked in a Jan. 7 letter to Green Bay general manager Ron Wolf. No, and just ask Chan Gailey, who went 8–8 with the Cowboys and made the playoffs and got a boot in the gluteus for his troubles. Where's Jackson's March on Dallas? Since 1960, 17 NFL coaches—all of them white except Rhodes—lasted a year or less on the job, including San Francisco's Monte Clark, who was rewarded for his 8–6 season with a pink slip. Nobody's seeing color here but Jackson.

Ain't that a kick in the bicuspids for Wolf? He pulls Rhodes off the Salvation Army pile after Rhodes was canned in Philadelphia (the Eagles went 6–9–1 and 3–13 in his last two seasons as coach), and now Wolf's getting his cerebellum beaten in for it. Jackson isn't helping black coaches' NFL prospects, he's hurting them. You hire a black coach, you get Jesse on your butt—no extra charge.

Exhibit B: In November, Jackson went barging into Decatur, Ill., hunting mice with an elephant gun. Following a brawl in the stands during a football game at Eisenhower High, six black students were expelled from the Decatur school district. According to police, the Sept. 17 fight was tied to an incident that occurred two weeks earlier between members of two rival gangs. Jackson slapped down the race card, alleging that the Decatur school district's "zero tolerance" policy on violence targeted black kids. He pooh-poohed the melee, calling it "a silly thing. Something children do." Except video showed these children rampaging through the stands, beating the bejesus out of each other and terrifying fans. The little darlings.

Didn't matter to Jackson. He organized marches, backed a lawsuit filed by the six kids and their parents against the Decatur board of education, and even made sure he got arrested during a demonstration in front of Eisenhower High. He had the gall to liken Decatur to Selma, Ala., and compared his efforts with Martin Luther King Jr.'s. Bull. Still, Decatur held firm. For some crazy reason it doesn't feel like tolerating violence. Last week a U.S. District Court judge in Urbana threw out the lawsuit. Didn't matter to Jackson, who called for more demonstrations.

Can you imagine all the good Jackson could do if he didn't go around trying to wrong rights? What about keeping the heat on South Carolina, where the rebel flag still flies above the stadiums, not to mention the statehouse? What about going to Washington, where Chief Justice William Rehnquist hasn't hired a black law clerk in 28 years on the bench? Why is Jackson wasting his time and ours, playing to the biggest crowds on the smallest issues?

And I call on Foot Locker to explain why the black shoelaces are stacked behind the white ones!

When the handcuffs finally went on Jackson during that ludicrous scene in Decatur, he pronounced, grandly, "It's an honor to be arrested in a righteous cause!"

Yes, Reverend, it is. Now go find one.

Save Your Prayers, Please

FEBRUARY 4, 1991—Harry Truman once said that when you hear someone praying real loud, that is the time to lock up the smokehouse. Well, the praying was deafening during this NFL season.

It's the latest thing: Ringed by TV minicams, a dozen or so fervent Christian players from both teams join at midfield after the game, drop to their knees, clasp hands, bow heads and pray. A stadium full of people and a national television audience are in attendance, whether they like it or not. You saw some New York Giants do it during the postseason, with a delegation of Chicago Bears. And you saw a group of Buffalo Bills do it with some Los Angeles Raiders after their AFC Championship Game.

I have a Jewish friend who is a big Giants fan, but these heaven huddles are getting to be too much for him. "I come to the game, and I root for the Giants, but that doesn't mean they have a right to shove their religion down my throat," he says. "Why can't they do that somewhere else?"

Why *can't* they do that somewhere else?

Howard Cross, the Giants' backup tight end and one of the team's Christians, says that doing it somewhere else would blow the whole message. "It's a testimony," he says. "We *want* people to notice. People hold athletes so high. We have the money, and we have the press, and if we want, we have the girls. But we want to show people that we need more than that. When we bow down, we're showing them that we're looking for more than this world has to offer. Some people think it's weak, but some people say, 'Boy, I'm really touched by that.' And if we touch one person, then it's worth it."

Personally, I think it's weak. I don't think your average fan goes to football games to be touched. I don't think that when he loads up the thermos and pays $10 to park, he's looking to get proselytized. The only conversions he cares about are extra points.

Sure, athletes are entitled to freedom of religion like anybody else. But let them exercise it on their own time. When Giants quarterback Jeff Hostetler, who is not among the midfield huddlers, came off the field after New York's NFC championship win over the San Francisco 49ers, he ran to his locker, knelt in front of it and prayed. Fine. He was keeping it private. It wasn't his fault that a television camera followed him. In fact, athletes have been crossing themselves before at bats and free throws for years, and I can live with those fleeting, more or less reflexive displays of faith.

What I resent are elaborately orchestrated 50-yard-line religious sales pitches. I believe in my God as surely as you believe in yours, but I don't use my last paragraph to mention it, and my plumber doesn't inscribe it on his U joints. He simply fixes my sink and lets me worry about going down the spiritual drain. When you signed up to be a Giants fan or a Bills fan or whatever, you never figured that the players were going to try to reroute your allegiance toward their own version of the way God works.

Promotional prayer is wholly inappropriate to a sporting event, even if, as the players say, they are offering thanks that athletes on both sides survived the game without serious injury. But an outrageous Sunday service happened not after a game but during one. Two weeks ago, against the 49ers, Giants kicker Matt Bahr was lining up a 42-yard field goal try with four seconds left. A successful kick would put New York in the Super Bowl. During the timeout that preceded the kick, seven Giants knelt together and prayed hard for Bahr to split the uprights, which, as it turned out, he did.

Then a *really* outrageous service was held at Sunday's Super

Bowl, where a group of Giants knelt and prayed as Bills kicker Scott Norwood attempted a 47-yarder, as time ran out, to win the game. Is praying for somebody to blow it very Christian? Does the Lord have something against Norwood?

Now, I don't know about your God, but I'm not sure mine has time to consider wind direction and trajectory at NFL football games. It has been kind of a busy month.

I hope that the NFL will have the good sense to curtail these huddles—and, if not, that television will have the sense to ignore them—for the simple reason that imposing one's beliefs on a captive audience is wrong—irreligious, even. It would be just as inappropriate for Jewish players to conduct services at the far hash mark or for Muslim players to place prayer rugs under a goalpost and face Mecca.

I can put up with athletes who, when asked for their views, start out by saying, "First, I'd like to thank the Lord Jesus Christ." They have the right to reply to questions as they see fit. But I object to these noisy "testimonies" I always figured God had time for you whether you were sitting in the front pew or the last.

Besides, just because you rant and rave about how tight you are with God, doesn't necessarily mean it's true. I'm reminded that in World War II, German soldiers had a phrase inscribed on their belt buckle: *Gott mit uns*. The translation: "God is with us."

POSTSCRIPT: According to reaction to this column and the next one, I am either going straight to hell with a seat next to the furnace or I'll be Pro-Am partners with God the rest of my days. Usually, born-again Christians hated it and priests, brothers and nuns loved it. Go figure.

Two Men, Two Flips of Fate

FEBRUARY 7, 2000—Two NFL stars. Two days. Two seat belts unbuckled. Two horrible accidents.

The police who arrive at the first wreck say they've rarely seen a car so crushed after flipping. They're sure the occupants are goners. But the first star, St. Louis Rams Pro Bowl wide receiver Isaac Bruce, crawls out of it, hardly needing a Band-Aid. His girl-friend is also fine.

The police who arrive at the second wreck are surprised the car isn't more damaged after flipping. But the second star, Kansas City Chiefs Pro Bowl linebacker Derrick Thomas, is carried away by ambulance, no feeling in his legs. His best friend is dead.

Same two men, Sunday's Super Bowl, each with the sound of the crowd ringing in his ears, each in a room with colorful banners on the walls and tension in the air, each needing a personal triumph in the worst kind of way. The first man, Bruce, sprints down the side-line in Atlanta's Georgia Dome, turns for a spiral, catches it in front of one defensive back, ducks under another and flashes into the end zone to give the Rams the winning touchdown in the most thrilling Super Bowl finish ever. He's covered in hugs. "That wasn't me," Bruce says later. "That was all God. I knew I had to make an adjustment on the ball, and God did the rest."

The other man, Thomas, knows he has to make an adjustment, too. After six hours of emergency surgery on Jan. 24 at Miami's Jackson Memorial Hospital, he woke to find himself paralyzed from the chest down. His Super Bowl Sunday goal is to find the courage to let himself be lifted out of his bed and into a wheelchair for his first ride into a future he never dreamed of. Surrounded by his new teammates—his mother, his surgeon, his therapists—in a room papered with banners from well-wishers, it's too much. He decides not to try. His head sinks back into the pillow. He's covered in hugs. "Tomorrow," says Barth Green, the University of Miami spinal-cord specialist who operated on him. "Tomorrow he gets in the wheel-chair. Today, with the game on and everything, it's very tough."

In Atlanta, Bruce's tomorrows are all limos and roses. He wears a Super Bowl championship hat, a Super Bowl championship T-shirt and a smile you can't buy. "Coach [wide receivers coach Al Saunders] told me to work hard and good things will happen," Bruce says. "He was right."

In Miami, Thomas wears a rigid collar around his neck, a plastic shell around his chest and a deadness in his eye you can't miss. He hasn't shaved, and he's hardly eaten in a week. He's listening to a pep talk from two more new teammates—Nick and Marc Buoni-conti. Nick is the bustling former All-Pro linebacker for the Miami Dolphins; Marc, his son, is in a wheelchair, left crippled by one play with The Citadel in 1985. Together with Green, they helped start the Miami Project, a 120-scientist dream to cure spinal paralysis.

The Buonicontis tell Thomas that if he's ever going to walk again, it will be through the Miami Project (800-543-WALK). They tell him if he works hard—raising cash and hope—good things will happen. Thomas hopes they're right.

Two men. Two flips of fate.

"Do you ever think about Thomas and say, 'That could be me'?" I ask Bruce.

"Oh, no, not at all," Bruce says.

"Why not?" I ask.

"Because as I was flipping, I threw my hands off the wheel and called Jesus' name."

"Does that mean God doesn't love Derrick Thomas?" I ask.

"Oh, no," Bruce says. "I don't know what Derrick said as his car was flipping."

"What about Payne Stewart? He was a Christian man. Does that mean God didn't love Payne Stewart?"

"I have no idea what Payne Stewart said in that plane that day."

"Well, are you saying if Payne Stewart had invoked the name of

Jesus Christ, he'd be alive today?"

"Oh, definitely."

"What about the Columbine High student who was asked by one of the killers if she believed in God? She said yes, and he blew her away. How can that be?"

"You don't *know* what she said, do you?"

"There were witnesses."

"But you weren't there, right?"

Two men. Pray for them both.

CHAPTER TWO: RAVES

CHAPTER TWO: RAVES

—————◆—————

Quick, Before You're 30

JUNE 22, 1987—With its June issue, *Gentleman's Quarterly* is celebrating its 30th anniversary of showing American men clothes they cannot afford. To pop the cork for the occasion, the editors of GQ took it upon themselves to list 99 musts for the cultured 30-year-old male, besides, of course, owning a dozen $300 belts. By the time a man is 30, GQ insists, he should, among other things, own a power drill; be able to make dinner for eight; have spent the night in a jail, a monastery, a youth hostel or a Motel 6; be able to speak another language; and have a periodontist.

But why only 99 musts? Why not 999? Why not 9,099? In the age of the information explosion, the 30-year-old man needs more specific guidance. And cab fare, if possible. Ever helpful then, we offer up our own musts for the male sports sophisticate. By the time he's 30, he should:

1) Have stopped wearing metal spikes to softballs games;
2) Have eaten a bratwurst with sauce at Milwaukee County Stadium, a burrito at Jack Murphy Stadium or a Dodger Dog;
3) Own season tickets;
4) Have coached the Knicks at least once;
5) Have ruined at least one promising relationship over sports;
6) Have stopped after *Rocky II*;

7) Have thrown at least one hellacious knuckleball;

8) Have stopped doing the Wave;

9) Have run with the bulls at Pamplona, imbibed a cocktail at a Georgia-Florida game or tasted strawberries and cream at Wimbledon;

10) Own a hat from a defunct pro sports league;

11) Admit he bowls;

12) Have stopped bringing a glove to major league baseball games;

13) Be able to explain Bobby Knight;

14) Tell the truth on line calls;

15) Have tossed his baseball cards;

16) Have had one childhood sports idol who has died;

17) Be able to name all the teams in the Smythe Division;

18) Have attempted a putt for more than $100;

19) Know how to turn the wheel during a fishtail;

20) Have won an amusement park stuffed animal at least the size of Ian Woosnam;

21) Know what Bevo Francis was;

22) Be able to name four players who wore No. 32;

23) Know the difference between 501, 301 and cricket;

24) Be able to let a professional athlete eat his dinner in peace;

25) Have attended a World Series game;

26) Have a good explanation for why the only time he watches figure skating is when Katarina Witt is on;

27) Have hit an opposite-field home run;

28) Be able to name the current holders of the World, Ryder and Davis cups;

29) Have been to Fenway, Wrigley and Chavez Ravine;

30) Have thrown out his Jack Kramer model;

31) Have a line to lay on an umpire other than, "Hey, Blue, you gained a little weight—or did you swallow a Fotomat stand?"

32) No longer own any clothing with his name on the back;

33) Be throwing most of them back;

34) Have stopped reading the sports section first;

35) Own copies of *Ball Four*, *The Boys of Summer* and *The Dogged Victims of Inexorable Fate*;

36) Be able to make a lefthanded layup, a crosscourt topspin shot or a mint julep;

37) Be able to hit a one-iron;

38) Have given up saying, "The opera's not over till the fat lady sings";

39) Have a nagging injury from some glorious sports experience;

40) Have one good sports impression (besides Marv Albert);

41) Have been shown the exit by an usher;

42) Be able to recognize Grant Fuhr;

43) Remember Floyd Little, Gates Brown and Red Klotz;

44) Have lunched with Howard;

45) Know the symbol for "called out on strikes";

46) Be unable to remember a single O. J. Simpson movie;

47) Know how much to tip a caddie;

48) Have become less militant about pro wrestling;

49) Have a nickname that embarrasses him;

50) Have hurt his hand on the rim;

51) Have been in traffic school with Leon Spinks or an elevator with George Steinbrenner or been spilled upon by Tommy Lasorda;

52) Have sworn off ever seeing another movie starring a former Olympic gymnast;

And, of course . . .

53) Have given up all hope that someday, somewhere there is a scout waiting to discover him.

Naturally, there are a few musts on this list that I haven't checked off. But I have eight months until my 30th birthday, and that's a long time. Why, in eight months, I may even *be* a periodontist.

POSTSCRIPT: That worked well enough that I thought I'd sneak basically the same column by the editors ten years later. Only this time, with a little twist . . .

Hey, This Turning 40 Ain't So Bad After All

APRIL 13, 1998—Turned 40 recently. Asked what I wanted, I said, "The Perfect Day."

6 a.m.—Alarm rings.

6:01—Smash alarm with two-iron.

9:15—Wake up on own.

9:16—Reintroduce self to Heather Locklear.

9:20—Gabrielle Reece brings breakfast in bed—wearing only sports page.

9:21—Open sports page.

10:21—Read sports page. See that Bobby Knight and Albert Belle hospitalized after freak revolving-door accident.

10:30—Enjoy wholesome breakfast of BBQ chicken wings, chili-cheese fries and Guinness. Forget to eat anything good for colon.

10:42—Wipe face on guest towels.

10:43—Forget to do crunches. Forget to shave. Take one-hour shower.

11:53—Put on fleece sweatpants, favorite ratty Valparaiso sweatshirt and prized BUFFALO BILLS WORLD CHAMPS hat.

11:55—Dealership delivers silver Porsche Boxster. Custom set of Callaways in trunk. Vertebra-snappingly gorgeous redheaded caddie riding shotgun.

12:01 p.m.—World Cup canceled.

12:20—Exhilarating drive to airport on state highway patrols' National Give a Warning Day.

12:30—Board private Gulfstream V for flight to Cypress Point Golf Club. Met on board by commissioners of major pro leagues.

1:05—Satisfying accords reached onboard: Patrick Ewing to be called for traveling every time he touches ball, clichéd dumping of Gatorade on NFL coaches outlawed, bicuspid-bashing goons banned from NHL but made mandatory at major league baseball owners' meetings. Commissioners praise wisdom, parachute out.

1:37—Track canceled.

1:38—Field canceled.

1:55—Greeted at airport by Cypress Point chairman, who compliments me on adhering to club's new no-collared-shirt rule.

2:00—Lunch of BBQ wings, chili-cheese fries and Guinness.

2:08—Wipe face on club blazer of nearby member.

2:30—Enjoy leisurely warmup. Certain rich cablinasian pays up on long-drive contest.

2:45—Tee off with Sultan of Brunei, Bill Gates and Tom Lehman. Tom and I agree to take bastard sandbaggers on, $100,000 a hole, straight up, except Tom gets one floating mulligan on par-5s.

2:47—Katarina Witt and entire cast from *Hooters on Ice* drive up in golf cart and ask if we need anything from their roving, complimentary, single-malt-scotch bar.

4:15—After playing front nine in 90 minutes and 35 shots, agree to let Sultan and Microchip Boy press the back.

6:00—Sign for satisfying 64, highlighted by aces on tricky 15th and 16th. Score qualifies for this week's Masters.

6:05—Bets settled, I graciously buy a beer for losers to share. Sultan leaves somewhat abruptly but not before signing over deed to Florida panhandle.

6:10—Plane departs. Lawrence Phillips sucked into engine upon takeoff.

6:15—On flight back caddie gives relaxing casaba-oil massage; then a nap.

7:30—Arrive refreshed in Seattle for Bulls-Sonics game. Get seated courtside between Alan Greenspan and Warren Buffett, who exchange insider stock tips.

8:01—Bryant Gumbel canceled.

8:45—Have lucky seat number, swish million-dollar half-court shot, sign 10-day Bulls contract and suit up immediately.

9:57—Make move that twists Gary Payton into Picasso painting, then nail jumper to win game.

10:45—Dinner with Michael Ovitz, who interrupts enjoyment

of BBQ wings, chili-cheese fries and Guinness with plan for multi-million-dollar Bic pen endorsement.

11:01—Wipe face on Ovitz's Joseph Abboud suit.

11:05—Meet Charles Barkley for postgame relaxation.

11:06—Barkley graciously allows me to throw first fan through plate-glass window.

1 a.m.—Swimsuit model Heidi Klum begins foot massage in par-5-length limo, suggests strip poker. She's not holding any cards.

2:30—Discover 432 unpublished columns by Damon Runyon in bottom dresser drawer.

2:35—Watch highlights of Pat Riley going bald in single day.

2:36—Forget to floss.

POSTSCRIPT: *Believe it or not, I'm writing a movie based on this column. So far, it stars John Cameron Swayze.*

———•———

Superspectator: My Olympic Feats

AUGUST 17, 1992—I cannot vouch for the authenticity of all I am about to tell you. The incredible ordeal I endured, combined with the heat and a foolishly chosen mayonnaise-and-shrimp sandwich from a street vendor, addled my mind to a state from which I am only now recovering. But I remember that it began with my walking into the boss's office, asking to go to the Olympics and walking out with the worst assignment in the history of journalism.

I was to see if it was possible to go to every single sport at the Olympics without a ticket, for under $2,000—hotel, meals, scalped tickets and bail money included. No reservations, no press credentials, no press buses. I was to see at least one competition in all 28 full-medal sports: archery, badminton, baseball, basketball, boxing, canoeing, cycling, diving, equestrian, fencing, field hockey, gymnastics, handball, judo, modern pentathlon, rowing, shooting, soccer, swimming, synchronized swimming, table tennis, tennis, track and field (counts as one, dammit), volleyball, water polo, weightlifting, wrestling and yachting; plus the three demonstration sports: roller hockey, taekwondo and pelota. I was to do it in 13 days. I was to keep a diary as I went along, and take my own photographs to prove I did it. I was to go out of my mind.

And yet, after a while, I actually started looking forward to the adventure, mostly because it was going to give me a chance to visit the one European sight I had always wanted to see—the Sagrada Família, the spectacular, unfinished modernist cathedral by Gaudí.

This might not be so bad after all.

DAY I

This *is* going to be very bad after all. Everything in Barcelona is twice as expensive as I had figured. A ham sandwich is $8. The only hotel rooms for under $50 are so cramped you have to go outside to sweat. I rented a tiny room off the Ramblas, the wildest, loudest street in the city, and I am sweating now. This is the room the feds should have given Leona Helmsley. It is no bigger than a Volkswagen and has one tiny bed with a mattress that is nearly two inches thick and one window the size of a toaster oven in the corner. It makes up for that, though, with a lack of amenities, including no TV, no phone, no air-conditioning and no French-milled soap. And this is the best deal I could find.

The lady running the place, a fire hydrant of a woman named Rosa, wanted 5,000 pesetas a night (about $53, U.S.) but we settled on 4,100. I asked her if I would be automatically enrolled in the hotel's honored-guest program. She did not seem amused.

I have mapped out exactly what day and what time I will go to each sport by using the Official Olympic Schedule. Today I was supposed to see volleyball, weightlifting, basketball, roller hockey and soccer. Of course, that was before I found out about the Official Olympic Bar Closing Time, which is 5:30 a.m. So I slept right through volleyball. Then weightlifting was misprinted on the schedule ("It is wrong, no problem," said the man at the gate, after I had walked a half hour to find the venue), and roller hockey looked like it was halfway to Portugal, so I rescheduled it. One man's opinion: This is not possible.

I did make it to basketball. It was the Dream Team's opener, and I wanted to be there for the greatest upset in the history of sport—Angola stuns the U.S. team. After a 30-minute subway ride out to the Palau d'Esports de Badalona, I found $38 tickets going for $300.

I finally found a ticket for $200 and made it inside just in time to see Angola come out and blow kisses to the crowd. Then they took basketballs and started hoisting up treys. No layup drill, no weave, just every man for himself. My kind of team. They gave the Yanks all they wanted, too, tying the score 7–7. Then the Americans went on a little 46–1 run. Any coach will tell you: Anytime you get a 46–1 run against you, it can be a difficult mental thing.

It took me two hours on the subway to get from Badalona, the site of the basketball arena, to the west side of Barcelona for a soccer game. Don't ask. It just did. I bought a ticket from the window for $9.90 to see Paraguay versus Sweden. The stands were one-quarter full, but the Swedish fans were cheering and drinking and carrying on as if it were the finals of the World Cup. They kept chanting the same cheer over and over again, so I asked the guy next to me if he knew what it was. "They are cheering about themselves," he said. "They say, 'We are friends from Sweden, going through Europe.'"

Now that's the kind of cheer that will kick-start a team to triumph. What will they holler at tomorrow's game? *We had chicken for lunch and will probably take a nap later!*

I've already spent more than $300. Plus, Rosa forgot the mints for my pillow.

Money left: $1,689.50. Events left: 29.

DAY II

Can I tell you how hot it is in my hotel room at night? It's like sleeping in Saran Wrap under the engine of a Chevy Blazer in Americus, Ga. If I don't buy a fan sometime soon, I may throw myself out the window. Soon, I will be skinny enough to fit through it.

Still, Barcelona is an unforgettable city, sort of Paris on two nights' leave. I can't remember ever being on a street like the Ramblas anywhere in the world. Today I saw a rock band, a harpist, two violinists, a juggler giving free lessons, a man standing on his head on a pile of broken glass, chipmunks for sale, two couples making out and Charles Barkley. I love this city already, and I still haven't seen the best—the Sagrada Família. If I do one thing here, let it be that.

Today I bought a wrestling ticket behind a tree and a swimming ticket behind a port-a-potty. I had expected to see Spain, but not this much of it. These transactions have to take place well out of sight of the Guardia Civil who, it turns out, are the toughest *policía* in Spain. They are the descendants of Generalissimo Franco's bloodiest henchmen. One seller told me that the Guardia had already confiscated the tickets and money of two scalpers. The wrestling ticket was $26.30, but the swimming ticket was expensive—$131—because it included some finals. I think I saw Pablo Morales win his gold and Nicole Haislett win hers, although I couldn't tell, since some lady kept holding up her Japanese flag in front of me the whole time. It was important that she do this so that she could root a Japanese swimmer on to eighth place.

The wrestling I saw was Greco-Roman, which was good but not as good as we used to watch in our basement with Killer Kowalski and Bobo Brazil. Since you are not allowed to use any leg holds in Greco-Roman, it's mostly just one guy trying to push the other guy out of the way. I get that on the subways here every day.

After the wrestling I went to judo, a 40-minute journey, and got stiffed. Not a ticket or a scalper to be found. My feet were howling, but on the way back to the hotel I saw in a window the answer to my aching back and feet—a motorcycle. Well, not exactly a motorcycle. A scooter. Actually, a Honda Scoopy 50, about the wimpiest excuse for a cycle that ever grew pipes. Still, with that puppy, I could knock off five or six venues a day. Two problems: 1) the price—$74.50 a day; and 2) Doug, my friend from the States who lives here now, says I'll be dead in a day and a half. Apparently, he does not know how a good Honda Scoopy can *own* the road.

Every day I ask Rosa to please turn up the air-conditioning in my room. She does not seem amused.

Money left: $1,408.60. Events left: 27.

DAY III

Went to tennis. Wished I hadn't. I was one of 500 people watching Boris Becker play some Norwegian I had never heard of in the Spanish sun, and it almost killed all 502 of us. The clay-court temperature was 108°. The two of them went five sets. I, however, lasted 20 minutes. I would not watch tennis in 108° if it were Bush–Clinton, loser shaves head.

Then I scratched another scorcher, yachting, in favor of volleyball. Volleyball is the best sport yet, thrilling, well played and, most important, air-conditioned. I should have gone to badminton then, but instead I stopped and had lunch. I had lots to choose from, including, according to the English on the menu, broiled macaroni, potato ships and squid in your ink.

From there I hoofed it to the subway, took that to the funicular, went up Montjuic and paid absolutely nothing for one of the greatest views I've ever seen: the diving venue, with the city of Barcelona as a backdrop. I paid zilch because there was a fence to the side of the main gate and you could see through it. One man's opinion: I may just pull this off.

Then it was on to women's team gymnastics, where the Unified Team's prepubescent girls whipped our prepubescent girls. I paid only $55 for a $77 ticket, and the lady from Boston sitting next to me paid $120. Rookie.

Tonight in a bar I met an Australian cyclist who was bandaged up like he had just come from Gallipoli. He had wiped out while warming up before his first race. Still, some good came of it. His father sold me two basketball tickets he wasn't going to use for face value, $77. One of them was to a Dream Team game. Was it up to me to remind him of this fact? I think not. If I get only $200 U.S., for it, I've cleared $123. That's enough for almost two glorious, fun-filled days on the scooter. My legs stopped cramping.

I thanked the two Aussies, and we drank a frosty *cerveza* and toasted the next Summer Olympics, in Atlanta. "Here's squid in your ink," I said.

They were not moved.

Money left: $1,132.95. Events left: 23.

DAY IV

I picked up the scooter today. I think I will be dead within a day and a half.

Drivers here are certifiably crazy, and the road signs are unreadable. I am wearing a helmet the size of Buzz Aldrin's, and girls in cocktail dresses and no helmets are zipping by me on their Honda Scoopys like I'm a lamppost.

Today I overslept and missed table tennis but made weightlifting, where almost nobody was. I just bought a ticket and walked to the front row. That's my new strategy now. Walk to the front row until somebody either stops me or pulls an Uzi. Then make haste for my Scoopy.

No time to enjoy it, though. I was off to modern pentathlon. Modern? Shooting, riding, fencing, swimming and running combined? Sounds like Errol Flynn Week on TBS. After a half hour of not coming even close to finding it, I realized that I was already covering the five sports of the pentathlon. Wouldn't it be overkill? I mentally checked it off and headed to a far better-known Olympic sport, pelota.

In America, pelota is known as jai alai and is supposedly as fixed as the tossing of the bride's bouquet. Spain was playing the Philippines, which, in pelota, is like the Washington Redskins playing Jake's Auto Parts of De Kalb, Ill. One of the Filipinos was so awful he had a difficult time catching—simply catching—the pelota in his cesta. He must have booted it 25 times. It was the equivalent of watching an outfielder drop 25 fly balls. Spain won 40–11.

On the way home I thought I'd try to see the Sagrada Família, but I got lost three times and gave it up. An hour more of searching and I found my hotel. I don't know how much more convenience I can stand.

Money left: $869.50. Events left: 20.

DAY V

Today, me and Scoopy almost got turned into an oil spot. Somehow, I found myself on a four-lane superhighway, trying to find the city of Granollers, sight of that must-see Olympic sport, women's team handball. Suddenly, 20-ton trucks were jetting past us. When one nearly clipped us, I left the highway at the next opportunity. It is one thing to die writing war correspondence, quite another to die for team handball.

I drove on local streets for a half hour until I found a subway stop, parked Scoopy and took a subway to a train station, took the wrong train to Granollers, waited a half hour for a taxi and took it to the handball. The game was nearly over, but I sat down next to a lady with biggish shoulders and big blonde hair. The goalies had the unenviable job of trying to stop miniature soccer balls being heaved at them by huge, piano-lifting women.

"What sort of person would want to do that?" I asked aloud.

"My daughter," said the lady. "She's the American goalie."

Oh.

Once I got back to my scooter, it took only 2½ hours to find my way to cycling. The velodrome is great, but do not—*do not*—buy a ticket to team pursuit unless you enjoy watching a single marble roll down a funnel for three hours.

Next stop was judo, where I finally could buy a ticket at the window and, unfortunately, another godforsaken ham sandwich. All you seem to be able to get at the stadiums are ham sandwiches. And the only thing available in bars seems to be these weird open-faced ham sandwiches. I now rank fourth among the world's ham-consuming countries.

The judo fans were very organized and without concern for the future use of their larynxes. On the way home I ran out of gas. When I got to the gas station, they didn't have gas cans to loan out, so I had to rifle through the trash looking for a plastic water bottle with the cap on it. This is what my life has become.

As I was leaving the gas station, a policeman came toward me, holding an automatic weapon and looking concerned. I realized that he was wondering what I wanted with a plastic bottle full of gasoline at three in the morning in the heart of the Olympics. I did what I think was a very good impression of a motorcycle running out of gas. I think it was very good in that I am still alive as I write this.

Money left: $722.75. Events left: 17.

DAY VI

I figured that if I don't eat or drink another thing and average $20 a ticket the rest of the way, I'll make it. Right. Still, I am determined.

I started with an $8 ticket to table tennis, which has to be my favorite sport here so far. These people put so much spin on the ball it could tear the hair off your arm. Their problem is they need a union. They have no ball boys. Here was the French guy, who has got to be one of the best players in the world, and he's on his hands and knees trying to get a Ping-Pong ball that rolled under the table.

Then I left to watch archery, which is like sitting in the Superdome watching two guys in the middle of the field play cribbage. You can't see the arrows. Even the archers look through a telescope to see how they've done. Plus, it was hotter than summer car seats. Skip this one.

No visit to the Sagrada Família again today.

Money left: $636.80. Events left: 15.

DAY VII

I can't tell you how exciting the rowing and the yachting were today. I can't tell you because I don't know.

I was supposed to get up at 3 a.m. and catch a 4 o'clock bus to the rowing, which was three hours away. I didn't, partly because I was still drinking sangria on the Ramblas at 3. I was also still drinking sangria at 4. I believe it was about 4:30, just before more sangria came and just after the bus left, when I decided that rowing and canoeing are much too much alike and should either be combined or eliminated or both. I offer this up free of charge to the IOC. I checked off rowing.

I did go to yachting and saw nothing. The spectator boat had left and wouldn't be back for two hours. Sadly, I was left with nothing to do but rest at a topless beach.

Eventually I made it to fencing, where it is quite impossible to tell who got stuck, what the flashing lights mean or why one of the fencers rips off his mask on virtually every point and argues with the official. This gets old fast. Near as I can remember, Basil Rathbone didn't argue when *he* got stabbed.

Three rotten sports and four boring ones in the last two days, and my feet are begging for a press bus and my wallet looks anorexic. My money is going fast, and I hear the market on Dream Team tickets is dropping fast. My Australian investment is looking like Silverado Savings and Loan. Maybe I was wrong about this. Maybe the Olympics were meant to be viewed in a reclining position, in front of a 36-in. TV. Maybe they exist only for the love of a good remote.

Money left: $531.50. Events left: 12.

DAY VIII

There is nothing worse than being in a European country and seeing these lame, homesick Americans clustered at the McDonald's having their insipid quarter-pounders with cheese, large fries and a Coke while a whole undiscovered world of cuisine waits outside for them.

That is why today, when I went to McDonald's, I had a quarter-pounder with cheese, large fries and a beer. McDonald's serves beer. Is Spain a great country or what?

I actually took the right train for once—to the shooting, 40 minutes out to Paret del Vallès. After a 20-minute walk from the train, I was there just in time to hear the last shot shatter the last target. I'm counting it.

From there it was a 20-minute walk, a 40-minute train ride back to the Barcelona train station, a 30-minute search for the right train to the roller hockey town, a 45-minute train ride there and a sick feeling in my stomach when I realized I had gone to the wrong town. Turns out roller hockey was now being played in a town called Reus, 60 kilometers away. Tears very nearly came to my eyes. It was about then that I settled on the logic that roller hockey and field hockey are too much alike and should either be eliminated or combined or both. I checked it off.

I was totally drained in Spain, and yet I still had to go to boxing. Luckily, on the subway there I sidled up to a swank-looking guy from Chicago, who said he had just flown in from Mallorca and needed a ticket to the Dream Team game tonight.

Ahem, I said.

He bought the Dream Team ticket I'd bought from the Australians for 10,000 pesetas—$107. That was a $30 profit. Thank you, Jesus.

At almost every event now, tickets are easy to come by. I bought a boxing ticket for face value, $33, off a nonscalper who just wanted to go home. The boxing was at a terrific little venue, and I saw Raul Marquez of the U.S. win his fight. Up in the stands Norwegians were chanting wildly, and Evander Holyfield, the heavyweight champion of the world, was right in the middle of them. I think they were singing, "We are friends from Norway, but who is this black guy?"

I am really in trouble with money. If I don't start getting some free tickets, I'm going to have to start sleeping on the beach.

I hear Jack Nicholson and Michael Douglas are in town. You think they have an extra ticket to synchronized swimming tomorrow?

Money left: $508.92. Events left: 9.

DAY IX

Today I devised a brilliant, ingenious and, naturally, despicable plan. I bought a FREEDOM FOR CATALONIA T-shirt, some gauze and athletic tape, borrowed crutches from my buddy's friend and wrote out a cardboard sign that read, in Spanish, NEED ONE FREE TICKET PLEASE. I wrapped up my ankle as if it were sprained, put on the T-shirt, hobbled up on the crutches, sat down in front of the swimming venue and held up the sign. I had a free ticket in my shameless mitts within three minutes. It was from a volunteer Olympic worker. As he handed it to me, he said with a smile, "The child who does not cry, does not eat." You got that right, Pablo.

I got my comeuppance. As I started to get up to hobble into the event, an 85-year-old Californian named Glen Calloway decided to help. "I'll just keep you company," he said. "It's a long walk." I had planned to get through the gate, duck into a corner, rip off the tape, ditch the crutches and walk the rest of the way, but Mr. Calloway, bless his heart, insisted on escorting me on a 400-yard walk and up the 100 or so stairs to my nosebleed seat, with me doing it on crutches. Karma.

On the Ramblas tonight I saw some buddies from the press. They told me about the press buses (air-conditioned and on time) and what they do with their mornings off (like visit the Sagrada Família). "Amazingly cool," said one guy.

May they all start writing like Dick Vitale.
Money left: $396.73. Events left: 8.

DAY X

I was at badminton, trying to buy a cheap ticket—my conscience couldn't bear the guilt of the crutches scam again—when a guy said, "You want to come in with my mate?"

Turns out his mate was a British badminton player named Nick Ponting. The competitor's credential got Ponting four free passes, and he was looking for four people to go in with him, at $53 each. He'd been eliminated in the second round. He took me, his Aussie pal and a couple from Finland right through. Twenty feet inside the gate we gave him 5,000 pesetas each and never saw him again. Do they give medals for capitalism?

Badminton is a terrific sport, easy to follow, packed to the ventilator grills with screaming fans and thrilling to the last shuttlecock. Playing flawlessly, an Indonesian named Susi Susanti flicked, dived and smashed her way past Bang Soo Hyun of South Korea in three sets. Juan Antonio Samaranch put the medal around Susanti's neck, and I was close enough to see her tears. I guarantee you nobody with a remote will get that.

While I was there, a guy handed me a ticket to the field hockey final three nights hence. Since I was going there next, I took it. You never know. Sure enough, I found somebody there who traded me straight up—and why not? My ticket was worth three times as much. I was in.

I wished I had been out. Field hockey is another one of these sports in which the ball is maddeningly easy to steal. That means that the game is constantly played in the middle 30 yards of the field, two subway stops from the nearest goal. I saw the German women beat the English women 2–1, an event on the thrill scale equal only to watching Irving R. Levine get his ear hairs clipped.

I was supposed to go from there to baseball, two hours away, when my body simply refused. I got a nasty headache, stomachache, fever and, uh, infirmity. I was sick as a rat, sitting on a lonely train. And it was *still* more fun than watching field hockey.
Money left: $241.93. Events left: 6.

DAY XI

If I hadn't dragged my sorry carcass out of the sick bed and gone to the 9 a.m. equestrian event called individual dressage today, I would have blown the assignment. You gotta play hurt. I went. I nearly threw up on a horse, and I spent bazillions in cabs, but I went.

Dressage is an acquired taste that I hope I never acquire. Thousands of people watch in silent rapture as a horse and rider walk around on the dirt. In the background, light classical music plays softly, as if from a librarian's gardening radio two blocks away. The horses don't have to race, carry, jump, jog or even so much as canter—and some riders keep the same horse for 14 years. If I'm a horse, I'm asking where the line forms.

Taekwondo was every bit as good as judo, but I was the only one in the arena. After that it was an afternoon water polo game at the same site as the diving. My table was waiting. *Fence for one?*

Then I collapsed on my bed. I've only got about $85 left, and I still need canoeing, and track and field. Getting a track and field ticket tomorrow is going to be like trying to buy the Magna Carta. Plus, when am I going to catch baseball?

Money left: $84.63. Events left: 3.

DAY XII

Never. That's when I'm going to catch baseball. I have lost. Turns out they played the baseball finals last night. That means I won't see all 31 sports. I will be at least one short. History must do with me what it will.

With little money left, my scruples shrank and my ankle swelled again. I dug out the sympathy act. Scalpers wanted $110 to see the night's track and field finals, but after 10 minutes of holding up my sign in front of the Olympic Stadium, I was handed a ticket. The seat was magnificent, 28 rows up from the long jump pit, hard by the Olympic flame. This crutches thing is scary good.

I was privileged to witness legend: Kevin Young setting a world record in the 400-meter hurdles, Gail Devers falling one step from gold, Carl Lewis taking the long jump by three centimeters. Lewis celebrated by throwing his sweatshirt, shoes and shirt at us. I guess throwing your clothing into the crowd is some kind of track tradition. I am glad it is not a wrestling tradition.

Money left: $13.58. Events left: 2.

DAY XIII

I can't think of a more poetic final sport to witness than kayaking. Canoe? Well, I could, so I deputized my buddy Doug to take the train out to Castelldefels to watch the paddling and fill me in on it. Don't look at me like that. He was going there anyway.

After listening to Doug's report for a full 11 seconds, I had the rest of the day to finally see the city. Where else was I going to go? The city *was* my hotel room now. I know I will miss Barcelona. And I know I will miss the Ramblas. With the planet looking especially bloody lately, you could do worse than the Ramblas these last two weeks as an example of how peace could work.

At last, at 1 a.m., I turned the corner and saw the eight whimsical melting rockets of the Sagrada Família. And as I lay down on a bench to stare up at it, I decided that it was only fitting I bed down here tonight, at the foot of my towering Holy Grail. And I thought, as I marveled at it, that if Gaudí himself were with me, he wouldn't mind that I fell one sport short in my task.

Hey, some of the world's greatest works are unfinished, right?

POSTSCRIPT: The funniest part of this piece was the photos. I took a photo of my feet sticking up in the air at every venue to prove I was there. I still don't know how I didn't get a Keds contract out of it.

———— •—•—• ————

Speaking of Class to the Class of '98

MAY 25, 1998—Thank you, graduates. Please be seated. It's an honor to address the college athletes who are going on to the pros this year. If I may, I'd like to offer just a few pieces of advice.

Every now and again turn off Nintendo, shut off Spectravision and open a book. We already have enough jocks who think the Brothers Karamazov are the WWF tag-team champs.

If you ever hear yourself saying, "They offered me $81 million? That's an insult!" find a tire iron, go into a quiet room and hit yourself very hard on the shin.

Marry someone who has never heard of you.

Now that you've made it, practice twice as long as you did in college. The hardest worker in the NBA is Michael Jordan. What does that tell you?

If you write a book, read it before it comes out.

Be careful with your money. Write your own checks. None of this power-of-attorney crap. Get an agent *and* a lawyer, and tell each the other's a crook.

Shock the world: Apologize when you screw up.

Don't buy a Vanderbilt mansion just because you can. Do you know how many 50-room jock palaces I've been in with two rooms' worth of furniture?

Never, ever rip a teammate.

Spread the jing around. There's nothing uglier than a man in a $3,000 Armani stiffing a coat-check girl.

O.K., so you didn't grow up with a father. Then go *be* one. Make a difference in the life of one kid who is not your own, and it'll give you more joy than a lifetime shoe contract.

Just a reminder: You *will* die someday.

Stop thumping your chest. The line blocked, the quarterback threw you a perfect spiral while getting his head knocked off, and the *good* receiver drew double coverage. Get over yourself.

Give the bodyguard the night off once in a while and wade into the people. Some are sort of cool.

Loosen up a little with the quotes. This isn't a congressional budget hearing. Why say, "I really was shooting well today" when you could say, "I was hotter than a three-dollar pistol."

Once a season, let your offensive guard spike the ball.

See the woman up there in section 595, row WW, seat 29? She makes $26,000 a year, paid $22 a ticket for her family and just plunked down $17 for three Cokes and a warm beer. Treat her nice. Without her, you're a 320-pound bouncer with half a P.E. degree.

Go easy on the tattoos. By the time you're 60, that hula girl on your biceps is going to look like Don Knotts.

This just in: You can do community service without being sentenced. Try it. Have somebody leak it to the media. There are worse things than people seeing a millionaire painting an old lady's house.

Learn the piano. Try another language. Take up origami. It's hard for you to believe now, but someday people are going to get sick of hearing about the crosscourt forehand that beat Sampras.

Once a year take your free tickets, walk through the stands in your uniform, go outside the ballpark and give them to the kids hanging on the fence.

Remember, these are all just games. Hale Irwin missed a two-inch putt that cost him the British Open. What are you going to do? Go soak in your Olympic-sized hot tub and laugh about it.

This is the career *you* picked. If you can't handle public scrutiny or deal with strangers graciously, become a taxidermist.

Read everything written about you, good or bad. Then forget about it. No matter what you do, half the people will worship you and half will detest you. You can't fight it.

Help your opponent up. He'll probably be your teammate next year.

No offense, but when you're setting off the airport metal detector from the back of the line, you might have on too much jewelry.

For the next 10 years or so, you'll travel the world first class, laugh yourself sore on the team bus and get paid half of Zurich, so let's not hear a lot of whining, O.K.? So what if your Oakley deal fell through? We'll start a telethon.

One last thing. Remember when you were a kid? All you dreamed of was playing centerfield for the New York Yankees. Soon, you'll be there. Don't forget to tingle.

POSTSCRIPT: *After I wrote this, I was invited to give an actual commencement address to my own high school in Boulder, Colo. Many of them immediately went out and became taxidermists.*

The Heavenly Hundred

MAY 22, 1989—Suppose there came a telegram from Heaven that read:

Sorry Stop Running out of space up here Stop Jammed to the rafters Stop From now on can handle only one athlete per jersey number Stop Doesn't matter which sports Stop You decide Stop Fax list soonest Stop

This could happen. So we need to be ready, and I've taken the liberty of drawing up the list. Each jersey number shall honor one athlete and one athlete only. That's the law. And I *don't* want any guff. . . .

0   GEORGE PLIMPTON Paper Lion.

00 JIM OTTO

1/8 EDDIE GAEDEL

1   JACK NICKLAUS The number worn by the caddie of the defending Masters champion.

1A SECRETARIAT The 1973 Kentucky Derby winner's entry number.

2   LEO DUROCHER

W2 JOAN BENOIT She wore it when she broke the women's world mark in the 1983 Boston Marathon.

3   BABE RUTH

4   LOU GEHRIG Over Bobby Orr.

5   JOE DiMAGGIO

6   BILL RUSSELL Sorry, Dr. J.

7   MICKEY MANTLE

8   CARL YASTRZEMSKI

9   GORDIE HOWE With a nod to Ted Williams.

10 PELE

11 NORM VAN BROCKLIN

12 TERRY BRADSHAW Four rings.

13 WILT CHAMBERLAIN

14 ERNIE BANKS

15 FRANZ KLAMMER Won the 1976 Olympic downhill wearing it.

16 JOE MONTANA

17 DIZZY DEAN I don't want to hear about no Hondo.

18 JACKIE ROBINSON Wore it as a UCLA basketball player.

19 JOHNNY UNITAS

20 JOSH GIBSON

21 JIM THORPE

22 ELGIN BAYLOR

23 MICHAEL JORDAN Forever.

24 WILLIE MAYS

25 FRED BILETNIKOFF

26 SATCHEL PAIGE

27 JUAN MARICHAL

28 YALE LARY Detroit Lions.

29 KEN DRYDEN Over Rod Carew.

30 JIM CRAIG The USA's Olympic goalie in 1980.

31 JIM TAYLOR

32 SANDY KOUFAX With apologies to Jim Brown, Magic Johnson and Elston Howard.

33 LEW ALCINDOR Edging out Kareem Abdul-Jabbar.

34 WALTER PAYTON

35 DOC BLANCHARD

36 O.J. SIMPSON In his first pro year.

37 CASEY STENGEL

38 RAY DANDRIDGE Of the Negro leagues.

39 ROY CAMPANELLA

40 VINCE LOMBARDI Wore it at Fordham. Over Crazy Legs Hirsch and Gale Sayers.

41 ROGER BANNISTER The day he broke the four-minute barrier.

42 SID LUCKMAN

43 RICHARD PETTY

44 HENRY AARON Over Jerry West, Pistol Pete and Reggie.

45 BOB GIBSON

46 LOU GROZA Wore it for a short time.

47 MEL BLOUNT

48 GERALD FORD At Michigan.

49 TOM LANDRY Wore it as a player with the New York Giants.

50 MIKE SINGLETARY

51 DICK BUTKUS

52 MIKE WEBSTER

53 DON DRYSDALE

54 GOOSE GOSSAGE

55 OREL HERSHISER

56 JIM BOUTON

57 JOHNNY (Blood) McNALLY Four Green Bay championships.

58 JACK LAMBERT Next to ...

59 JACK HAM

60 CHUCK BEDNARIK

61 BILL GEORGE The meanest Bear ever.

62 BUD WILKINSON Wore it at Minnesota.

63 GENE UPSHAW

64 JERRY KRAMER Author.

65 LES BINGAMAN Lions' lineman.

66 MARIO LEMIEUX

67 SIXTEN JERNBERG Won four Olympic cross-country ski golds.

68 L. C. GREENWOOD

69 LARRY COSTELLO Of the NBA.

70 SAM HUFF

71 ALEX KARRAS

72 CARLTON FISK With 27 taken in Chicago, he reversed himself.

73 LEO NOMELLINI A pro wrestler, he wore it with the 49ers.

74 MERLIN OLSEN

75 DEACON JONES

76 LOU GROZA Wore it the rest of the time.

77 RED GRANGE

78 BUBBA (Kill) SMITH

79 ROOSEVELT BROWN

80 JERRY RICE Over Tom Fears. How's that for recognition?

81 NIGHT TRAIN LANE

82 RAYMOND BERRY

83 RENALDO NEHEMIAH Hurdler. When he played for the 49ers.

84 ANDY ROBUSTELLI

85 NICK BUONICONTI

86 BRUD HOLLAND 1930s Cornell All-America end who became ambassador to Sweden.

87 BILL CARPENTER The Lonely End.

88 LYNN SWANN

89 IRON MIKE DITKA

90 BOB (Foothills) KURLAND The first great seven-footer.

91 OLGA KORBUT At the Montreal Games.

92 LES HORVATH

93 This space available.

94 RANDY WHITE Wore it at Maryland after fans stole all his 74's.

95 RICHARD DENT

96 BILL VOISELLE From Ninety Six, S.C., he wore it with the Boston Braves.

97 ART STILL

98 TOM HARMON

99 WAYNE GRETZKY

POSTSCRIPT: *More than a decade later, there wouldn't be many pink slips. For sure you'd have to replace Fred Biletnikoff with Mark McGwire at 25, Jim Craig with Ken Griffey Jr. at 30, and Jim Taylor with Greg Maddux at 31. But neither Sammy Sosa nor Roger Clemens replaces Jim Thorpe at 21 and Pedro Martinez is no Bob Gibson yet at 45.*

—•—

An Easy Choice

NOVEMBER 4, 1996—When Daniel Huffman quit football, did exactly what his mom told him not to do and started messing around with needles, folks in tiny Rossville, Ill., shook his hand. How else was he supposed to save his grandmother's life?

Still, if there was one kid in town you hated to see quit the high school team, it was Daniel. "That kid *lived* for football," says his grandfather, Daniel Allison. Young Daniel would count the days from the end of school to the start of summer two-a-day practices. He was the screamer on the team, the human pep rally. O.K., so maybe he wasn't going straight to Florida State, but at 6' 2" and 275 pounds, Daniel was where a lot of enemy tailbacks ended up. "He would just engulf them like some huge amoeba," recalls his former coach, Dave McDonald. "And then he'd yell some more."

This is Daniel's senior year at Rossville High. He is an honor-roll student (A-plus average), a member of the school chorus, the class vice president, a writer of poetry, a part-time cleanup boy at a discount store and a onetime shot-putter on the track team, but none of those things have made him as proud as being a co-captain, starting defensive tackle and occasional offensive tackle on the football team. In a town such as Rossville (pop. 1,400), a hiccup of a place 118 miles south of Chicago, your senior year of football is precious, and Daniel had planned to make this season a doozy.

Though he played primarily on defense, he had the soul of an offensive lineman. He had no designs on stardom. Of the team's star running back, Zeb Stephenson, Daniel once said, "It will be my privilege to block for him."

Daniel is very big on making other folks' paths a little easier. When diabetes left his grandmother Shirlee Allison legally blind for a while, 14-year-old Daniel and his 13-year-old sister, Kristina, did the dishes and folded the laundry. Daniel became Shirlee's eyes, helping her walk, reading the mail to her. When Shirlee's husband had his quintuple bypass two years ago, Daniel got his grandmother through it. "Sometimes we raised them," Shirlee says of her grandchildren, "and sometimes they raised us."

Daniel is just as attentive to his friends. "He'll do anything for us," says Lisa Masengale, a high school classmate. "He writes me poetry when I'm down. He can always make me laugh."

Hard to figure where he got all the spare sunshine. Daniel's mother, Alice, left the family when he was four. His father, Barry, remarried, and an evil-stepmother/ungrateful-stepkids thing broke out. Daniel and Kristina were miserable, but Barry wasn't one to interfere. "He's kind of a partyer," Daniel says. So the summer after Daniel finished seventh grade, he and Kristina moved to Florida to live with Alice. That didn't work out either, so after a year everyone agreed that the kids would be best off living with their grandparents, the Allisons.

"My grandparents kinda saved me," says Daniel. "There's a whole lot of drugs and stuff around here. I probably would've ended up all messed up." Kristina eventually moved back to Florida, which left Daniel and Shirlee as the oddest couple in town. Sure, they shared a love of books and a certain hardheadedness, but he was a 17-year-old growing uncontrollably, and she was a 60-year-old disappearing before the town's eyes. After a time her diabetes-ravaged kidneys were producing almost no urine. All that poison the kidneys were supposed to filter out was circulating through her.

As last spring grew warmer, Shirlee's trips to the hospital in nearby Danville for dialysis got more frequent, and her condition worsened. Her muscles were atrophying, her heart was enlarged, and her blood pressure was dangerously low. "We all figured there was no hope for her," says her neighbor Madge Douglas.

But then Daniel had this crazy idea. He was sitting at a Burger King with Shirlee after another brutal day of watching her on the dialysis machine ("the metal and plastic vampire," he called it in his diary). He had been thinking about how much he missed her. Where was Gran, the kidder? Gran, the one you couldn't get to shut up? Who was this 101-pound ghost? Who was this clothes hanger of a woman, all bone where he used to plant his good-night kiss? "Mrs. Allison," the doctor had told her, "many people can live years on dialysis, but you aren't one of them."

Well, that made the situation sticky. She refused to take a kidney from a relative. She was on the waiting list for a cadaver kidney. That was good enough for her. "I'm not imposing on anybody," she said. Daniel was so scared that he couldn't watch her undergo treatment anymore. He started picking up medical handbooks about dialysis. He talked to Shirlee's doctors. He learned the dangers of becoming a kidney transplant donor. He knew that if he gave Shirlee one of his kidneys, he would have to give up contact sports forever—one hard hit from behind, and he could end up on life support. On the other hand, he learned that eight people die each day in the U.S. while waiting for an organ. The wait for a cadaver kidney can be two years. At the rate Shirlee was shrinking, that would be a year and a half too much.

And so, somewhere between the Whopper and the onion rings, Daniel made up his mind. "Gran," he said, "I can't take it anymore. I want you to take my kidney."

"No, no, no," she said. "You're too young. What if something happens?"

"Gran, I don't care what happens to me. I'm doin' this!"

"Absolutely not," she said. "Besides, when I think about you giving up football, it makes me sick to my stomach."

Daniel got good and mad. He yelled, "Gran, you always told me, 'Stand up for what you believe in.' Well, I'm standin' up! You're takin' my kidney!"

You do not hear that every day at Burger King. Every head in the joint turned. "Well," Shirlee whispered, sliding back in her chair, "we'll see if we match."

Getting around Daniel's mother was even dicier. Alice was foursquare against the donation. When Daniel decided to go ahead with the operation anyway, Alice took action. She wrote a letter to the University of Illinois Medical Center, where Daniel and his grandmother wanted the transplant to take place, and asked how the surgeons could take organs from minors. The center, which had not known Daniel's age, declined to allow the operation.

Daniel was dogged. If he waited until his 18th birthday—Dec. 24—Shirlee might be too weak to survive the operation. "He was ready to go to court on this," says Jeff Miller, transplant coordinator for Dr. Frederick K. Merkel, who performs surgery at the Illinois Medical Center and Chicago's Rush Presbyterian Hospital and accepts living-relative transplant donors as young as 16. The operation was on, at Rush.

The night before the July 9 surgery, Daniel was scared for both Shirlee and himself. "Gran," he said, "I gotta ask you one thing: Is this worth risking your life for?"

"Oh, honey," she said, laying her withered hand on his huge one. "I have no life without this."

When she woke up in the intensive care unit, she already had her color back. "My stars!" she said to a nurse. "Now that I've got this 17-year-old kidney in me, I hope I don't feel like going out and tackling somebody!" Across the hall, though, Daniel was hurting. After a kidney transplant the donor gets months of tests—the constant blood work, the working knowledge of the hierarchy of hospital needles. Shirlee's scar is small and on her pelvis. Daniel's is 18 inches long and wraps from his navel nearly to his spine. It was Daniel who was in pain long after the surgery, not Shirlee. Who said it's more blessed to give than to receive?

But a lot of wonderful things also started happening. Daniel had quit the football team, but the football team refused to quit him. The players insisted that he wear his football jersey each Friday. He went to every practice when he wasn't working at the discount store. He rode on the senior players' float at homecoming and made the speech at the pep rally before the game. And on Friday nights you could hear his voice all over the field: "C'mon, everybody! *Clap!*" Funny, how somebody who wasn't even playing could be the toughest kid on the team.

Daniel is almost completely recovered. In fact, the doctors say his remaining kidney will soon be twice the size it used to be. They still haven't figured out how to measure his heart.

Daniel wants to be a writer, and he's applying for college scholarships like crazy. As for Shirlee, her weight is up to 128, she rarely uses her cane, and her vision has improved. She has even gone to some of Rossville's football games—something she couldn't do before the surgery. You should have seen her there, bursting with pride. "The boy loved his grandma more than football," she marveled, wiping a tear from the corner of her eye. "Whaddya think a that?"

Folks in town seem to think a lot of it. Folks out of town too. Governor Jim Edgar wrote Daniel to say how proud he was of him, and the story of Daniel's donation was on national as well as local TV programs.

The Rossville football team didn't do too well, finishing the season last Friday at 3–6. "We sure could have used Daniel to put a body on somebody," said lineman Chad Smith. With 24 seconds left in Rossville's final game, a 28–3 win over Palestine High, Rossville's Shaun York asked to leave the game and be replaced by Daniel—who, with the coach's permission, had put on shoulder pads, a helmet and a borrowed pair of cleats. Daniel lined up 20 yards behind the line of scrimmage, and as his quarterback took the snap and downed the ball, Daniel raised his hands in a V for victory. "It was," he says, "the single best memory of my life."

Now Daniel hopes for a victory for his friend Lisa. When she was sick for two weeks last month, doctors discovered that she had a badly infected kidney. Now Lisa, too, is learning all about needles and even transplants. Luckily, she's got a 17-year-old Mayo Clinic encyclopedia to talk to on the phone, to keep her calm—and make her laugh. "He's getting me through it," she says.

Shirlee Allison knows how well Daniel can do that sort of thing. After she went home from the hospital, she ran a two-inch-by-one-inch ad in the Danville paper expressing her love for her grandson. She says, "Every morning I wake up, I get on my knees and thank two people: God and Daniel."

POSTSCRIPT: *A lot happened to Daniel after this ran. Florida State coach Bobby Bowden—knowing full well that he could never play a down for him—offered Daniel a full-ride scholarship to be on the Seminoles sideline and Daniel took it. "I just never heard of anything so valiant," Bowden said. Daniel's grandmother is doing fine, too. In fact, Debbie Reynolds played her in the 1999 Showtime movie* A Gift of Love: The Daniel Huffman Story. *Hey, who says lineman isn't a glory position?*

———————

An All-Consuming Hunger for Victory

JULY 6, 1998—The most fearsome competitive eater in the world stands only 5' 8". He weighs 135 pounds. His waist is 30 inches. You look at him and you think, *I spot this guy a pork shank and I still beat him.* Yet this polite waif has made giant men bury their faces in their napkins in agony, struck terror in the stomachs of sumo wrestlers and given all-you-can-eat noodle-shop owners facial tics.

He is Hirofumi Nakajima, of Kofu, Japan, and he's coming to Coney Island on July 4th to defend his title in the 83rd annual Nathan's Famous Fourth of July Hot Dog Eating Contest. Please, keep pets and small children away.

Winning again won't be easy. He will have to beat a man who can eat 150 jalapeño peppers at one sitting. The world haggis-eating champ will be there. So will the American pickle-eating champion. One beast goes 6' 7" and 360. None of them can carry Nakajima's fork.

Last year, he ate 24½ hot dogs (and buns) in 12 minutes, or enough to kill Babe Ruth three times over. He has put away 50 sushi in one minute; 14 bowls of *soba* in 30 minutes; more than six and a half pounds of sweet potatoes in half an hour. But he is not merely a speed-eater. He is a classic distance eater as well. He inhaled 15 bowls of noodle soup, 100 pieces of sushi, five plates of wheat noodles, five plates of beef over rice, and five plates of curry over rice in a single lunch. Plus the mint. Another time he slurped down 58 bowls of rice-cake soup in a sitting. There is nobody the dreaded Black Hole of Kofu can't outeat.

"Excuse me," he says, bowing apologetically. "But this is not true. I lost once."

You did?

"Yes. To an elephant."

O.K., there is no *human* the dreaded Black Hole of Kofu can't outeat, unless maybe you're counting Gilbert Brown. Men travel days just to quiver at the terrible things he can do to a menu. Shop-keepers see him coming down the street and immediately start hand-cranking down the steel shutters.

You look at him, this 23-year-old man, not even filling out his shirt, born without benefit of a butt, his belt notched lightly at the first hole, and immediately you think, *Two Happy Meals, he's done.* When Nakajima humiliated the 360-pounder, former champ Ed (the Animal) Krachie of Queens, New York, at last year's Nathan's Famous contest, Krachie was reduced to crumbs. "I'm dumb-founded on how someone that small can do it," Krachie declared.

"It is a secret," Nakajima says of his gift. "If I told you, you might beat me." The mind shudders. What could it be? Japanese microtechnology? He is a black belt in judo. Maybe it's a Zen thing. "Concentration, yes, is most important," he says.

Maybe it's his training. Before a contest, he will eat a lunch of 10 to 12 bowls of ramen every day for two weeks—yet he can't put on weight. There were rumors that he had a surgically installed super-stomach, until he was examined on the steps of New York's City Hall. "It is only that I hate to lose," Nakajima says.

We couldn't resist. We bought him a Jethro Bodine–sized bowl of ramen and asked for just a glimpse of his greatness. We handed him some chopsticks. We took a step back. As he broke them apart and began feeling their weight in his hands, a tingle came over us. This was Ted Williams with the pine tar, Horowitz warming up on scales, a Kennedy fingering the drink list.

Suddenly, he summoned a huge glob of noodles to his over-sized maw and Hoovered them down with sickening speed, as though some-thing horrible deep inside him were pulling furiously at the noodles, hand over fist. There was no chewing. There was no swallowing. The noodles were just *gone.* The bowl was empty in 30 seconds. He dabbed at a small droplet on his chin, smiled and bowed slightly in apology. If you want just a quick bite for lunch, Nakajima-san is your man.

Me, I'd bet the kitchen that on the Fourth somebody at Coney Island will be placing a mustard-yellow belt around the waist of the Black Hole of Kofu.

If I were the presenter, I would take off my rings and jewelry first.

POSTSCRIPT: *I've only seen Mr. Nakajima once since that day. It was on an MTV rock video. The producers filmed him devouring a jaw-dropping quantity of food, then used it in the video—backwards, so that this incredible string of food comes flying out of his mouth, emerging whole and intact. Hey, it's good work if you can stomach it.*

What's Not to Like?

JANUARY 10, 2000—My 12-year-old came down to breakfast, stole the sports page from under my eggs and said, "So, Pops, who you dissin' this week?"

I gave him my hurt-and-stunned look.

He stuffed a half box of Frosted Flakes in his mouth and said, "Yurnghh alghays rippinngh smmmbundy."

That's not true! Well, other than cheerleaders, hunters, baseball, the NBA, the BCS, the INS, the IOC, the NCAA, college jocks, pro jocks, Detroit, France, Little League and the 20th century. I told him he had me all wrong. I told him I love sports.

I told him I love the penalty box and starting blocks and "Rock, chalk, Jayhawk!" and NFL Films spirals and eye black and ear holes and slobbermouth tackles and multimillionaires piling on each other with glee and dignified CEOs sitting behind huge mahogany desks wearing Slippery Rock boxers and how the diamond explodes on you coming out of a stadium tunnel and long walks to the green with your putter and crossover dribbles so quick a mountain lion would gasp and broken bats and salt-stained hats and Minnesota Fats and Wrigley ivy and Fenway monsters and every blade at Augusta and DODGERS jerseys and IRV'S DELI jerseys and Crosley and Ebbets and Shibe and reverse 1½ somersault with 3½ twists from platforms most people wouldn't even climb and par out of the spinach and 30-second pickles and Saratoga mudders and the Albert brudders and super slo-mo and goal-to-go and "Yajustneverknow!" and the soft leaner in the lane and the 8 ball the hard way and how nobody eats peanuts in the shell except at baseball games and passing the hot dog eight seats down and the money eight seats back and "Hey, ump! Move around, yer killin' the grass!" and bloop singles and mixed doubles and triple OT and marathoners who run 4:48 *per mile* and 78-year-old women who average 4:48 per block but finish anyway and appreciative coyote hoots from the chair lift above and the strut of women sprinters and the way athletes just can't stand still for the national anthem and Student Body Left and Wide Right and Nebraska players diving for cover as Ralphie comes snorting by and women on bikes in flowing hair racing the bus to the corner and 85-year-old men in white playing tennis at one mph for the price of half an egg-salad sandwich and kids going, "How come you always get to be Jagr?" and the way a new Wilson Jet basketball feels straight out of the box and Stickum and pick 'ems and "Who needs one?" and two-hand touch and three-and-out and four-baggers and "Through the five hole!" and seeing the breath of everybody in the stadium at once and "Thanks for stopping by the booth" and "Dadgum, I just gotta thank this Fram filter Champion spark plug Goodrich tire crew of mine" and "My second favorite team is who's ever playin' Texas" and bricks and bombs and bullets and the freshman fall football banquet and trap blocks and swim moves and alligator arms and the way the holder catches it, sets it down and spins it perfectly in one eighth of a second *every time* and how you still play Beat Bill Bradley in the driveway and it has nothing to do with the New Hampshire primary and hangin' the net and coffin corners and Madden and Summerall and a big bowl of Cheez Doodles and the Packers' logo and a 165-pound punt returner under a 50-foot-high, 50-yard punt in horizontal rain with half the nation watching and half a dozen 230-pound greenied-up men very anxious to see the inside of his neck and "Who's your Daddy?" and "Hi, Mom!" and catching a foul ball with one hand without spilling the beer in the other and writers banging out a 14-inch lead and a 12-inch sidebar in 25 minutes in a meat-locker-cold press box and "Red hots!" and orange segments and the Green Sheet and suicide squeezes and sudden death and the 100-yard war and everybody gets to go home anyway and Tour juice and the amazing thrill of a McGwire pop-up to short and "He's got *absolutely* no shot here, Jimmy" and four tires, 20 gallons and a ham sandwich in 18 seconds and "Thaaaaare goes Rusty!" and "gunga galunga" and the bell and the buzzer and the beep of the Olympic downhill starting gate and all the stuff that makes you forget the Visa bill and the leaky radiator and the second mortgage long enough to tingle.

My son gave me his hurt-and-stunned look.

"Dad?" he said.

"What?"

"You still hate the Yankees, right?"

"More than ever."

We hugged.

POSTSCRIPT: *Slippery Rock University sent me a pair of Slippery Rock boxers after this ran. Tragically, I've heard nothing from the Cheez Doodle people.*

CHAPTER THREE: REALITY

CHAPTER THREE: REALITY

The Big Hero of Littleton

MAY 3, 1999—As usual, coach Dave Sanders spent Tuesday of last week at Columbine High hanging around the kids.

One kept constant pressure on the gaping gunshot wounds in Sanders's shoulders, using T-shirts off other kids' backs. Another made a pillow from kids' sweatshirts for his head. Others covered his shivering body with more shirts.

Outside the science room bullets and shrapnel were still flying, but inside, where Sanders lay, the kids were quietly keeping him talking, conscious, alive.

"Who's this?" they whispered, going through his wallet, showing him his own pictures.

"My . . . wife . . . Linda," he said with what little breath he had. They asked him about the pictures of his daughters Angela and Coni. They asked him about coaching the Columbine girls' basketball team. They asked him about coaching the girls' softball team. They asked him about all of the boys' and girls' teams he used to coach. A man coaches just about every team at a school over 25 years, there's a lot to cover.

Every high school has a Coach Sanders, the giving one, the joking one, the one who sets up the camps, sacrifices his nights to keep the gym open, makes sure the girls have the weight room to themselves twice a week. RUN, GUN, AND HAVE FUN is what the girls' basketball team T-shirts said last season and it worked. The Rebels had their best record in a decade. So when he ran into the cafeteria on Tuesday morning at 11:30, his face bright red, and yelled, "Get out! Get out! They're shooting!" the hundreds of kids in there took him seriously.

Some people believe Sanders saved the lives of more than 200 kids that day. Witnesses say he led many to the kitchen, to the auditorium, to safety. "He saved my life," says Brittany Davies, one of his jayvee basketball players, "and then he kept running, cutting across the lunchroom, telling people to get down. He left himself in the open where he could get shot."

Columbine English teacher Cheryl Lucas told the *Rocky Mountain News*, "He was the most responsible for saving a bunch of lives. . . . They would've been sitting ducks if not for Mr. Sanders." But that wasn't enough for Sanders. There must have been a dozen ways out of the cafeteria to safety. Instead, he ran upstairs to warn more kids.

"I was standing in the science room, looking out the window [in the door leading to the hall]," says Greg Barnes, a varsity basketball player. "Then I saw Coach Sanders turn around, take two shots, right in front of me. Blood went flying off him and he fell."

Sanders got up and staggered into the science room. Teeth were knocked out when he fell. Blood was pouring from his shoulders and chest. A roomful of kids leaped back. Eagle Scout Aaron Hancey, a junior who videotapes boys' basketball games, began applying pressure to the wounds.

An hour went by. The gunmen had tried to enter the room next to the science room but couldn't. Hancey talked to police on the science room phone, telling them where he and the others were, that Coach Sanders was badly wounded. The police said a SWAT team was coming.

A second hour went by. Someone crept to a science room window facing the parking lot and held up a sign that read 1 BLEEDING TO DEATH. Still, no SWAT team. No fire ladder to the window. No chopper.

Three hours and nothing. The kids in the science room weren't hearing explosions anymore, but they dared not run for it. They figured the killers could be anywhere. How could they know that the killers had been dead for more than an hour?

Somehow, Sanders stayed alive, despite losing body heat, blood and breath. "He was a brave man," says Hancey. "He hung in there. He was a tough guy."

Finally, after 3½ hours, a SWAT team burst in. One member said he'd wait with Sanders until a stretcher came. "Even if they'd gotten him out then," says Hancey, "I think he would've made it."

Outside, in the hollow-eyed afternoon, there came a rumor that Sanders was in surgery at a Denver hospital. For hours Linda and the girls frantically called area hospitals. Nothing. Finally, at about 9 p.m., Angela went live on a Denver TV station and pleaded, "Does anybody know where my father is?"

Her father was still in that science room. He died by the time paramedics reached him. He died a couple hundred yards from 300 cops and dozens of ambulances. Only the kids in that terrifying room heard his last words: "Tell my girls I love them."

Everybody said Dave Sanders lived for kids.

Should've known he'd die for them, too.

It Doesn't Get Any Tougher Than This

AUGUST 23, 1999—The toughest coach who ever lived is not Rockne or Lombardi or Parcells.

The toughest coach who ever lived is skinny as a foul pole, won't step on spiders and wears pigtails.

The toughest coach who ever lived is a 110-pound wisp, Dawn Anna, who twice now should've died on the operating table, only to live through something tenfold worse.

Anna, 49, the girls' volleyball coach for the past seven seasons at Columbine High, has something in her brain that makes her world spin every waking hour. A divorced mother of four who has remarried, she has coached while holding an IV bag in one arm as it dripped medication into the other. She has coached when she couldn't feel half her face, when the gym went black, when she felt like throwing up. But those weren't the tough days.

The tough days started on April 20. That's when she found out that last year's captain, Lauren Townsend, the school's 4.0 valedictorian, had been murdered while studying in the school library. Lauren was Dawn's youngest child.

"You know, I always told my kids to be careful crossing the street, and I told them to be careful riding their bikes," says Dawn, "but I never thought to tell them to be careful studying in the library."

That Dawn even had Lauren pretty much broke the bookmakers. Two times during the pregnancy doctors told Dawn they feared she had miscarried. In the delivery room they said extensive hemorrhaging should've killed her and her baby. Didn't. A year later Dawn was teaching Lauren to walk, urging her on, arms wide open.

In 1993 Dawn's world started rolling like a fun house barrel. Doctors found a jumbled mass of blood vessels in her cerebellum. During a preoperative procedure her carotid artery was inadvertently cut, and Dawn could see blood pooling fast on her shoulder. The doctors said she could've died. Didn't. As part of her recovery from brain surgery, Dawn had to learn to walk again. This time, Lauren taught *her*, urging her on, arms wide open.

Even though the dizziness remained, Dawn went on to become one of the better volleyball coaches in the state. Four years ago Columbine won its first girls' volleyball conference championship in 20 seasons. After that, with Lauren as their best blocker, the Rebels didn't finish below fourth in the 10-team conference.

Last summer, just before Lauren's senior season, doctors cut Dawn open, hipbone to hipbone, to remove ovarian cysts. That should've stopped her. Didn't. Two months before she was supposed to start coaching again, she was coaching again. Columbine didn't win it all last season, but Dawn's players got the award for the highest combined GPA of all 5A girls' volleyball teams in the state: 3.89. "I kept coaching because I wanted to be with Lauren," Dawn says. Yeah, well, who didn't? Lauren was everybody's friend. Honors Society. Worked daily at a small-animal hospital, even on Christmas and Easter.

Then came that morning in April: Lauren and her friends sitting at the front table in the library, explosions shaking them, Lauren saying, "This is a *wicked* senior prank," finding out how wicked it really was, hiding under the table but not nearly well enough and taking 11 bullets from both gunmen. *This* was the jock the shooters wanted?

This week Columbine started practicing under a new coach and a new captain. After last season Dawn had decided to quit to help Lauren during her first year at Colorado State. This was the week she was going to move Lauren into her dorm. Instead, Dawn, tougher than a Woolworth steak, is finding new ways to cope. "It's life," she says, red-eyed. "It's not supposed to be smooth. Everything bad that's happened has always had something good come out of it. It's just, with Lauren, we're still trying to figure out what that is."

Well, how about this?: There are plans to use a memorial fund in Lauren's name (303-778-7587) for a college scholarship to be given annually to a Columbine student. And Dawn has dedicated herself to helping make other people's kids safe in other libraries. "There're too many guns out there," she says. "*Way* too many."

Meantime, there's another mass of vessels, this time on Dawn's brain stem. Maybe it will kill her, but probably it won't. She's ready either way. "Those first two times, I think God was preparing me for Lauren's death," she says. "I found out death is calm and peaceful. That's why I know Lauren didn't suffer."

When the toughest coach finally goes, may she arrive in a place that sits perfectly still. And may her captain be waiting there, urging her on, arms wide open.

POSTSCRIPT: *Columbine was personal for our family. We lived a half mile from the high school for six years. I played softball with guys who had kids at the school that day. We know emergency room nurses who had to try and save those kids' lives. Cops who had to push parents back. During this interview with Dawn Anna, I wept. It's the only time it's happened in more than 20 years of journalism. May it never happen in your town.*

The Longest Yard for Doak Walker

MAY 18, 1998—Before there was *Dateline, Nightline, Outside the Lines, Inside Edition, 60 Minutes* and *48 Hours,* there were heroes.

They were handsome and swift, and we knew just enough about them to keep them as gods. They played offense and defense and kicked and punted and dated the homecoming queen, and that was enough. They didn't go on Leno or Oprah, and they never cried on Roy Firestone. You only saw them on magazine covers and in newsreels, and on the back of your eyelids when you slept because all you wanted to be was them.

That man, lying so still there, learning how to talk again, he was one. He's Doak Walker, and he was as golden as golden gets. He had perfectly even, white teeth and a jaw as square as a deck of cards and a mop of brown hair that made girls bite their necklaces. He was so shifty you couldn't have tackled him in a phone booth, yet so humble that he wrote the Associated Press a thank-you note for naming him an All-America. Come to think of it, he was a three-time All-America, twice one of the Outstanding Players in the Cotton Bowl, a four-time All-Pro. He appeared on 47 covers, including *Life, Look* and *Collier's.* One time, Kyle Rote, another gridiron golden boy, saw a guy buying a football magazine at a newsstand. "Don't buy *that* one," Rote said. "It's not official. It doesn't have a picture of Doak Walker on the cover."

Fifty years ago they gave Doak Walker the Heisman Trophy because who the hell else were they going to give it to? That season he was among the nation's finest in rushing, passing, punting, punt returning, kick returning, field goals, extra points and interceptions. The Cotton Bowl added more than 20,000 seats just so more people could see him. He led SMU to two straight Southwest Conference championships. After a game he'd come out of the locker room in a coat and tie, hug his girlfriend, who really was the homecoming queen, and take her for a malted. Thirty million mothers sighed.

That's why Doak Walker, *motionless*, can't possibly be. Are you saying that the man who won two NFL titles with the Detroit Lions, who was inducted into the college and pro football halls of fame, is a *quadriplegic*? Are you saying somebody finally stopped Doak Walker?

What gets you is that it was an intermediate ski slope. Doak Walker never did anything intermediate. He was a wonderful skier, one of the best at Steamboat Ski Resort, along with his wife, the former Skeeter Werner, an Olympian. But there he was, on the last day of January this year, on a slope called Rainbow, carving those beautiful giant arcs of his, when he hit a change in the rolling terrain and traveled 20 to 30 feet in the air. He fell forward and tumbled, severely bruising his brain stem. When the first skiers arrived, he had no pulse. Luckily, one of them was a dentist who knew CPR.

Doak Walker is at Craig Hospital in Denver now and, at 71, working harder than ever. He speaks through a tube and he's up to four words now: *yes, no* and *thank you*. But the eyes are still bright, and when he disagrees with you he sticks out his tongue. Here's a guy who in college and the pros gained close to 10,000 all-purpose yards—most of them effortlessly—yet you wonder what he'd give now to run just one foot of that.

Doak Walker doesn't want people to make a fuss over him. He never was much for fusses. Still, it's unthinkable. One of the most vital, virile men in American sports history, a guy football barely left a mark on, will have to learn how to sip and puff on a straw to get his wheelchair around. Some Rainbow this turned out to be.

There's a little hope that he might get back some movement. But he's going to have to have his house redone—lower sinks, wider doorways, showers he can wheel into. Long-term care is going to cost a small mutual fund, so proceeds from this year's Walker-Lundquist Steamboat Invitational golf tournament will go to the Doak Walker Rehabilitation Fund.

Anyway, the point of all this is just to let you know that every day isn't Saturday in the open field anymore for number 37. A lot of days are fourth-and-11, actually. So, if you think of it, write

Doak Walker. The fax machine is right down the hall, 303-789-8330, and he reads every message.

Tell him he's still your hero. After all, everybody likes a thank-you note.

POSTSCRIPT: *Craig Hospital received so many messages, that fax machine broke. Whatever good it did, it wasn't enough. Walker was released a month or so later and started to stare into a future that he could never live with. His closest friends knew he was terribly depressed. They say he just gave up. He died only weeks later—on September 27, 1998.*

When Your Dream Dies

DECEMBER 26, 1994–JANUARY 2, 1995—On a refrigerated, color-less Saturday morning in the no-McDonald's town of Walnut, Ill., Kenny Wilcoxen walked along the street carrying the letter he had waited for his whole life, the one that meant that after 20 years he was finally going to ref the state high school football finals. On the other side of the letter, written neatly in blue ink, was his suicide note.

Unblinking, Kenny made his way past the simple little white two-story houses with the big backyards, turned right at Main Street, walked a block and then turned left, passing the one-story Walnut Grade School, where all the kids, K through 8, knew him as the gym teacher, as Coach. Every kid he taught got a nickname: Gerdie for Sharon Gerdes's kid; Tuffy for Brandon Rhodes, his cen-terfielder; Sarge for Chris Tornow. Kenny was also head coach of the three boys' basketball teams and assistant coach of the track team, the man in charge of the summer baseball programs and the coach of his son's Little League team. When he was dead, personnel was going to have a real headache trying to replace him.

He was handsome and sturdy, 36 years old, with a mustache and a wrestler's build. The cold didn't bother him, but he did keep checking the righthand pocket of his Chicago Bears windbreaker for the 98 penicillin and 50 ibuprofen pills he had put there. He was wearing his lucky Chicago Cubs hat. In his right hand he carried a half-empty bottle of Mountain Dew to help the pills go down.

He walked around the front of the school, past the basketball courts, past the baseball field, the one he had helped to till and flatten, and back to the maintenance shed that doubled as the concession stand. He unlocked the door with his key, closed it behind him, turned on the light and sat on the big John Deere mowing tractor, the one he used all spring and summer to cut the soccer, football and baseball fields. Maybe it was weird, but dying on top of that tractor didn't seem so bad. Of all the things he did in Walnut, population 1,200, it was riding the mower that he loved best. Maybe it was because that was the only time he could sit and think without hearing the phone ringing or a mom ragging him about her son's playing time or some dad screaming at him because the man figured his kid gets 2½ steps on a layup. Besides, Kenny loved the smell of cut grass, and he loved the perfect lines the mower made, back and forth, forth and back. And if he made a mistake, if the lines weren't quite parallel, he could always go back and fix them.

That was the problem with Kenny Wilcoxen. He liked things perfect. The Magic Markers in his drawer at work all had to face the same way. The pencils had to go the other way. He was a card-carrying double-checker of locks. Close it. Lock it. Check it. Step back. Check it again. At home the washing machine was in perpetual use because Kenny hated to have dirty clothes just *lying* there in a hamper. The family calendar was done up in glorious, fastidious Technicolor—red for Kenny's coaching, blue for his refereeing, black for his school meetings. Everything under control.

But in the last week, life just seemed to spin out of control. It seemed there was no way to go back and fix things. And that's how he came to be in the shed, taking a deep breath and then a big glug of the Mountain Dew and dropping the pills in his mouth, fistfuls at a time. He went through all the soda to get them down. Then he started up the tractor and waited to die.

And all because he blew a big call.

When he was asked why Kenny did it, Randy Rimington, his basketball refereeing partner, said, "You've got to understand Kenny. For some of us, refereeing is just kind of a strange way to relax. For Kenny, it was his whole life. He was *born* into it." Kenny's father, Larry, is a renowned ref in the world of north-central Illinois high school sports. Get this: Larry has made it to the finals in four sports. Four sports! It takes at least 20 years for a ref to get to a final in any *one* sport. Most guys spend a lifetime and never get asked at all. But Kenny's dad made it in football, boys' basketball, girls' basketball and baseball. He is in the Illinois Basketball Coaches Hall of Fame. This year he got a plaque, presented by Kenny, for reffing his 5,000th high school varsity game for the Illinois High School Association (IHSA). Even Larry's license plate echoes his legend: IHSA SF 4.

Most guys try officiating when they can't play anymore, but even when Kenny was still playing he wanted to be a ref. He started umping Little League games at 16. He stayed with it until one day he looked up and he was officiating one sport or another 250 to 300 nights a year. He kept all his ref bookings in neat little datebooks—where he had to be, when he had to be there and exactly what time he could expect to get home. When each year ended, he saved the little datebook in a box, just like his dad did.

Kenny's pretty blonde wife, Melissa, could go weeks without seeing him anywhere but at the breakfast table. She tried everything to keep him home—tears, anger, aloofness—but nothing helped. The pull of the legend was too strong. "I've always thought games were too important to Kenny," Melissa says. "Not just state tournament games. Any game."

He had driven his little 1985 sky-blue Chevy Nova to games in ice storms, through snowdrifts and despite tornado warnings. One night it took him four hours to get home. "I've never called [a school] and said I couldn't make it," Kenny liked to say. "Never once." Nor did he call and say, "I forgot—I have the kids' recital" or "It's my wife's birthday" or "I'm sick." The gym teacher never *got* sick. For crying out loud, even as he lay overdosed in the hospital and the nurses searched madly for a single medical record of his, none was found. The man never even had a regular doctor.

In early November, the day Kenny got that letter from the IHSA, Melissa knew what it was from 100 yards. Didn't even have to read it. She saw Kenny coming up the street, making the block-and-a-half walk from their home to Hardware Hank's, where she works. He was bouncing along like a kindergartner, the letter in his hand.

He flung himself through the door with a grin on his face, holding the letter in front of him like a steering wheel, tilting it giddily from side to side, making it dance.

"Is that it?" she screeched.

"Yeah!" he yelped.

His football crew's ratings were among the best of the 175 crews in the state, and that meant they were "going downstate," which is what Illinois high school sports fans call making the state finals. Kenny had never made state as an athlete, but now he would as a ref. He would do a championship game. Might be Class 1A, the smallest schools. Might be Class 6A, the biggest. Didn't matter. He and the crew were going to "walk on the carpet," which is what refs call working a game in Normal, on the AstroTurf field at Illinois State's Hancock Stadium. Paradise found.

Kenny had been there only twice, and he had put his nose up to a fence and looked at the turf. He could have gone in the stadium. The gate was open. But it wouldn't have been the same. When he took his walk on the carpet, he wanted it to be in his black-and-whites.

Now he would have one more playoff game to do, Durand at Stockton, Class 1A (fewer than 313 kids), both teams undefeated, and then he would do a semifinal game, and then—can you believe it?—*downstate*. He made his hotel plans.

It was a 65-mile drive to Stockton that Saturday, Nov. 12. Kenny never minded the long drives. "When you coach, you get all the complaints afterward. You never leave it," he told his old high school coach, Dave McFadden. "But when I ref, I get in my car and drive home. It never follows you home."

He took his 11-year-old son, Kris, along to be the ball boy.

This was Kenny's 25th playoff game—he kept track of that, too. Unfortunately, this would be the worst. There were five or six very tough calls in the game. Once Durand fumbled and Stockton fell on the ball, only to have the crew rule that the ballcarrier had been down. Most of the tough calls, though, seemed to go against Durand.

With Durand leading 14–8 and 45 seconds left to play, Stockton quarterback Jesse Brandt heaved one about 50 yards toward the corner of the end zone and wide receiver Matt Leitzen. Leitzen was actually a backup quarterback who was filling in at wideout because of an injury to the regular starter. Fact is, Leitzen had never caught a pass in a game. Durand's man in coverage was Jason Smith. "I thought he was two or three feet out-of-bounds," Smith said later. "I didn't even think of jumping for the ball, he was so far out. I knew the referee was there." The ref was Kenny, in perfect position. He thought he saw Leitzen extend his arms fully and make the catch with his left foot inbounds. Kenny signaled touchdown. Stockton missed the extra point. Tie game, 14–14.

"Whew, boy," Kenny yelled to his crewmates as they set up for the kickoff. "He was lucky he got that one foot in. If this was pro, it wouldn't have counted."

In the overtime a Stockton running back broke through left tackle at the Durand 10-yard line, was hit at about the three and dived for the end zone. Linesman Andy Yowell signaled touchdown. Game over. Stockton wins.

There was the usual screaming, and the walk to the officials' changing room got a little dicey, but it was nothing unprecedented. Nor was there anything unusual in the postgame wrap-up on FM 92 in nearby Freeport, which Kenny and Kris heard on the car radio. Two of the hosts discussed Kenny's touchdown call but didn't make much of it. Sixty-five miles and a $70 paycheck later, Kenny told Melissa, "It was crazy tonight."

Meanwhile, in Rockford, near Durand, three TV stations showed Kenny's touchdown call, and two ran a slow-motion replay. The replay showed that Leitzen never did get his foot down and was, in fact, out-of-bounds by eight inches. One station also showed a replay of Stockton's overtime touchdown that suggested the runner was down at the two and lost control of the ball before recovering it in the end zone. The TV sports reports mentioned that several other calls by the officials had been close.

At about 11:15 that night Durand's athletic director, Jeff Pinker, called Kenny's crew chief, Don Cook, at home to ask if he had seen any of the replays. Pinker also wanted to let Cook know that at Durand's Lakeside Oak Rail Lounge, where patrons had seen the replays on TV, there was a lot of grumbling going on. "I don't think anybody is going to do anything stupid," Pinker told Cook. "But you never know about people these days." Just trying to be helpful.

Kenny didn't see the replays, but by Monday he started hearing things. More important, the phone started ringing in his little white two-story in Walnut, and it kept ringing over the next couple of days. Usually Melissa or one of the kids answered it, since Kenny was often out teaching or coaching. The rest of the messages ended up on the answering machine.

"I have a problem with your husband's blatant calls," one woman told Melissa. She told the woman to call the IHSA and hung up. The next caller said Kenny was "incompetent." The next call was much worse. Melissa tried to laugh it off. "You know, I'm havin' *fun* hangin' up on these people," she said. But the calls kept coming.

By Tuesday, Pinker had fired off a bulky package to Don Robinson, the IHSA's head of officials, including tape from two of the TV stations plus a long letter citing, among other things, evidence that a Durand touchdown that had been disallowed in the second quarter probably should have been allowed. Pinker, who has been involved in high school football for more than 20 years, including 10 as a ref, wrote, "In my entire career, on any level, I have never seen this many major mistakes in one game." He strongly urged Robinson to yank the crew off its assignment downstate. "I would feel it a real injustice if any other team or town would have to go through what we have," he said. The letter was also signed by Durand's superintendent of schools. Meanwhile, Durand's principal began looking for a counselor to deal with the emotions of distraught players. Parents of eight of the nine departing seniors wrote a letter of protest to the IHSA and sent copies off to a few local newspapers.

On Wednesday things seemed much better for Kenny. The packet came from the IHSA with his parking pass and tickets and I.D. tag for the state finals. His dad visited him at the school to look at the tag and beam. Larry had worked the very first state football finals exactly 20 years earlier. Now his boy was going to walk on the carpet too.

But that morning, down in Bloomington, Robinson was undoing all that. The head of officials had looked at the tapes, read the complaint from Pinker and decided to take Cook's crew off the finals. "If this had been one call, it would have been a reprimand," Robinson said. "But it was three calls that were clearly in error, and they all led to scores or elimination of scores." Robinson called Cook, who was shaken by the news. Cook had been reffing for 27 years and never been to a final. Robinson told him the decision had been made "for the good of the playoffs."

Cook agreed to call the rest of the crew. Fun job. Kraig Kniss, who had been reffing for 15 years, was rattled when he got his call that same morning. Andy Yowell, a ref for 21 years, said the news hit him "like a brick alongside the head." Since Cook couldn't get hold of Kenny, he called Kenny's parents and told his mom, Judy. She couldn't bring herself to tell her husband until midafternoon, and then the two of them got in the car and went looking for Kenny.

It was about four o'clock, which meant that Kenny and Melissa were on their daily walk. When Larry's car pulled up, they stopped. Larry got out of the car and looked at Kenny a second and said, "You're off."

"What do you mean?" Kenny said.

"You're not going downstate. You're not working this Saturday or the state finals."

They all climbed into the car to talk about it. Before long Kenny and Melissa got out, and Kenny just started walking. Fast. Hard as she tried, loud as she yelled, Melissa couldn't get him to slow down.

That night Kenny didn't eat. That was very weird, for him not to eat. He was an eater of prodigious proportions. He liked to mix his salad dressings—ranch, Catalina and Thousand Island—into a phantasmagoria of flavors. Or he would glop Heinz 57, A-1 and Worcestershire sauces together and move in on a steak.

Now, nothing. Melissa got so worried she called Durand's football coach, John Schwab, and asked if there was any way he could get his fans to get off Kenny's back. He said he would. Oh, and one other thing. "I think Ken got followed home that night," he told her. "Two men." Word was, the men sat outside the Wilcoxens' for two hours before finally driving off. What do you know about that? Refereeing finally followed Kenny home.

The rumor, which would later turn out to be false, terrified Kenny. He remembered going on a walk with Melissa that night and leaving the kids home alone for half an hour. Were the men out there then? He would later tell Melissa that he "kept having visions of coming home some night to a family shot to death," she recalls.

After that, Kenny seemed to go into a small, dark place where you just couldn't find him.

Officials in the area complained to Robinson about his decision to remove Cook's crew. "If it were a rules interpretation or we were out of position, we should get our butts chewed," said Kniss, the umpire on the crew. "But these were judgments. You see it and you respond. That's it."

Nothing could lift Kenny's spirits. He told Melissa he might just quit officiating altogether. "Honey, don't let them win," she said. "If you quit, they'd win." She unhooked the phone and the answering machine, but she couldn't unhook the mailman. On Thursday a letter arrived from a woman in Durand. Kenny opened it. "She said he must not have any feeling for kids," Melissa remembers. "She told him maybe he should retire from officiating. That letter hit him the hardest. Every one of those words were like knives to Kenny, stabbing him."

He began to kick off his shoes and leave them in the middle of the floor, a previously unthinkable act. There was *laundry* undone. Melissa called four of Kenny's friends and asked them to try and talk to him. "Please," she said. "He's not himself."

On Saturday, Melissa left for work at seven. Kenny ate no breakfast. He sat and read the Peoria *Journal Star* sports page, where he saw the matchups for the day's big semifinal game, Byron at Rock Ridge, the one he was supposed to call, the one he had *earned* the right to call. *This isn't right*, he thought to himself. *I should be leaving right now for Rock Ridge. Hour-and-a-half drive. Get there an hour and a half early. I should be going. I should be on the road right now.* Then he put down the paper, went upstairs and got out his packet from the state office—the parking pass, the I.D. tag, the ticket for Melissa. He stared at them, fingered them, studied them. He realized it would be the first time in his life that his little datebook had lied. The lines weren't parallel anymore. Everything was coming out crooked.

It was then that something inside him just gave in, just sort of clicked off. He got the IHSA letter that he had filed so neatly in his filing cabinet in the bedroom, sat down, picked up a pen and turned the letter over.

"To everyone I love," he wrote. "I'm sorry for what I've put you through. All this harassment is my fault. When I'm not here, it will stop." He apologized to "the whole crew, for getting us pulled off state." He told his family how much he would miss them. He told Melissa, "I love you more now than the day we were married." He told his parents he loved them. Then he thanked Rimington and the football crew and a whole lot of other officials and signed the letter, "I love you all, Ken."

He walked to the bathroom closet. He opened the door and stared. He thought to himself, Should I do this or not? What good was he now to his family? To his town? An embarrassment. What good was he to his crew? To himself? To his dad? A disappointment. What was he to his wife? To his kids? A danger. He saw a bottle of penicillin and a bottle of ibuprofen. He flicked off the caps and emptied both bottles into his pocket, flipping the empties into the trash can. He walked downstairs and found the open Mountain Dew in the fridge. He walked by his daughter, eight-year-old Anna, and told her he was going out for a walk.

He slipped out the back sliding glass door and off the porch and hurried down the block, late for the cemetery.

The ref is a bum. He is a sightless, soulless, gutless bum who needs to be told that One Hour Optical stays open late now. You pay for your ticket, you get to scream at the ref. That's half the fun. He is a brainless oaf who ought to move around a little out there because he's killing the grass. He should be booed when he walks on the field, and he should leave under a shower of ice cubes. He is a no-good wannabe jock who usually requires a state-trooper escort off the field and into a little room somewhere, where we forget about him until the next time.

Across American sports, across towns, across generations, that is one thing that never changes, and it didn't change for Kenny Wilcoxen. As a kid he once saw a man go on the basketball court and smash his dad on the shoulder with an arm wrapped in a cast. "You're the reason we have juvenile delinquents in this country!" the man yelled. Kenny's father had been spat upon, jeered at, booed and ridiculed. One time Kenny asked, "Dad, why do you do it?" And his father said, "That's their right, son." And so Kenny grew to accept hate as part of the job, and the hate never seemed to bother him. He pursued officiating with every ounce of obsession inside him.

When the obsession was stifled, when the hate finally got to him, Kenny found himself in a little shelter, trying to poison himself and escape from the fans and parents and coaches, from purple screaming faces and the mailman and the answering machine. Things would get back to normal soon. He figured they would find him by dusk. The services would be Monday at Walnut Methodist. Rimington would get someone to fill in for him on Tuesday at the Kewanee–Wethersfield basketball tournament.

After about 25 minutes he started feeling dizzy, and his legs started getting numb. His skin got cold and clammy. He could feel himself going, and it scared him a little.

And then, for no reason at all, he heard Melissa's voice.

"Don't let them win," she was saying. "Don't let them win."

It was so clear that he looked around the shed to see if she were really there. Suddenly, the reality of what he was doing hit him. *This is dumb*, he thought. He slid queasily off the tractor and made his way to the door, staggering out into the late-November sunshine, heading toward that voice at Hardware Hank's, about a quarter mile away.

His right leg wasn't cooperating. He was having to drag it along. The park was circling around him like a carousel. After a while he realized he could never make it all that way, and he turned in another direction, toward the soccer field and maybe the houses up on the hill.

Who knows why Dave McFadden decided to take his dogs out back just then? The dogs had been in the front yard, where McFadden was helping his wife put up Christmas lights, but suddenly he got the urge to go out back and let the dogs run. When he went around the house, he caught sight of somebody out of the corner of his eye, an elderly person having trouble walking. He turned his attention back to the dogs. No, wait, it's a drunk. A drop-dead drunk on Saturday morning. What a world. No, wait, it's Ken Wilcoxen. And at that moment Kenny fell straightforward into the grass, still holding the letter in his hand.

McFadden's wife called emergency while McFadden ran down the hill and turned Kenny over. "God, Kenny, what have you done?" he screamed. He began to cry. He yelled at Kenny the way he had yelled at him when he coached him. "You're tougher than this! You're a fighter!" Kenny was incoherent, except for one thing he kept repeating: "I don't think I locked it." The shed door.

Walnut has no hospital and no paramedics. There is only a loud emergency whistle that pierces the town. But Walnut has volunteers like Skinny Andersen, who sells ambulances, and Sharon Gerdes, who lives up by the Tastee Freeze, and Mike Howlett, who ran to the fire station and jumped in one of the town's two ambulances. In less than five minutes Gerdes and Andersen and Howlett and about a dozen other volunteers came flying up the street and got Kenny on a stretcher. They set off for Perry Memorial Hospital in Princeton, a 20-mile drive. They all knew Kenny. Hell, he'd coached two of Mike's kids. And now, with no doctor and not much equipment on hand, they had to get him to the hospital before he died.

At Hardware Hank's the whistle made Melissa's heart lurch. When she saw the ambulance go past her window, she felt a cold wind inside her chest. But when the ambulance didn't turn down her street and instead headed toward the school, she relaxed and let her shoulders down.

Within five minutes, though, Kris had called and told her that two men had come rushing through the door of their house, gone upstairs and come down with two empty pill bottles. "Where's your father?" Melissa asked.

"Oh, he told Anna he was gonna go on a walk," Kris said.

Melissa felt a pain in her stomach.

As the ambulance sped out of town, Gerdes started trying to save Kenny's life. Her 13-year-old, Nick, was on Kenny's eighth-grade team. Nick was kind of like Kenny, actually—the kid with All-Pro expectations for himself and All-Pine talent. Kenny could relate. He had spent so much time on the bench during his high school basketball career that when the bench broke and was going to be thrown out, he asked for a piece of it, used it to make a plaque and hung it in his office. "Every time Nick did anything good, Kenny would praise him," said Sharon. "He'd always take the extra time to pat Nick on the back. Nick loved Kenny."

As Kenny drifted near unconsciousness, Gerdes slapped him, slapped him hard, shook him and pleaded with him. She knew she was supposed to keep him talking, and for some reason she knew exactly what to say.

"All the boys need you," she said. "*Nick* needs you." She said, "Don't you know what you mean to this town? Don't you know how important you are to us? Kenny, we all love you. The kids all love you, Kenny."

Come to think of it, inside most every house and store and machine shop and farmhouse they drove by on their way out of Walnut, there was somebody who had been coached or taught or reffed or helped by Kenny Wilcoxen. They sped past Mark Willis's old house. Remember? The awkward kid the other kids laughed at two years ago—until Kenny named him manager of the basketball team. And then of the track team. Who could forget graduation night that year, after all the big awards had been handed out, when Kenny called Mark up to the podium and gave him a surprise award? It was just an old shot that the shot-putters didn't use anymore. Kenny had inscribed Mark's name on it. Mark beamed like he had just lettered. Then he cried, right in front of everybody.

It was an idea that had never sneaked inside Kenny's brain before: *Don't you know what you mean to this town?* He had seen himself as a ref, the 250-nights-a-year man, the son of the great ref. He had forgotten what else he was—a teacher, a coach, a father, a friend to nearly every kid in town. It's funny, he had spent his whole life marking his calendar in three different colors, but he had really seen only one.

"After that," Kenny says now, "I wanted to make it."

At the hospital he was treated to prevent his kidneys from giving out because of the combination of the ibuprofen and all the potassium in the penicillin. His heart rate was flying. Outside, in the hall, his father was trying to get up the nerve to go in and see him. When Larry finally walked in the room, Kenny looked up with his face full of tubes and tape.

He whispered, "Sorry, Dad."

It took 26 hours in ICU and a whole lot of pacing and praying and hoping by Kenny's friends and family, but slowly his heart rate came down. And then a nurse told him a remarkable thing. "Mr. Wilcoxen," she said, "We want you to know something. You've broken all our records."

"For what?" he asked.

"Most people in the waiting room."

For they had jammed that tiny waiting room at Perry Memorial and spilled both ways down the hallway besides. Parents of kids he taught. Uncles of kids he coached. Refs and umps and back judges. Relatives. People Kenny had known his whole life. People whose kids he had taught to dribble and bunt and slide and run the down-and-out and pole-vault and skip rope. Kids on his teams. Families of the kids he taught every day. Grown young men he'd had in eighth grade. Mothers who never thought twice about turning their kids over to him summer after summer to learn to hit the cutoff man and to eat Popsicles after practice.

There was more when he went home on Monday: hundreds of

cards and letters, people thanking him for all he had done for their kids, feeling bad that they had never thought to thank him before. All the kids drew pictures for him, too, and nearly all of them signed the names he had given them. Gerdie. Little Willy. Tuffy.

"I guess I'd forgotten what all the kids meant to me," Kenny says today. "I was really amazed. I was amazed by everything, the cards and the people who called and all the nice things they wrote. You know, you go through life and you never think you make a difference in the lives of that many people. And then it just *hits* you."

It is a wonderful thing to be hit with. And in the stack there was the following letter from a 12-year-old:

> *Dear Coach,*
> *I have had you for a coach almost all of my years in school. . . . You are the one teacher who has meant the most in my life. You are also the teacher I respect the most. You are the teacher who, when I look back on my life, I'll say, "That's who I want to model my life after." You have taught me a lot not just about sports or school but about life.*
>
> *Derek Young*

Not bad for somebody with no feeling for kids.

Out in the north-central Illinois countryside, where the plains are so great and the towns so tiny that any little hillock can look like a mountain, losing your one dream can be too much to bear. Since that chilly Saturday morning when Kenny Wilcoxen tried to kill himself, two women in the area have succeeded, both with guns.

But Kenny is still looking down on the grass and loving every minute of it. The other day he woke up to a sleet storm, and he looked out his bedroom window and said, "What a terrific day!" Says Melissa with a smile, "I think he's going to be O.K."

There has been some fallout. Kris asked him, "Daddy, why did you want to die?" It's a good question, and the therapist they're seeing is working with the whole family on it. The answer is coming, bit by bit.

People in Durand are thinking things through a little, wondering how important games have become to them. Pinker insists his school did nothing wrong. "We *had* to report errors in judgment," he says. But the woman from Durand who wrote the wounding letter says she'll never write another. "Now when I go to games," she says, "I keep my mouth shut."

Maybe if there is a lesson in all of this, it is that there are real men under those black-and-white stripes, and they hear everything you say and feel every ice cube you throw. There are real hearts under there too. Some are even breakable. Maybe that's it. Maybe everybody just forgot that Kenny Wilcoxen was more than just something attached to a whistle. For sure, that is what he forgot.

"I'm going to start taking things one day at a time," he says. "Enjoy the mornings. Look up and see the sun shine. Enjoy every meal."

He has discovered that there are things his father did that he will never do. And vice versa. "One of my Babe Ruth teams went 17–0 and went to the county tournament," Kenny says proudly. "Dad never did *that*."

He sees all the colors on the calendar now. He knows what he means to his town and what the town means to him. The first day back at the school, a little kindergarten girl came running through the double doors, hugged his leg and said, "Coach, don't you ever try to leave me again."

"My wife was right," Kenny says. "If I'd have given up, that would have meant they won. It was a game. It's over. Life goes on. Her voice saved my life. And now I get to hear her voice all the time."

Well, not all the time. Kenny's little datebook is full through 1996, and Robinson has hinted that Kenny's crew may go to state next year. "If it happens, it happens," Kenny says. "I know right now that even though I didn't make it down there, I was *supposed* to be there. I've got my letter."

Kenny left the hospital that Monday and was working basketball games with Rimington on Tuesday and Wednesday night. Somebody at one game hollered, "You're so bad, you should have taken more pills!" but Kenny just tried to laugh it off. *That's their right, son.*

Yeah, reffing is still a Wilcoxen tradition. In fact, Larry is thinking now that someday all three Wilcoxen men could be on the football field together. After all, when Kris is 17, Larry will be only 64. "Wouldn't that be something?" says Larry. "Three Wilcoxens on one crew?"

Could happen. Lately, Kris has been slipping out the back sliding glass door and off the porch and hurrying to school wearing his grandfather's faded old referee's jacket.

[additional reporting by Lester Munson]

POSTSCRIPT: *To me, Ken Wilcoxen is George Bailey from* It's a Wonderful Life. *He's fine now, taking things easier, making this the happiest story I've ever written.*

Just Trying to Make an Indecent Wage

NOVEMBER 9, 1998—In Madison, Tenn., where 1,200 Peterbilt truck workers have been walking the picket lines for six months, they love the NBA labor dispute. It gives them something to finally laugh about.

They hear New York Knicks center Patrick Ewing walk up to the microphones and say, with a straight face, "We're fighting for our livelihood. We can't survive if we sign this contract," and it breaks them up. Last season Ewing made just under $100,000 per *basket*. When he still had a job, the average Peterbilt guy didn't make that much in two years.

They see where Boston Celtics guard Kenny Anderson whines that if things get any worse, he may have to sell one of his eight cars, and it tickles the workers' ribs. As the Peterbilt strike turned lockout continues, ribs are something the picketers are seeing a lot more of lately.

Every NBA gazillionaire with the gall to feel one gram sorry for himself needs to cart himself and his jewelry to Madison. According to union members, many of the workers have been evicted from their apartments or have lost their homes. People are living in relatives' basements, moving in with their kids, sleeping in shelters. "We've got families with five and six kids that we have to send down to United Way for meals," says Donna Dotts, a welder, "so I guess it's kind of hard to see how these basketball players need *more*."

Not that the players and the workers don't have a lot in common. NBA players want the minimum salary for veterans raised to around $1 million, superstars to be able to re-sign for upwards of $15 million without their teams' having to pay a luxury tax, and they want 60% of the league's gross revenues. The Peterbilt workers have outrageous demands, too. They're asking for a cost-of-living allowance, the company to kick in on some health insurance for pensioners and the chance to retire at a livable wage before 65.

Anderson let *The New York Times* get a look at his money woes last week. He was supposed to make $5.8 million this season, which works out to about a measly $3 million after taxes. But, hey, he's got expenses, don't forget, including $75,000 a year just to insure his fleet of Porsches, Range Rovers and Mercedes, and $150,000 yearly rent on his Beverly Hills crib (pool, tennis and basketball courts, four-car garage). Plus he helps support four children he has had by three women, including his wife, and he's *got* to have his $120,000 "hangin' around money," as he calls it. That leaves him with only $2 million a year to invest. "I have to start getting *tight*," Anderson said.

You'll forgive Larry Haynes if he doesn't throw Anderson a telethon. Haynes is a truck-cab assembler who's getting $405 a week in strike insurance and unemployment. Oh, he doesn't have Anderson's car-insurance problems, mostly because he has pawned two vehicles to pay his $500-a-month rent. He has a wife and two small kids, and he has already gone through his savings. Not that he doesn't have "hangin' around money." He allows $40 every two months so the family can have a big night out. "Like, we might go eat at Applebee's," he says.

C'mon, Larry, you have to start getting tight.

"I hear the NBA players talking about *struggling* and *barely surviving*," Haynes says. "Man, they don't know what real life is."

I think for most of us, the most difficult part of the NBA lockout is deciding which side we'd most like to see crushed by a comet. It's like a death match between Michael Bolton and Julio Iglesias. It'd be wonderful if, somehow, both sides could lose.

Until it's over, the owners and players need to shut up. They need to come out of their meetings, head for the microphones, smile hugely and say, "It's going pretty well. And even if it isn't, who cares? We're all richer than Oprah!" They need to stop bragging about how "united" they are. Yeah, it's easy to be united while on your cell phones in four-button Italian suits around the baccarat tables at Bellagio.

Try being united every morning down at the little union hall in Madison, where men try to hold their heads high without three bucks in their wallets and women try to hang on to hope wearing the same dress for two weeks straight.

There are two major labor disputes in America right now. One of them is a joke.

The Inconvenience of Being Human

NOVEMBER 16, 1998—Somewhere between making TIME and the *ABC World News Tonight* and getting turned into the kind of cuddly American hero people want to hang from their rearview mirrors, Doug Flutie lost his baby.

It's all right. He handled it. His wife, Laurie, handled it. It happened two weeks ago. She miscarried at three months, and they grieved at 10 cents a minute, and he missed two nights' sleep flying back and forth between his home near Boston and football practice in Buffalo, but they got through it. Then he went out and beat the Miami Dolphins and smiled for the cameras the way a good little legend is supposed to.

It's just that while America was getting giddy over how Flutie snatched the Buffalo Bills quarterback job from a guy to whom he gives up six inches, 11 years and $24 million, he was having to deal with the slight inconvenience of being human. What was weird was that he and Laurie knew this pregnancy was going to be worrisome. When you have a severely autistic six-year-old who has to be watched 18 hours a day, nonstop, you think hard before you have another child. "We knew we were going to worry," says Flutie. "We were going to watch that kid like a hawk until he was 21. I guess all the worrying started six months early."

Some autistic kids whine and wail and shriek. Not Dougie. Dougie is happy and smiling "100 percent of the time," says his father. But another autistic child would mean the end of Flutie's football career. He nearly quit after last season to stay home and help Laurie with Dougie. "He's a six-year-old with the maturity of an infant, but he can open doors and unlock windows and get out," says Flutie. "So, he's a handful."

It's bittersweet to see Dougie on the living room carpet, eating his frosted Flutie Flakes by the handful, having no idea how much he and the cereal mean to others. A portion of the proceeds from sales of Flutie Flakes goes to Flutie Jr. Foundation for Autism, which raises awareness and support for those affected by the disorder. Sales didn't figure to be $5, but then the Bills' 25-year-old starting quarterback, Rob Johnson, who has a $25 million contract, went down with Buffalo's record at 1–3, and football's favorite lawn gnome took over. Defensive ends couldn't seem to find Flutie and defensive backs couldn't seem to find his spirals, and pretty soon he had the Bills at 5–3 and the starting job for keeps.

So it became the feel-good story of the season: The man who won three Grey Cups in Canada is the littlest big man in America, but he's not one bit suckered. "Everybody's saying, 'Well, of course. He's always been a winner,'" Flutie says, "but what were they saying two months ago? 'He's too short. If Johnson goes down, Buffalo's in big trouble.' Crap like that. I've heard that the last 10 to 15 years, and it's never been valid."

If Flutie seems a little bitter toward the NFL and the media, it's only because it's true. The league has treated Flutie the way Calista Flockhart seems to treat a ham sandwich: 1) ignore it, 2) maybe nibble at it or 3) spit it out entirely. In 1986 the Chicago Bears took this Heisman Trophy winner and set him next to the door to the toilet. Jim McMahon called him Bambi. A year later Flutie was traded to New England, where he was allowed to throw the ball every other autumnal equinox. Then the Patriots cut him after the '89 season.

"They can write all the Flutiemania stories they want, and they can talk all they want," Flutie says. "I don't read them, and I don't listen to them."

Flutie understands life's divine balance. He's lived it, as have other NFL quarterbacks. To the gifted Dan Marino was born a mildly autistic son, Michael. To the athletic Boomer Esiason was born a son, Gunnar, with cystic fibrosis. To Mark Rypien was born a son, Andrew, who died of brain cancer in August at three. To Jim Kelly was born a son, Hunter, who is terminally ill with Krabbe's disease at 21 months. To Flutie, Dougie. Why?

"When you see kids like Hunter and what they and their families have had to go through," Flutie says, "you're so grateful to have someone like Dougie."

Who knows? Maybe Flutie and his Flakes will wind up in the Big Bowl. Maybe not. But one day soon Flutie will have a Sunday when he'll throw three interceptions or fumble twice or trip over his own size 11s and people will grumble, "Told you. Too short," and Flutie will slump home and there will be Dougie, laughing and smiling and happy.

Maybe *that's* why.

POSTSCRIPT: *Six weeks after this ran, Miami coach Jimmy Johnson got up on a table and stomped a box of Flutie Flakes to death after a game with Buffalo.*

—•—

Funny You Should Ask

APRIL 12, 1999—So we were lying on our backs on the grass in the park next to our hamburger wrappers, my 14-year-old son and I, watching the clouds loiter overhead, when he asked me, "Dad, why are we here?"

And this is what I said.

"I've thought a lot about it, son, and I don't think it's all that complicated. I think maybe we're here just to teach a kid how to bunt, turn two and eat sunflower seeds without using his hands.

"We're here to pound the steering wheel and scream as we listen to the game on the radio, 20 minutes after we pulled into the garage. We're here to look all over, give up and then find the ball in the hole.

"We're here to watch, at least once, as the pocket collapses around John Elway, and it's fourth-and-never. Or as the count goes to 3 and 1 on Mark McGwire with bases loaded, and the pitcher begins wishing he'd gone on to med school. Or as a little hole you couldn't get a skateboard through suddenly opens in front of Jeff Gordon with a lap to go.

"We're here to wear our favorite sweat-soaked Boston Red Sox cap, torn Slippery Rock sweatshirt and the Converses we lettered in, on a Saturday morning with nowhere we have to go and no one special we have to be.

"We're here to rake on a jack-high nothin' hand and have nobody know it but us. Or get in at least one really good brawl, get a nice shiner and end up throwing an arm around the guy who gave it to us.

"We're here to shoot a six-point elk and finally get the f-stop right, or to tie the perfect fly, make the perfect cast, catch absolutely nothing and still call it a perfect morning.

"We're here to nail a yield sign with an apple core from half a block away. We're here to make our dog bite on the same lame fake throw for the gazillionth time. We're here to win the stuffed bear or go broke trying.

"I don't think the meaning of life is gnashing our bicuspids over what comes after death but tasting all the tiny moments that come before it. We're here to be the coach when Wendell, the one whose glasses always fog up, finally makes the only perfect backdoor pass all season. We're here to be there when our kid has three goals and an assist. And especially when he doesn't.

"We're here to see the Great One setting up behind the net, tying some poor goaltender's neck into a Windsor knot. We're here to watch the Rocket peer in for the sign, two out, bases loaded, bottom of the career. We're here to witness Tiger's lining up the 22-foot double breaker to win and not need his autograph afterward to prove it.

"We're here to be able to do a one-and-a-half for our grandkids. Or to stand at the top of our favorite double-black on a double-blue morning and overhear those five wonderful words: 'Highway's closed. Too much snow.' We're here to get the Frisbee to do things that would have caused medieval clergymen to burn us at the stake.

"We're here to sprint the last 100 yards and soak our shirts and be so tired we have to sit down to pee.

"I don't think we're here to make *SportsCenter*. The really good stuff never does. Like leaving Wrigley at 4:15 on a perfect summer afternoon and walking straight into Murphy's with half of section 503. Or finding ourselves with a free afternoon, a little red 327 fuel-injected 1962 Corvette convertible and an unopened map of Vermont's backroads.

"We're here to get the triple-Dagwood sandwich made, the perfectly frosted malted-beverage mug filled and the football kicked off at the very second your sister begins tying up the phone until Tuesday.

"None of us are going to find ourselves on our deathbeds saying, 'Dang, I wish I'd spent more time on the Hibbings account.' We're going to say, 'That scar? I got that scar stealing a home run from Consolidated Plumbers!'

"See, grown-ups spend so much time doggedly slaving toward the better car, the perfect house, the big day that will finally make them happy when happy just walked by wearing a bicycle helmet two sizes too big for him. We're not here to find a way to heaven. The way is heaven. Does that answer your question, son?"

And he said, "Not really, Dad."

And I said, "No?"

And he said, "No, what I meant is, why are we here when Mom said to pick her up 40 minutes ago?"

POSTSCRIPT: *Sometimes, you write a column and never hear another word about it—not from friends, not from strangers, not from anybody. But this one seems to have pierced a soft spot on people. To this day, I still get people telling me they faxed it to their kids, their parents and their 20 best friends. People wrote their own columns about why we're here and sent them to me. I even turned it into a speech. If there's one column I'd like to be remembered, it's this one.*

CHAPTER FOUR: ROOTS

CHAPTER FOUR: ROOTS

Let's Get World Serious

SEPTEMBER 6, 1999—Went to Williamsport, Pa., last week and saw the Phenix City (Ala.) team win the U.S. Little League championship.

Well, *la-dee-da*!

They never played the Nuts. Actually, the team of 11- and 12-year-olds that I coach in the Denver Catholic Youth Recreation Association is the Good Shepherd Grizzlies, but we call ourselves the Nuts because our first and foremost goal each season is to learn how to eat sunflower seeds without using our hands, indoors or out. (Very big with the mothers.) We even have a cheer we holler before each game:

Elbows, knees, ankles, butts!

No one beats us!

We're the Nuts!

Near as I could see, there was nothing about Phenix City or any other team in the series this year that would crack the Nuts. True, the worst player on any of the eight Little League regional champions would possibly be the best on my team. And the smallest kid on Phenix City would be one of my biggest. (I had two kids this year who could sit on first and dangle their feet.) And, true, one kid on the Latin American champions was six feet, 170 pounds and had a second mortgage. I didn't even have *parents* who were six feet, 170.

But can the players in Williamsport do what my kids can do? For instance, could any third baseman there name the make, model and year of any car that drives by? "That's a 1991 Honda Civic CRX in the metallic burgundy with the optional roof package," our third baseman, Grant, would tell me during a game.

"Amazing, Grant!" I'd say. "Now, will you be getting the grounder that just rolled by your feet, or should I ask the leftfielder to come in?"

The Phenix City coach, Tony Rasmus, said his third pitcher had a "good fastball and a good changeup." But what would he give to have my third pitcher, whose fastball *is* his changeup? Yeah, his outfielders go down on one knee for every grounder, but so what? My outfielders go down on one knee, too (but only for worms). I bet his kids don't steal bases like we do. Of course, we *have* to steal. We only have two helmets. Can Phenix City players hit while backing out of the batter's box? Can they field line drives matador style? Can they apply a tag with both feet in the air, eyes closed?

Nope, I wouldn't trade teams with Rasmus, and, to be honest, I wouldn't want my son to play for him. For 10 weeks Rasmus had the Phenix City team practicing four hours a day, every day but one, sometimes past dark. The families of his players had to promise to take no summer vacations during that time. He even quit his job— he was supposed to teach 11th-grade chemistry starting Aug. 16—so he could devote more time to coaching this team. *Quit* to focus on Little League. God forbid the guy ever coaches Pony League.

I won't let my pitchers throw curves yet, but every pitcher I saw in Williamsport did. In our league all 16 kids on my team are in the batting order and each plays at least three innings in the field every game. Not in Williamsport. A kid only has to get one at bat *or* be on the field for three outs in each game. The Japanese team, which ended up beating Phenix City 5–0 for the world championship, had one boy who batted only once all week.

After the loss Rasmus said that nearly every kid on his team was crying. The Nuts get over losses immediately, and sometimes they are not even aware they've lost. "What's the score, Coach?" my second baseman, Eric, would ask.

"Seventeen to four," I'd say.

"Who's ahead?"

But mostly, I wouldn't switch places with Rasmus because every year I get a kid or two who has never played baseball. This year it was a stone-quiet kid named William, who wore wire rims and was no higher than a mailbox. He showed up with a brand-new, board-stiff, ottoman-sized glove, and every practice we worked on making the glove a little softer and William a little better. Eventually, he not only learned to hit but also to run to first afterward, instead of third. And in the last game of the year, he stuck that frying pan out in front of him as if he were trying to stop a train and caught his first fly ball.

In nine years of coaching, that was my favorite moment. You would have thought we had just won the Little League World Series. First we hoisted William up like Lindbergh and then let him drop and made a giant dog pile on top of him.

We lost that game to end our season, probably my last, but near as I can remember, there was only one set of moist eyes.

Mine.

POSTSCRIPT: I tell college kids, "Forget cereal boxes." What it means is, forget the athletes and the events that always appear on the Wheaties boxes. Try the littler events, the places people forget to look. And every time I remember to take my own advice—as in this column and the next one—it seems to work out. This column seemed to touch people. They either remembered a) how much fun their Little League teams were or b) how little fun their Little League teams were, on account of a General Patton coach who wanted to win at all costs. At least a dozen parks and recreation directors said they were copying the article and including it in the information packs that go home with the kids. See? The nuts always make good in the end.

Bringing Parents Up to Code

FEBRUARY 28, 2000—There's only one place in the galaxy where kids' sports is sane.

Jupiter.

Jupiter, Fla., that is, where on Feb. 15, the town's athletic association did something we should've done in America 20 years ago. It took the *parents* out behind the woodshed.

If you wanted your kid to play on one of the Jupiter association's zillion teams this year, you had to file into a minor league baseball stadium, watch a video on sportsmanship and then vow not to insult, cuss at, holler at, spit upon, push, punch, body-slam or otherwise abuse a coach, referee, team mom, scorekeeper, fan, player or another parent.

You think it doesn't happen? In Port St. Lucie, Fla., a youth soccer coach head-butted a referee, breaking the ref's nose. In Wagoner, Okla., a 36-year-old coach started choking a 15-year-old umpire in a tee-ball game for 5- and 6-year-olds. In Palm Beach Gardens, Fla., a baseball game for 7- and 8-year-olds ended in a parents' brawl. In Boca Raton, Fla., one of the managers in a baseball game for 9- and 10-year-olds mooned the opponents' parents.

And you thought pro sports was mayhem.

Jupiter parents had to sign the code of ethics, which included such pledges as "I will remember that the game is for youth—not adults" and "I will do my very best to make youth sports fun for my child." Break the code and they're banished from the association's games for as much as a year.

Problem was, that code didn't go nearly far enough. As a poor slob who has coached kids' sports for 10 years and gone to more kids' games than Mr. and Mrs. Osmond combined, I would've made the parents sign this—in blood:

• I'll keep in mind that, in case I hadn't noticed, my kid isn't related to the Griffeys. There's probably no college scholarship on the line, to say nothing of a $116.5 million guaranteed contract with the Cincinnati Reds. In fact, right now my kid is filling the inside of his baseball glove with ants. He looks happy. I'll shut up.

• I won't dump my kid out of the Lexus 20 minutes late to practice and then honk the horn when I pick him up 20 minutes early, as though the coach is some kind of hourly nanny service. If my kid has to miss a game, I'll call the day before. It doesn't cost any more to be decent.

• I'll remember that this isn't the seventh game of the NBA Finals. This is the 6-year-olds'YMCA Lil' Celtics finals, and by supper time not one of these kids will remember the score. They will remember that I tried to ride the other coach bareback, and possibly they'll remember the incident in the squad car, but not the score.

• I'll realize that the guy behind the umpire's mask, whom I've been calling "José Feliciano" and "Coco, the talking ape," is probably just a 15-year-old kid with a tube of Oxy 10 in his pocket, making $12 the hard way. I'll shut up.

• I'll stop harrumphing out of the side of my mouth about how much the coach stinks, unless I want to give up my Tuesdays, Thursdays and Saturdays every week, call 15 kids every time it rains and spend $200 every season on ice cream, catcher's throat guards and new seat covers. I'll shut up. (Oh, and once a year, I'll tell her thanks.)

• I won't rupture my larynx hollering nonstop directions. For one thing, my kid can't hear me. For two, because I'm shouting, he can't hear the coach, either. For three, I really have no idea what I'm talking about. Screaming at little Justin to "Tag up! Tag up!" when there are two outs is probably not very helpful. I'll shut up.

• Win or lose, I won't make the ride home the worst 20 minutes in my kid's life. "You played great" should about cover it every time. Then I'll shut up.

• One season a year, even if it kills me, I won't make my kid sign up for an organized sport. It's probably not necessary to have him play 91 hockey games in three leagues from September to June and then send him to Skating Camp, Slap Shot Camp and Orange Pylon Camp all summer. I'll try to remember that Be a Kid Camp isn't so terrible once in a while. Neither is Invent a Game Involving a Taped Sock, a Broom and Old Lady Winslow's Fence Camp, come to think of it.

• Most important, I promise I'll do everything in my power, no matter what, to remember to arrive at games with the single most important thing of all . . . the orange slices.

A Warm Ending to a Cold Story

MARCH 29, 1999—About the time they were laying a garland of yellow victory roses around the lead dogs of this year's Iditarod winner, the cement finisher was trying to snuggle up to a snowbank to sleep, 712 icy miles and almost a week behind.

About the time the winner was tucking in for a 12-hour snooze after a hot bath, the cement finisher was trying to find enough kindling in 90°-below windchill to make a fire.

About the time the winner was giving his victory-banquet speech, five days after mushing his team up Front Street in Nome, Alaska, to an adoring five-deep crowd, the cement finisher was alone, trying to decide which ached worse: his freeze-dried 46-year-old body or his heart, from knowing he'd probably never get to run the Iditarod again.

The winner was the well-sponsored Doug Swingley, who was awarded more than $60,000 in cash and a new truck. He's the owner of one uncatchable dog team, two Iditarod feeder teams and the race record—just under nine days, three hours, set in 1995.

But a lot of people figured the cement finisher for the real hero of this Iditarod: twice-divorced loner Shane Goosen, an unsponsored, wind-gnarled Alaskan, winner of the same sum, $1,049, that all the way-back-in-the-pack racers got for finishing the race, owner of a beat-up house, a truck that doesn't work and—

after blowing his last $20,000 on this race—*bubkes* in the bank.

"Shane probably won't ever have this chance again," says one bush pilot. The pilot, two mushers and a friend say Goosen has cancer. "Agghhh, I got some health things," Goosen said last Saturday as he fed his team pork in tiny Koyuk, 171 miles from Nome. "But it ain't cancer, and it ain't for publication."

O.K., so it's a coincidence that after breeding, driving and loving Alaskan huskies for the better part of 30 years, Goosen finally scratched up enough dogs and gear and cash to try mushing's Le Mans. "Well," he grumbled, "I *had* to do it once, didn't I?"

Put it this way: The cement finisher wasn't a heavy Vegas favorite. Where Swingley's sled cover bore big-corporation logos, Goosen's had GRETA'S GRILL GOODIES, CLAM GULCH, AK. Where Swingley dined on a seven-course gourmet meal at the Yukon checkpoint, Goosen ate one of the bags of pale spaghetti he'd sealed and shipped more than a month earlier. Where Swingley was greeted at stops by roars and schoolkids and documentary crews, Goosen would pull in to the resounding crescendo of one town dog barking. "Hell," Goosen said. "One time I got to a checkpoint and they'd already packed up the check-in tent. I had to wake up the checker."

Goosen wrecked his sled. Twice. One day his team took him a mile off course, chasing caribou. Another time he turned his head just long enough to get thumped off his sled by a low-hanging limb—and had to run a mile in the pitch black to catch his team. Exhausted, he fell asleep and off the runners "too many damn times to count." And he relished every second of it. "I didn't do this so much to race," he said. "I did this for me and my dogs."

The Iditarod will tell you more about yourself than a month of MRIs. No event in sports makes you feel less significant and yet so wildly human. Spend two weeks trying to keep you and 16 dogs alive out there with the whipping winds and wolves, and your other worries get small real quick. "Will I miss it?" Goosen said. "Hell, I'm already crying."

See, there's just no more money left. Upon finally hitting Nome, he planned to sell most of his dogs and all his gear and get on with his life—however long that is—by flying to El Paso and seeing the

24-year-old son and the five-month-old granddaughter he has never met, by fixing the holes in his roof, by defrosting. "Do you know I've never once stood on a sandy beach?" he said.

Goosen didn't do this to get his picture in the paper. He runs from attention. There was only one thing he wanted when the race was over: the red lantern that goes to the last-place finisher. "I want to set that on my fireplace mantel so one day my grandkids can look at it and say, 'Lookit there! Grampa really *did* finish the damn thing!'"

So, on Monday, a hunched-over hero too tired to quit finally mushed the 1,161st mile into Nome, but not so you'd notice. The streets were quiet, the race headquarters mostly closed and the banquet long over. Goosen didn't get the red lantern—he had the bad luck to beat two others to the line—but just finishing made him feel like it was a greater glory than Swingley's.

Hell, maybe it was.

Putting It in Writing

JANUARY 16, 1995—After we gave up the first touchdown in our Fourth Annual Touch Football/Pulledgroinathon, the guys on the other team sneered and said, "Suckers walk."

"Says who?" asked our left tackle, Cementhead.

"It's an unwritten rule," explained the other side's captain.

"Oh, yeah?" said Cementhead. "Show me where."

Which is exactly my point. Why are sport's unwritten rules unwritten? Say no more. Get a Xerox machine under these puppies and have a copy on everybody's desk in the morning:

The coach always sits in the first row on the team bus. If he is out sick or dead, the seat remains empty.

Apologize for a point won on a net cord.

Take two or three pitches if your pitcher just made the second out of the inning.

Never, ever put your finger in someone else's bowling ball.

The starting goalie is always the first player on the ice.

If a line judge makes a bad call in your favor, purposely double-fault the next point.

A manager never drinks at the same bar as his players.

Never knock in the tying run in the ninth inning of an exhibition game. Far better to lose than go extra innings in spring training.

No NBA player attempting a layup in the fourth quarter of a tight game should go unfouled.

In a losing clubhouse you must act as if there has been a death in the family.

Hand the manager the ball when he comes to the mound to take you out.

Never shoot the puck into the net after a whistle blows.

Do not talk to or sit near a pitcher with a no-hitter going.

And never bunt to break one up.

A first base coach never stands in the first base coaching box.

Never bet a horse that defecates during the post parade.

Never blow your nose before a fight. (It makes the eyes swell easier later on.)

Stand as far away as possible from a skeet shooter with a perfect score going.

Hockey goons fight hockey goons. And no fighting Gretzky.

Never walk on a player's putting line, including the two feet on the other side of the cup.

Always clear the inside lane for faster runners.

Never stand behind the pool table pocket your opponent is shooting for.

Never let the interviewee hold the mike.

A catcher may complain to the ump all he wants about balls and strikes, as long as he doesn't turn around and do it face-to-face.

Never hit the quarterback during practice.

Never start a decathlon 100 meters into a wind. Trade false starts until the breeze is favorable.

If your golfing opponent asks, his ball is always out of round.

When a soccer player is hurt, the opponents must kick the ball out of bounds.

Except for Rocky Marciano, the challenger always entered the ring first—and always will.

Never leave the field with a clean uniform.

Throw a handful of salt into the air before your sumo wrestling match begins.

It's true: Suckers walk.

The bus may be delayed by superstars only.

When the coach finally wraps up a long meeting with "Any questions?" nobody better ask one.

Rookies shag balls, whether they are millionaires or not.

Never shoot high on the goalie during warmups.

The back nine is always pressed.

You must admit it when you hit a forehand on the second bounce.

On the playground, offense calls the fouls.

Never write down the score of a bowler who is on a run of strikes.

Never admit you trapped the ball while trying to make a catch.

No overhead smashes at women in mixed doubles.

The caddie of the last player to putt plants the flag.

NBA refs will take some trash from head coaches but not a word from an assistant.

Never steal with a five-run lead after the seventh inning.

You must alter your course to help a boat in distress.

Boxers never blink during a ref's prefight instructions.

When a receiver drops a pass, go back to him on the next play.

Card games are played in the back of the plane.

Scrubs stand during NBA timeouts.

Winners buy.

Got it, Cementhead?

—•—

The Lipinski Who Was Left Behind

MARCH 2, 1998—Four years ago Jack Lipinski's family left him for a gold medal. His wife, Pat, and his only child, Tara, then 11, went to Delaware for the summer to take figure skating lessons from a hot new coach, and they just never quite came back. Since then Pat and Tara have made what amounts to three trips around the world, become famous and moved again, this time to suburban Detroit, but Jack is still by himself, knocking around like a pinball in the family's 5,000-square-foot house in Sugar Land, Texas. He shuffles among the only three rooms he uses, dutifully calling his wife and daughter twice a day, sending out the checks, being the good dad.

He has law and engineering degrees and is vice president of refining for a Houston-based oil company, but he still had to refinance the house to pay for the condo outside Detroit and the coaches and the ballet teacher and the tutors and the trainers and the travel and the clothes. Pat and Tara are grateful, but they don't call him in Houston and ask him what he thinks about adding a triple toe loop or more sequins, or the competition in Munich. You ask longtime skating writers about Lipinski's father, and they say, "Are they together?" or "Whaddya mean, father?" You open Tara's autobiography and see the dedication to her mom: "You have . . . sacrificed so much. . . . Without [you], I know I couldn't have gone this far."

No mention of you-know-who.

He knows they love him, and he loves them, and to prove it, 40 Fridays a year he trudges onto a 5:30 p.m. flight from Houston to Detroit, lands at 9, rents a car and drives to the condo, where he spends as much of Sunday as he can with Tara, since it's her only day off from skating. They maybe take in a movie before he has to head to the airport by 4 p.m. to make the flight back to Houston, where he flops into bed by 11, ready to wake up the next day and start funding Operation Tara again.

But he doesn't complain and he doesn't regret and he doesn't even call it a sacrifice. He figures a certain fireman and seamstress from Bayonne, N.J., worked like dogs to get him his two degrees, and now it's his turn. "The hardest part is the loneliness," he says. "But thank god for phones." The phone bill is almost $1,000 a month, but sometimes the calls only make him lonelier. He and Pat had been together 27 years when she and Tara left. All of a sudden he's supposed to be happy with a cozy fiber-optic line? "We can't even talk about the loneliness," Pat says. "It only makes us sadder. He gave up his family for this. I'm not sure I could've." When Pat gets into this sort of mood, Tara will sense it and bounce into the kitchen, going, "Mom, how 'bout I make dinner tonight?"

Jack flies in for competitions whenever he can, and he found himself in Nagano with two wonderful weeks to spend with his daughter, except that she didn't have two weeks to spend with him. She was staying in the Olympic Village, its youngest citizen. You come nearly 7,000 miles to see your little girl only to find out she had already grown up.

At the Olympics a lot is made about what these tiny dancers give up—their youth, their innocence, their prom. But does anybody ever mention what the Jack Lipinskis give up?

After Tara almost knocked down the boards in Nagano last week with her will and nearly jumped out of the joint with the kind of single-mindedness family friends see in her father, the Lipinskis finally had that precious medal, fair and square, and were on their way to the doping control station to prove it. As usual Jack tailed along at the end of the entourage—escorts, officials, coaches, Tara and Pat. All of them were allowed in. Except one.

"It's O.K.," he said, "I'm her dad."

"*Nai*," said the Japanese guard.

"Father," he argued. "Daddy."

"*Nai*," said the guard.

"Pop. Poppy."

"*Nai, nai, nai!*"

He gave up and collapsed on a bench. Alone, as usual, with his sense of joy and exhaustion and duty, he must've thought how many more years of cold sheets and burned salads he had to go. He glanced at his watch. It was well after midnight, which meant it was his 47th birthday.

You wonder if he made a wish.

POSTSCRIPT: *I never heard from Mr. Lipinski on this column. But I heard from a few other fathers who wished they could have their daughters back.*

The Missing Links

JUNE 13, 1988—The most important man in golf has a ball retriever in his bag, a score counter on his belt and a loop in his backswing. He buys three balls for a dollar and shows up at the course in jeans, Reeboks and a golf shirt that's so old it has no emblem. He's the foot soldier of the game, the guy who's up at four in the morning to pay $12 to wait three hours to play a six-hour round to lose $6 in bets.

No company wants him to wear its name on his visor, and nobody shines his cleats. Yet he's the guy who keeps the sport alive. He's the guy who lines up three deep to hit a bucket of almost-round balls off AstroTurf mats, which stain his irons an unnatural green. That's him in the back of the clubhouse, lying about his round and playing gin rummy on a white Formica table that hasn't seen a busboy's rag since Easter.

Lately he's been forgotten. Lately people have thought of golf as some kind of 18-karat Aaron Spelling production, people driving up in expense-account Cadillacs wearing La Mode du Golf shirts and tipping doormen 10-spots. Every new course is more glamorous and exotic than the last. And "greens fees" mean you have to buy a Jack Nicklaus lot overlooking the 18th green.

But golf can't change neighborhoods on us. Truth is, underneath all that, the heart of the game is still the shot-and-a-beer hacker, the golf guerrilla, the guy playing courses that move about as fast as a Moscow meat line, and smiling about it. Fuzzy Zoeller may shoot 66 at Augusta and then gripe about the greens, but the essence of golf is still the 14 handicapper who doesn't mind if the tees are rough, the fairways look like the aftermath of a tractor-pull and the greens aren't. He loves the game *for* the game. It's Saturday. He's playing golf. He's gonna gripe?

At Bethpage State Park on Long Island, golfers arrive at 2:30 in the morning in hopes of getting on the first tee by 6:30. Golfers who arrive at 7:30 are lucky to be planting a tee in the ground by noon. At Forest Preserve National in Oak Forest, Ill., players begin lining up at 3 p.m. *the day before* for a 6 a.m. tee time. They sleep in their cars. In Los Angeles, if you haven't called by 6:30 a.m. on a Monday for a tee time the next Saturday, you're usually shut out for that day on all 13 public courses. The switchboard opens at 6 a.m.

It's not uncommon for a round of golf to take almost seven hours. If you get around at all, that is. At Pelham Golf Course in the Bronx a few years ago, youths hiding in nearby woods robbed a man on a green of $65 and his credit cards. It is not known whether he then made the putt. When American Golf, a course management company, took over at Pelham, employees were surprised at what they found—dead bodies. Because of that, Kimble Knowlden of American Golf told *The New York Times*, "I try not to be the first one out on the course in the morning."

But warm bodies, too, keep flooding the Bronx's public links. Same as they do in Chicago and L.A. The country is four quarts low on reasonably priced golf courses for John Q. Public to play. The National Golf Foundation estimates that the number of golfers has grown 24%, to 20.2 million, over the last two years. To keep up with that pace, the foundation says, a course a day would have to be built between now and the turn of the century. Last year only 110 opened, and more than a third of those were private.

Still, for all of that—the ordeal of getting a tee time, the 20-minute waits between shots and the ungroomed greens—the public course golfer pursues the game as if he had invented it. And nobody's more loyal than the regulars at Ponkapoag Golf Club in Canton, Mass., known, for better or worse, as Ponky.

Overheard at a Ponky lunch table:
 Ralphie: "You know what my problem is?"
 Pete: "No, what?"
 Ralphie: "With you fishes, I need a bigger wallet."
 Pete: "Slob."
 Herbie: "What'd everybody make on that last hole?"
 Ralphie: "Four."
 Brooklyn: "Five."
 Pete: "Other."
 Herbie: "Whaddya mean, 'other'?"
 Pete: "Other. Like on TV, when they put up what all the pros have been making on the hole, right?"
 Herbie: "So?"
 Pete: "So it says something like, '181 birdies, 300-something pars, 98 bogeys, 42 double bogeys and seven others.' Well, I had an 'other,' O.K.?"
 Juice: "I'll guarantee you, tomorrow I'm not shootin' any 'others.' Tomorrow, I'm throwin' a 72 at you slobs."
 Tommy: "Right. And I'm Seve."
 Juice: "Bet me?"
 Tommy: "Sawbuck?"
 Juice: "You got it."
 Tommy: "So, how do you guarantee it?"
 Juice: "After I hit it 72 times, I'm pickin' it up."

For the third time in history, the U.S. Open, which begins June 16, will be held this year at The Country Club in Brookline, Mass. For the 88th time in history, the U.S. Open will not be held at Ponky. Still, the two courses are only 20 minutes apart in Greater Boston, and it's easy to get them confused.

At The Country Club, for instance, you drive up to the clubhouse, where the boy meets you and takes your bag. At Ponky, you give a boy your bag only at gunpoint. At The Country Club, you change shoes in the locker room. At Ponky, most people don't change shoes. At The Country Club, the men's room is stocked with colognes, hair dryers and jars full of combs rinsing in blue disinfectant. At Ponky, you comb your hair looking into the metal on the front of the paper towel dispenser. At The Country Club, the greens are truer than any love. At Ponky, the greens look like barber-school haircuts. At The Country Club, lunch in the Men's Grille might begin with the vichyssoise, followed by an avocado stuffed with salmon salad. At Ponky, you can get a fried-egg sandwich for a buck and a quarter.

At The Country Club, the most esteemed tournament is The Country Club Gold Medal. At Ponky, it's the TV Open. (Each member of the winning foursome gets a TV—color, no less.) At The Country Club, the names are Wigglesworth, Peabody and Coolidge. At Ponky, they're Papoulias, Sullivan and Tomasini. At The Country Club, the members peruse *The Wall Street Journal*. At Ponky, they read the *Racing Form*. At The Country Club, most of the families came over on the *Mayflower*. At Ponky, most of the guys came over on the bus.

Ponkapoag endures 120,000 rounds a year over its two courses, and a whole lot of these are played by the regulars. Among them are Bluto, a construction worker with a high resemblance to Olive Oyl's suitor; Ziggy, who looks like the doorman in *The Wizard of Oz*; Little Eddie, a slightly pudgy accountant; Jimmy, a postal worker; Cementhead, a cement-truck driver; Socks, a contractor; Pappy, a high-tech engineer; and the Can Man, a retired cop who collects plastic garbage bags full of aluminum cans during rounds and hauls them saddlebag-style over his golf cart.

Then there is Bob DePopolo. If The Country Club has Francis Ouimet, winner of the 1913 U.S. Open, then Ponky has DePopolo, 57, inventor of the Triple Tripod Leg-Log putting stroke. To do the Triple Tripod, you get a five-foot putter that reaches up to your sternum (DePopolo insists he invented this extra-long putter, now popular on the Senior tour), stand with legs crossed, use a cross-handed grip and whack away.

DePopolo was a master of all things technical about golf, but he was most obsessive about the wind. In fact, the only ball he would play was a Titleist 8. He said the symmetry of the 8 caused less wind friction than other numbers. "For years," says Paul Bersani, a Ponky regular, "you could not buy a Titleist 8 in the pro shop. DePopolo had 'em all."

DePopolo gave up golf to tend to an ailing mother, but he had long since become a legend. One year he played the Catholic Youth Organization tournament, still held annually at Ponky. After winning his semifinal match on a Friday, he was eating a cheeseburger when a priest admonished him. "Son, what do you think you're doing?"

"Having a cheeseburger, Father," said DePopolo.

"Don't you know it's Friday?"

"So what?" said DePopolo. "It's a free country, ain't it?"

DePopolo, thus rooted out as a Protestant, was immediately disqualified.

Ziggy, a short, sturdy man in his mid-50's, gets constant abuse at Ponky for: 1) his toupee, and 2) the fact that in 25 years, he has never gotten the clubhead past his waist on the backswing.

Socks: "O.K., Ziggy, this is the one, Baby. Get those hands way up high this time. Way up!"

Bluto: "Wait, Ziggy, wait! There's a divot on your head." (Despite making a perfect practice swing, Ziggy still strikes the ball with his usual foreshortened style.) "Beautiful, Ziggy. You did it that time."

Socks: "Ziggy, you could make a swing in a phone booth."

Pauli: "Without opening the door."

Rudy: "Remember that time Ziggy made that great shot out of the woods?"

Pauli: "Remember! I was *there.*"

Rudy: "Absolutely great shot. He was all bashed in there, in with the trees. Had no shot. Only he makes a great shot and he comes running out to watch it. Only his toupee is still hanging on one of the branches."

Pauli: "The Parks Department came. They thought it was a wombat."

Ziggy: "Rot, you slobs."

Golf isn't the sport of choice at Ponky. The sport of choice is betting. Golf is just a convenient vehicle for it. At Ponky, they bet on whether the pro on TV will sink his next putt. They bet on how long it will take Russ, the cook, to make a two-minute egg. They bet with their partners, and they bet against their partners. They bet with guys playing two groups ahead and with guys three counties over. They bet while they're waiting on the tees. They bet on whether they can chip into the garbage can or off the ball washer. On a rainy day at Ponky, Pappy the Edgeman (so named because he always wants the betting edge) will take bets on a hole that consists of hitting a ball off the locker room floor, over a bank of lockers, out a door, onto the practice green and into a designated cup. Par is 3.

They'll bet you can't make a 4 on the next hole. They'll bet you can't turn the front nine in 42. Little Eddie will bet you that he can stack two golf balls, one on top of the other, ricochet the bottom one off a wall and catch the top one in his back pocket. (Don't take the bet.) Pappy, the snake, has bet people he can beat them putting with his wedge. (Don't take that one, either.)

Then there was the time Pappy bet Socks 10 bucks that Socks couldn't make a 4 on the next hole. Socks made a 3. "Pay up, Edgeman," said Socks.

"What for?"

"You know what for. I made a 4."

"No you didn't. You made a 3." Took a while for Socks to get over that one.

They bet for 27 holes on weekends, and they bet on their regular nine-hole game after work. They bet "sandies" (up and down out of the sand), "greenies" (closest to the pin on par-3s), "barkies" (hit a tree and still make par) and "Arnies" (make a par without ever being on the fairway). Afterward, they'll bet on hearts, gin, whist and poker until it gets dark, and then go outside, turn the car headlights on the putting green and have putting contests until somebody has won all the money or the Diehards start to wear out. In the winter, when the course is closed, they'll get a pound of bologna, some roast beef, a loaf of bread and some tonic and play cards in the clubhouse, although they're not supposed to have a key. Loser has to vacuum.

Golf is so much fun at Ponky that guys who are members at country clubs come over for a most un-clubby kind of golf game. Rudy Tomasini has been a member of Plymouth Country Club for years, yet every afternoon Rudy shows up to play a 5 o'clock round with the boys, and every day the boys give him the business.

Bluto: "Hey, Ziggy, what's Mr. Country Club doing here, anyway? Why does he want to play Ponky when he could be at the country club?"

Ziggy: "I'll tell you what he's doing. He's slumming, that's what he's doing. He's favoring us with his presence."

Bluto: "Must've run out of hors d'oeuvres over there or something."

Most of the gambling is $5 stuff, but some of it isn't. Herbie lost $18,000 one day at Ponky. Another gambler—we'll call him Nicky—plays golf, the puppies, the ponies, the games, the lottery, anything. "You can always tell whether Nicky's had a good week," says Bluto. "If he's ahead, he's playing golf. If he's down, he's mowing greens." Today, Nicky is mowing greens.

Bluto: "Whaddya think Nicky made last year?"

Jimmy: "I don't know. Hundred grand?"

Bluto: "Yeah. And he lost 110."

Sometimes the betting gets complicated. One day Georgie Conroy, a regular, was playing in a sevensome and had bets going with everybody. After madly scribbling down all his bets, he headed for the first fairway, where everyone found his ball. Everyone except Georgie, that is. They were just about to give up looking when somebody pointed back to the tee and yelled, "Georgie! There it is!" He had forgotten to tee off.

The boys have just found out that qualifying for this year's state amateur championship will take place at Ponkapoag.

Little Eddie: "Can you imagine a guy from The Country Club coming here to qualify?"

Bluto: "Man, wouldn't you love to get a three handicap from The Country Club out there for a little $50 Nassau?"

Jimmy: "I get a game with somebody from The Country Club, I start refinishing my basement."

Andy: "I'd just like to see the guy at the first tee. He's probably not used to guys yelling at him on his backswing."

Jimmy: "Yeah, I played at Brae Burn [Country Club] one time, and I couldn't concentrate on the tee. Too quiet."

Socks: "Wouldn't you love to see a guy from The Country Club try to get out of our rough? He'd come back into the pro shop with his attorney."

Cementhead: "I dunno. They got some pretty mean rough out there for the Open, you know."

Little Eddie: "How do you know, slob?"

Cementhead: "Didn't I tell you? I *played* The Country Club the other day. Played it even par."

Socks: "Get out! You never."

Cementhead: "I did. I was working on a job on some property that's next to it. And, you know, I always carry that four-iron and some shag balls in the truck with me, right?"

Socks: "So?"

Cementhead: "So I realize I'm standing right next to No. 2. It's a par-3, like 185 yards away. I look around and I see that nobody's watching me, so I hop the fence. I tee it up and I just couldn't believe it. Their tees are better than our greens, Eddie! So I hit it and I hit it pretty good, but it catches up on the left fringe. Still nobody's looking, so I figure, what the hell, I'll go putt out. Their greens, you can't believe. I felt bad just walking on 'em. So I make par putting with the four-iron, and I guess I could've kept going because nobody was out there, but I decided not to. So that means I'm par for The Country Club, right? Take that, you muni hacks."

Bluto: "Geez. Where do you play next week? Winged Foot?"

Sometimes the boys at Ponky hustle visitors, and sometimes the boys get hustled. One day Jimmy Sullivan, a 12-time club champ, and Pappy the Edgeman lined up a game with two guys from Franklin Park in the Roxbury section of Boston. One of the guys from Franklin Park walked with a limp and hit all his shots cross-handed. The Edgeman tried to keep from drooling. They upped the bet to $50 Nassau, with plenty of presses.

As they approached the 9th tee, Pappy was losing his bet, and Jimmy was two under par but still two holes down to his man. Pappy and Jimmy lost big. Jimmy's opponent turned out to be Charlie Owens, now a star on the PGA Senior tour, a lifetime cross-handed player and a man who has walked with a limp for 36 years.

The latest hero of the publinks player is Tour pro Jodie Mudd, who won the 1980 and '81 U.S. Public Links championships. (To enter the Publinks, you can't have had privileges at any private club during that year.) But public courses are more famous for forging the great minority players—guys like Lee Elder, Lee Trevino and current Tour star Jim Thorpe—players who, in their amateur days, could not afford a country club and who probably would not have been afforded membership in one even if they could. But on municipal courses, these guys were *good*. In 1967, Charlie Sifford, a former Tour player, came to Palmer Park in Detroit, a famous hustlers' track, and lost four days in a row. He then left and won the $100,000 Greater Hartford Open.

Thorpe's legendary days were at East Potomac Park in Washington, D.C., when he was in his early 20s. He was unbeatable at Potomac and, therefore, unbettable. So Thorpe had to take his game on the road. Wherever he went, he would show up late, with his clubs falling out of his dilapidated bag and his tennis shoes untied and wearing a shirt with a hole in it. "But I was ready to play," he says. "I could play *anywhere*."

Except at a country club. "I just didn't feel comfortable at a club," says Thorpe. "Everybody's shoes all spit and shined, clubs sparkling clean, everybody being so polite. Everybody saying 'Good shot.' I wouldn't say 'Good shot' to a guy if he holed out from 300 yards. I might say 'So what?' But I'd never say 'Good shot.'"

One time Thorpe set up a match with the best player in Flint, Mich. On the first day they played a public course, and Thorpe took him for $16,000. "I figured I'd catch a flight out that night," recalls Thorpe, "but at the end of the day, the guy says to me, 'What time we playing tomorrow?'" "So the next day he took Thorpe to the Toledo Country Club. Thorpe's game wasn't the same. "Chandeliers hanging everywhere, real thick carpet," he says. "I just wasn't dressed for the part." Thrown off, Thorpe got him for only $1,000.

Thorpe is convinced that, all things being equal, a public course player can whip a country club player every time. "You take a 15 [handicapper] from a public course and a 15 from a country club," says Thorpe, "and that public course 15 is going to walk out with that guy's ass. A public course golfer learns to play all the shots. He has to roll his putts true just to give them a chance to go in. When he gets on nice greens, he can make everything."

On a public course almost any kind of, uh, gamesmanship is fair play. "I'll jangle the keys, rip the Velcro on my glove," says Thorpe. "Anything to distract the guy."

Thorpe tells a story about a match in Tampa between the best local hustler and the famous Atlanta-based hustler George (Potato Pie) Wallace. The two men came to the 18th hole with about $20,000 on the line. Potato Pie had driven safely, but his opponent had hooked his ball into the rough, and even the 20 or so spectators following the twosome were having trouble finding it. "They'll never find it," Potato Pie whispered.

"Why not?" Thorpe said.

"Because I've got it in my pocket."

Just then, the opponent, standing 50 yards ahead of the search party, hollered, "Found it!"

Thorpe looked at Potato Pie and Potato Pie looked at Thorpe. "Well," Potato Pie whispered. "Looks like the man has got me this time."

Ponky etiquette: Jimmy is about to hit his drive on No. 10. The bets are flowing. The usual 10th-hole logjam crowd is hanging around. Just as he takes the club back, Socks, standing 20 feet behind him, interrupts.

Socks: "Hey, Jimmy. Am I safe back here?"

Jimmy: "Not if you keep that up." (Jimmy hits and now it's Wally's turn.)

Little Eddie: "Excuse me, Wally, but I just wanted to remind you—you haven't come over the top with your swing yet today."

Wally: "Thanks, Bum."

Little Eddie: "You're welcome, Wally." (Wally hits without incident and Socks steps up.)

Bluto: "O.K., everybody, pay attention. The pro from Dover is on the tee." (Socks hits it dead left into the woods.)

Little Eddie: "Now you got it, Socks. Those lessons helped." (Socks hits his provisional ball dead right into the woods.)

Cementhead: "Atta way to correct it, Socko."

Bluto: "Hey, Socks, ever thought of taking up boccie?" (Cementhead steps up and splits the fairway.)

Cementhead: "I'm hitting it so straight, all I need is one pass of the mower and I'm in the fairway."

Socks: "Hey, Cementhead, this is Ponkapoag. All you get is one pass of the mower."

Jimmy: "Yeah, unless it's a weekend or holiday. Then you get no pass of the mower." (Lee steps up and hits a perfect drive.)

Freddy: "What is it with this guy? Every time I bet against him, he swings like he's the poorest man in Boston. You need money that bad, you got to swing like Gene Littler, for Chrissakes?" (Now Little Eddie is up. He is partners with Socks today and has made two straight bogeys.)

Socks: "You're getting heavy, Eddie, you know what I mean? I'm not a frigging camel. I can't carry you forever." (Eddie shrugs, and then hits his drive into the trees.)

Socks: "Eddie, what the hell are you doing?"

Eddie: "I'm screwing up, what's it look like I'm doing?"

Socks: "Eddie, do you understand the term 'fairway'?"

Eddie: "Do you understand the term 'slob'?"

Playing Ponkapoag, says Bluto, is a distinct experience. "It's like you died and went to hell," he says.

Almost half the tees have no grass on them. Only a few sand traps have sand; the rest are overgrown with weeds. The 150-yard markers aren't 150 yards from anything in particular. The greens are a quilt of dirt patches, weeds and long grass, all of which can make a straight putt do a 90-degree turn. "I had one putt today actually back up on me," said Bob Stone, who has been playing Ponky for 25 years. And there's no such thing as a putt dying in the cup at Ponky. The crew members are so inexperienced that when they yank a hole out of the green, they don't flatten the ground around it back down, so every hole has a crown. Only regulars know that to make a putt at Ponky, you've got to allow for the hump of the hole.

All of this is not how it was meant to be. The first 18 holes at Ponky were designed by the famous golf architect Donald Ross in 1933. Ponky now has 36 holes, which require at least 12 crew members to maintain them properly. Ponky has only five.

Problem is, Ponkapoag is run by the Metropolitan District Commission, an archaic arm of the Commonwealth of Massachusetts that operates in 46 towns, patrolling beaches, skating rinks, swimming ponds and pools, and two golf courses. Why the towns can't maintain these facilities themselves is anyone's guess. The MDC hires employees for the courses from within the MDC. As a result, most Ponky staffers have about as much expertise in golf-course maintenance as they do in 747 repair.

Ponkapoag's greens fees are cheap as dirt: $7 on weekends, $6 on weekdays, $3 for seniors on weekdays and $3 for anybody after 3 p.m. Given those rates and the course's overall condition, Ponky is crying out to be leased to a private management company like American Golf, which would raise the prices a little and improve the playing conditions a lot. But the MDC won't do it.

"If there are 25 jobs in a year at Ponkapoag," says former pro Ken Campbell, "then 25 different politicans can give the jobs out. They don't want to give that up." So Ponky becomes, as one Ponkian put it, "a summer drop-off spot for every politician's son, brother-in-law, cousin and niece."

Ponky's members are left, more or less, to take care of the course themselves. Many of them spend their off-hours repainting 150-yard markers, digging weeds out of traps and using their own chain saws to cut down overgrown limbs and trees. They went so far as to buy flags for the pins and rakes for the traps. The rakes were stolen.

Even in the face of such ratty conditions, an act of sheer will is still needed to get a tee time. Unless you're a member of the Inner Club, whose members, for $30 a year, get guaranteed starting times, you must put a golf ball in a long green pipe to establish your position in the tee-off order for that day. Dropping a ball in the pipe at

6:30 a.m., when the pipe is first brought out, will get you a tee-off time at about 11. The only way to beat the pipe is to arrive at the course at 5 o'clock in the morning, sign in with the starter and wait for dawn. On some mornings the fog is so thick at sunrise that groups on the fairway must holler back when it is safe to hit.

So why put up with it all: the shabby conditions, the starting-time masochism, the six-hour rounds? Boston has public courses with shorter waits and better greens. Why do it?

Pete Peters, a dyed-in-the-polyester Ponkian, knows why. "If somebody came up to me right now," says Peters, "and told me, 'Pete, you can become a member of The Country Club today, free of charge. But if you do, you can't ever come back to Ponky,' I wouldn't hesitate a second. I'd stay right here. I'd stay here where I can get some action, have a lot of laughs, relax and be with my friends."

In fact, not only do hardly any of the guys leave Ponky once they become entrenched, they even aspire to what Al Robbins did. Al was a Ponky lifer, a man who played there on weekends when he worked and seven days a week when he retired. But for all his playing, he was still an ordinary hack. Then one day Al parred the 1st hole, picked his ball out of the cup, walked over to the 2nd tee, had a massive heart attack and died on the spot.

Nobody at Ponky grieved much for Al. If anything, the guys thought of him as a lucky stiff. Former pro Campbell remembers why.

"He always said if he ever shot even par on Ponky, he'd like to drop dead then and there," says Campbell. "He finally got his wish."

POSTSCRIPT: *I grew up playing muni courses in Boulder, Colo. Maybe that's why I never had more fun than the week I spent playing with the knuckleheads at Ponky. A month later, I played with some members of "The Country Club" in Brookline, blue-blood host for the 1988 U.S. Open a week later. I never had less fun. That's when it hit me: This is a novel. So I wrote* Missing Links, *which puts a course I called "Ponkaquogue" over the hedge from a snooty course I called "The Mayflower Club" and whirls around a bet made by the boys at Ponky over who can play The Mayflower first. Almost five years later, it's still selling, became a pilot for an ABC-TV comedy and then a movie on TNT. And yet when I went by Ponky on a*

book tour, none of them had read it. They wanted to, they said, but Socks
kept calling for a double-the-bets emergency nine, and well. . . . Maybe
they'll see the movie. If the TV in the lunch room ever starts working again.

Answer to a Young Man's Prayer

MARCH 23, 1998—No salary caps. No $100 million contracts. No
arbitrators. No agents. No lockouts. Just this: a buzzer blaring and a
basketball spinning near the rafters and two kids, two teams, two
towns about to get their lives changed when it comes down.

Of course, pretty much the entire town of Kimberly isn't even
watching the ball. Those folks are still hugging, screaming and
thinking they've just won the Idaho Class A-3 high school championship at the Idaho Center outside Boise. With only 2.9 seconds
left in the season, their hero, junior Rich Arrossa, swished a Hou-
dini of a jumper for a two-point lead. They figured it was over.
They were state champs for the first time in 46 years.

No wonder almost nobody noticed Mike Christensen, a hat-
rack-thin senior for Declo High, as he took the inbounds pass,
dribbled to just past the free throw line and heaved a 75-foot rosary
off his chest, trying to save a 25–0 season, his high school dreams
and the hopes of his town of 300. "Without our high school
sports," says Jay Fox, who runs Declo's only grocery store-gas sta-
tion-deli, "we don't have much."

Seemed like that basketball would never come down. "It was just
like in the movies," says Mike. "Everything seemed to go totally
quiet, and the ball just kind of hung in slow motion."

If anybody was going to make a shot straight out of *Hoosiers*, it
would be Mike. He's one of those kids who can sit in the backseat
of a 1976 GTO going 35 mph and bank a crumpled Doritos bag
off a 7-Eleven and into a trash can. A bow hunter, he has taken deer

at 75 yards. In practice he made 75-foot bombs now and again, though his coach, Loyd Garey, always made him stop. "You're not going to get that shot in the game," Garey said. One night at a Declo girls' game, Mike bought a one-dollar raffle ticket and won a chance at making a half-court shot for charity. *Count it!*

Now the crowd at the Idaho Center loosed the kind of gasp you hear when a Wallenda falls. Now there was this indoor thunder, and Mike's dad, Val, is crying, and Rich's dad, George, is crying, and Rich is crying, and Mike is somewhere in the middle of a scrum of arms and shoes and size-12 grins, and the little scoreboard reads DELCO 72, KIMBERLY 71, 0:00. *Didja hear? Some kid just banked in a 75-footer to take state!*

Sports today isn't easy. We suffer the agents and contracts and lawsuits because we know that at its center sports is heartachingly real. It doesn't come from Disney or Nike or somebody's convoluted scheme to gift wrap a school record. Sometimes there's utter joy, and sometimes there's utter sorrow. Sometimes it stays for only 2.9 seconds, and sometimes it stays for a lifetime. "I never felt anything like that in my life," says Kimberly guard Scott Plew. "To feel the highest high you've ever felt and then, in the next second, the lowest low, it was horrible. But I'm still glad I was a part of it."

What happened next was more amazing still. Nobody beat chests or pointed fingers or commissioned a new tattoo. No parents screamed at scorers or coaches or kids. The Kimberly players just stepped up straight and tall and took their runner-up trophy and medals and their ache as Declo became, officially, the state champ on a shot too big to dream.

Back home Mike and his teammates got to ride through town on the fire truck, and girls Mike hardly knows gave him hugs. The school threw a big assembly to celebrate its first boys' basketball title and asked Mike to try the shot again. Sure enough, he made it on the second try. Fox taped every newspaper clipping he could find by the cash register, where they'll probably hang for what, 50 years? "Tell you what," he says. "He's got free lunch in here the rest of his life, long as I can afford it."

In a small town much of who you are in life is worked out by your senior season. If he gets lucky, Mike might play some Division III college ball, but he's got to go off on his two-year Mormon mission soon. After that, he hopes to stay in Declo, maybe make a living working outdoors, while holding down a permanent job as the town legend.

As for Rich, he went home and played the tape of the end of the game over and over that night until it sank in. He got up early the next morning, went over to the gym and shot for an hour and a half, alone.

"How else am I going to go back next year?" he says.

——•——

A Team with Some Pop

MARCH 8, 1999—The best sub in college hoops has got to be the one who comes in for Issac Gildea at the College of the Redwoods. Not only does the guy pay Issac's tuition, room and board, but he also nearly bursts out crying every time Issac scores.

In return Issac lets the guy sleep with his mom.

That's because Issac's sub is usually his 41-year-old dad, Frank, a 6' 1", 172-pound sophomore guard-forward. Of course, Frank isn't as quick, strong or relentless as Issac. Frank is quicker, stronger and more relentless. At week's end Gildea & Son had helped Redwoods to a 21–12 record and the second round of the California community college tournament.

Frank not only plays like a 20-year-old, but he also *looks* like a 20-year-old. He has 2% body fat, a full head of hair, and he can still dunk, just like Issac, who was the Golden Valley Conference Player of the Year last season. "Girls always say, 'I didn't know you had a brother,'" says Issac, who is two inches taller than Frank. "I'll say, 'That's not my brother. That's my dad.' And they'll say, 'No, seriously!'"

No, seriously, Papa G, as Redwoods fans call him, was a stud football recruit at Kansas State in the late 1970s but blew out his knee before playing a down. He returned to the West Coast, enrolled in Redwoods in '81 and played one year of hoops for the Corsairs, bringing his baby boy, Issac, in a stroller with him to practices. Then he took 18 years off and tried it again. O.K., so he took a redshirt life.

"When he said he wanted to play again, my first thought was, Let's not steal Issac's limelight," says Linda, wife or mother of one-sixth of the Redwoods team. "But Issac knows how good his dad is. His dad still beats him one-on-one! Issac *wanted* him out there."

To become eligible, all Frank had to do was sign up for 12 credit hours. He took some personal-growth classes. In one of them the discussion was about "following your dreams." Imagine that.

"Sometimes, one of the kids will come up to me and say, 'Coach, I'm tired,'" says Redwoods coach Bill Treglown. "I always say, 'Look, Frank works in the mornings [as a middle school gym teacher], comes to class from 12 to 3, practices all out, goes home and plays father and husband, has dinner, then starts working on his second job [as a representative of a fireworks firm]. And he's 41 years old! *Now* tell me how tired you are.'"

Even with all that, the hardest-working player on the floor is Frank. Seventeen years ago he won Redwoods' Mr. Hustle Award, and he might win it again this year. Sometimes his game is as good as ever. One night he came out and hit three straight treys. "That's my dad," says Issac.

Still, Issac has been without a doubt the Corsair with flair, averaging 20.6 points a game to his dad's 1.4. In fact, Issac's been so good lately, Frank hasn't been getting much playing time. *If you don't sit down right now, young man, you're grounded.*

Nothing bridges a generation gap like sitting in the back of a bus with your son and all his friends, learning to get jiggy with it. "Every parent wants to spend quality time with his kid," says Frank. "It just so happens I get to spend quality time with my son on the basketball floor."

About a month ago, before a game at Shasta College, Frank was warming up when he realized a man was staring a hole in him.

The man was an old college teammate of Frank's. The man and his beer belly were so flabbergasted, he could hardly speak. "Frank? Frank, is that *you*?"

You know, sports could use a lot more Franks. Dennis Rodman whines at a press conference that he's *only* going to make $500,000 to play basketball? Introduce him to Frank. Superstar athletes make sons and never meet them? Tell them about Frank. I'm 41. The other day I got off the couch and went skateboarding with my teenage son. Thanks, Frank.

At Redwoods it's a tradition to start the outgoing sophomores in the final regular-season game. That meant Frank and Issac started together for the first time all season. Seeing them out there, Linda about lost it. "I really thought my heart was going to bust open," she says. "A heart can only contain so much."

Frank's still has room. After the last two wins, including Redwoods' first playoff victory in its history last Friday night, he slept with the game ball. "I'm savoring every moment of this," he says, "because it's all going to end soon."

Until then, Papa G, sweet dreams.

POSTSCRIPT: *I'm not sure I've ever known a finer man than Frank Gildea. His boss wrote me a letter six months after this ran. He said the company was at a convention at Disneyworld in Orlando, Fla. After one meeting, the whole group was going into the Magic Kingdom together, kind of a bonding thing. Frank refused to go. His boss insisted. Frank still refused. The boss, irked, finally said, "You better have a good reason." Frank did. He said he'd promised his family that someday, when he made enough money, he was taking them all to Disneyworld. He refused to go until they could all go together.*

—•—

Get the Message?

JUNE 21, 1999—My name is Frankie and I'm eight and I wanna be *just* like my dad.

Like, I used to hate Latrell Sprewell because my *dad* hated Latrell Sprewell. Dad used to yell at the TV about what a jerk Sprewell was, how the guy choked his coach, and how he never once even 'pologized for it, and how he kept pit bulls, and how one of 'em bit off his little girl's ear and chewed her face, and how he didn't even feel bad about it and even said, "These things happen."

But now Sprewell's on the New York Knicks, and they're my dad's and mine's favorite team, and now my dad yells, "Atta baby, Spree!" and "Take it to the hole, Spree!" And that's what I yell, now, too, cuz the Knicks're kickin' serious booty in the NBA playoffs. And now Spree even has a cool commercial out. In it, he calls himself "the American Dream" and acts like he's almost *glad* he choked that coach, and I turn the sound up for the commercial because Spree is *my* dream now, too.

And I seen a man on TV talkin' about Iron Mike Tyson and how things are really lookin' up for the champ cuz, after beatin' the crap out of two guys, he got out of jail *early*. The judge didn't even care that Tyson'd been to jail before for hurtin' that teenage girl, but like my dad says, "What's she doin' up in his room that time a night anyhow?"

And now the men who run boxin' in Lost Vegas say it's O.K. for Tyson to fight again, even though they took his license s'pos'dly forever after Tyson went totally *mental* in the ring, bitin' off a guy's ear like he was Sprewell's dog or somethin'. And the man on TV says that's good because now it looks like Tyson can fight not just once but prob'ly twice this year and make a whole buncha, buncha money, like a hunnert dollars, and it works out good for the boxin' men, too, because he'll prob'ly fight in Lost Vegas, it turns out.

And that's really cool because me and my dad watch a lot of paper view together, which is what best buds do. Like the *really cool* pro wrestlin' match when the man on TV told us a guy fell 80 feet down from a rope and landed right on the turnbuckle. We couldn't see it on paper view, but I bet everybody there thought it was just another crazy wrestlin' stunt, like maybe he'd lay there awhile and then jump up and eat the mike or somethin', but the guy was *really* dead. They stopped the show for a few minutes, but then it started up again, and that was cool, because, like my dad said, this was paper view and what're they gonna do, rip off the people?

My mom didn't like that one bit, but she's actin' funny about a lotta stuff lately. Like, after those two high school kids shot everybody, my mom made me throw away almost all of my cool video games like *Carmageddon*, like it was *my* fault, because she says they're too violet. I started to complain, but my dad told me to shut up because SportsCenter was just gettin' to the car racin', and there was a cool wreck, and when somebody dies in one of those they stop the race at least half the time.

I like to look over my dad's shoulder when he reads the sports, and just now he asked my mom what kinda gotdamn world is it when a guy like Darryl Strawberry is gonna just get a wrist slap for "doin' Coke and ho's," but I know he doesn't mean it because I saw him with both out in the yard today, and besides he never said anythin' mean about Strawberry when he was a New York Met, which is his and mine's favorite baseball team, acourse.

And sometimes my dad gets tired a me lookin' over his shoulder at the sports, and so now I'm down in my room playin' sock basketball and I'm Chris Webber of the Sacramento Kings, and I see the hated John Stockton of the Utah Jazz come down the lane, and it's only a minute into the game and I do exactly what Webber did, which is I just knock Stockton goofy. That's what my dad says you gotta do to earn a man's respeck, like when pitchers throw the baseball at guys' heads, which is just part of the game and doesn't hurt nobody, except if they're Mets heads, acourse.

And Stockton is layin' there, and Webber don't get kicked out of the game, and I say, "Chris Webber has sent a clear message to the

Jazz tonight!" just the way the man on TV did that night my dad and me watched.

O.K., I'm only eight, but like my dad says, you gotta send the right message.

———•———

Magic's Greatest Trick

NOVEMBER 15, 1999—Walter Payton is dead. Payne Stewart is dead. Wilt Chamberlain is dead. Joe DiMaggio is dead.

And Magic Johnson is alive.

He's happier. He's richer. He's stronger than he was on that unforgettable day, eight years ago this week, when he retired because he was HIV positive.

He can bench 325 pounds. Weighing 245, he's about 20 pounds heavier than he was in his prime, but now he's ripped. *Muscle & Fitness* asked him to be on the cover. He's ordered all new suits. He just had a triple-double in a Swedish league appearance, despite being at least 10 years older than any other man on the court. He says that his T-cell count is through the sunroof and that there are "no viral accumulations" in his bloodstream.

"I guess people thought I'd be dead by now," Magic says, "but I'm still here—and I'm still *going* to be here. I don't think about dying. I just live."

Nobody else I know squeezes more out of one day of life than Magic. What he did with his life in basketball—a state high school title, an NCAA title, five NBA titles—is crumb cake compared to what he's doing with it now. Magic is a better man now, a bigger hero, a greater agent of good.

He's one of the most influential black businessmen in America. He owns five Starbucks and has plans to open 10 more—nearly all of them in black neighborhoods, including one in Crenshaw and one in Harlem. He's got four Magic Johnson Theaters in inner-city neighborhoods. He owns a TV and film production company, a talent-management company (Vivica A. Fox, Steve Harvey, Mase are clients) and a record label. He's part owner of four shopping centers, a restaurant and Founders Bank. He's got a foundation that since 1991 has given away $15 million, primarily to community-based organizations dealing with HIV/AIDS education and prevention programs. He's making truckloads of money in neighborhoods in which white businessmen are scared to pull to a stop, much less invest.

He hires black contractors to build businesses that he staffs with black employees, many of whom are working for the first time. When he built one multiplex, in Crenshaw, he hired 12 gang-bangers to be part of the construction crew, and six of them stayed on in full-time jobs. He has gone into areas where there were mostly pawnshops and liquor stores, and put up gleaming palaces that have stayed as clean as they were the day they opened.

He's a player in politics. Bill Clinton has strolled Watts with him. Gore and Bush have met with him. Bill Bradley calls. Yeah, when you're a black businessman with a net worth of more than $200 million and you can move huge blocs of votes with one well-placed quote, your answering machine tends to fill up.

At the end of last season a reporter asked Charles Barkley why more multimillionaire athletes don't give back to their roots. Barkley responded by writing out $1 million checks to his college, his high school and an elementary school. But why are he and Magic exceptions?

"Black athletes forget their neighborhoods," says Magic. "They forget where they came from. They take their millions and move to the suburbs, but if they'd just invest in our own neighborhoods, they'd make more money there than anywhere else!"

Can you imagine the kind of change we'd see in the ghettos if a certain slick-headed former Chicago Bull would follow Magic's lead? "Oh, my God," says Magic. "Michael really *would* own the world then."

No, HIV hasn't killed Magic Johnson. In a sense the virus has been a gift to him. And to us. "It sounds funny," he says, "but it's been a joy. I've been able to teach and help people."

He opens his theaters to health seminars. At his Starbucks he has pamphlets that remind customers that AIDS is the No. 1 killer of American black women aged 25 to 44, that blacks suffer the high-est mortality rate for breast cancer. (His sister-in-law, Shirley John-son, is a two-time survivor.) He gives away 30,000 toys a year, arranges for computer systems to be set up at community centers, answers hundreds of HIV/AIDS-related letters a week. He always *was* good with an assist.

Sports is leaving this century in the world's slowest parade, marched to a dirge, in the worst kind of luxury box. But, thank God, Magic Johnson is alive. "No, Magic is dead," he says with that 10,000-candle smile. "They call me Mister Johnson now."

So nice to see you, Mr. Johnson.

Now Their Hearts Are in the Right Place

JANUARY 25, 1999—My mom always had a little crush on Dan Reeves. She liked his looks, loved his accent and admired how he always wore a coat and tie on the sideline during Denver Broncos games. "Doesn't he look so nice?" she'd gush. So when they both had quadruple-bypass heart surgery the same day five weeks ago, on Dec. 14, she felt as if they were in it together.

At first my mom took the recovery lead, even though she was spotting him 20 years. She spent eight days in a Boulder, Colo., hospital and was released. Reeves, in his typical double-parked way, was out of there in four and eager to get back to his job as coach of the Atlanta Falcons, only to be readmitted two days later with an accelerated heart rate.

My mom stewed about him. Then we watched together the day

he stepped out of that hospital the second time, weeping. It was a Reeves I'd never seen. Unlike my mom, who would cry if you gave her a Glad bag full of dirt, the Reeves I knew was about as sentimental as a right cross. He used to growl in triplicate, play golf as if he were attacking the German flank and was about as popular with his players as a lanced boil. He made them winners, true, but you never saw shorter postgame hugs. His quarterback with the Broncos, John Elway, grew to hate him, especially after Reeves accused assistant coach Mike Shanahan of drawing up plays with Elway behind his back and Reeves fired Shanahan but good.

But the Reeves on TV in December was overwhelmed by the mulligan he'd been given on life and the flood of support he'd received. "I just had no idea that many people cared," he says. He took a deep breath, cut his decibels in half and broke out a wonderful smile that had some very low mileage on it. He answered every card with his own that said, I THANK YOU FROM THE BOTTOM OF MY NEW AND BETTER HEART. By New Year's night, he was a new and better man.

By New Year's night, my mom was dead of a heart attack.

I wish I could say I took it bravely. I was en route to the Fiesta Bowl, got the news on the plane, wept worse than any baby on board and took the first flight home. I couldn't write a grocery list, much less a column. They found one in the vault from three years ago and ran it. I think. I never even looked.

Some guys are tougher. Miami Dolphins coach Jimmy Johnson, for instance. Two Sundays before, his mom died, but Johnson didn't crumble. He didn't book the first jet home to Texas. Instead, he prepared for and then coached a Monday night win over Denver. He worked Tuesday, too. Then, finally, he flew to the funeral on Wednesday morning and was back in Miami that afternoon. He wasn't around for the viewing. His sons were. But he wasn't. He wasn't there to comfort his sick father, either.

But Johnson paid for it. He figured out too late that you can lose a lot of games but only one mother. Outside, his hair was still perfect, but inside he was a mess. He decided to quit his job. Then he decided to unquit his job. He hired an assistant head coach. Somewhere in there, I hope, he's not the same Johnson. Definitely this isn't the same Reeves. And, come to think of it, this isn't the same Elway.

In the off-season John's wife, Janet, had complicated colon surgery at the Mayo Clinic. She came home but went back into the hospital a week later for emergency surgery when an infection put her life in jeopardy. John was beside himself with worry, and it didn't help when, praying on his knees with his four kids one night, one of them asked, "Dad, does Mom have cancer?"

She didn't, and when she finally recovered, third-and-12 didn't seem quite so big anymore. On Sunday night, after John won a fifth trip to the Super Bowl, he hugged Janet and cried. "I learned there's a lot more important things than a dang football game," John said.

"I think we both feel we got a second chance," Janet said.

Funny, there's a lot of that going around. Last spring Elway ran into Reeves at Augusta National, and they fixed the divots in their relationship. Reeves congratulated Elway on finally winning the Super Bowl that they never could together. Later, after the bypass, Elway sent a warm note and a donation to a Falcons charity.

So here we are at the biggest game of the year, and to two of the principal players it means everything and nothing at the same time. Sounds about right, doesn't it?

Me, I don't care who wins. All I ask is that Reeves wear a nice coat and tie.

You never know who's watching.

POSTSCRIPT: *I never knew how many people used sports to bond with their parents until this ran. I was flooded with people who said they read the piece and drove straight to their dad's house, or to their mom's assisted-living apartment, to tell them how much they loved them. I had one man tell me he was on a plane when he read it, landed, changed flights and flew to his dad's to spend the weekend with him instead. They say one person can't make a difference in people's lives, but in a way, my mom did.*

Seoul Searching

AUGUST 28, 2000—Eleven years ago, my wife, our two sons and I adopted a baby girl from Korea. As she grew up, she began asking questions. When she said, "I want to meet someone I'm related to," we went looking. Here's what we found.

After 11 years and 6,000 miles, we still hadn't met our daughter's mother. We had come only this close: staked out in a van across from a tiny Seoul coffee shop, the mother inside with a Korean interpreter, afraid to come out, afraid of being discovered, afraid to meet her own flesh.

Inside the van, Rae, our 11-year-old Korean adopted daughter, was trying to make sense of it. How could we have flown the entire family 6,000 miles from Denver to meet a woman who was afraid to walk 20 yds. across the street to meet us? Why had we come this far if she was only going to reject Rae again?

We were told we had an hour. There were 40 minutes left. The cell phone rang. "Drive the van to the alley behind the coffee shop," said the interpreter. "And wait."

When a four-month-old Rae was hand-delivered to us at Gate B-7 at Denver's Stapleton Airport, we knew someday we would be in Korea trying to find her birth mother. We just never dreamed it would be this soon. Then again, since Rae was a toddler, we've told her she was adopted, and she has constantly asked about her birth mother. "Do you think my birth mother plays the piano like I do?" "Do you think my birth mother is pretty?" And then, at 10, after a day of too many stares: a teary "I just want to meet someone I'm related to."

"When they start asking that," the adoption therapist said, "you can start looking."

We started looking. We asked the agency that had arranged the adoption, Friends of Children of Various Nations, to begin a search. Within six months our caseworker, Kim Matsunaga, told us they had found the birth mother but she was highly reluctant to meet us. She had never told anyone about Rae. In Korea, the shame of unwed pregnancy is huge. The mother is disowned, the baby rootless. Kim guessed she had told her parents she was moving to the city to work and had gone to a home for unwed mothers.

Kim told us the agency was taking a group of Colorado and New Mexico families to Korea in the summer to meet birth relatives. She said if we went, Rae's would probably show up. "The birth mothers almost always show up," she said. Almost.

We were unsure. And then we talked to a family who had gone the year before. They said it would be wonderful. At the very least, Rae would meet her foster mother, who had cared for her those four months. She would meet the doctor who delivered her. Hell, I had never met the doctor who delivered me. But meeting the birth mother was said to be the sweetest. A 16-year-old Korean-American girl told Rae, "I don't know, it just kinda fills a hole in your heart."

We risked it. Five plane tickets to Seoul for our two redheaded birth boys Kellen, 15, and Jake, 13—Rae, me and my wife Linda. We steeled Rae for the chance that her birth mother wouldn't show up. Come to think of it, we steeled ourselves.

At first, it was wonderful. We met Rae's foster mother, who swooped in and rushed for Rae as if she were her long-lost daughter, which she almost was. She bear-hugged her. She stroked her hair. She touched every little nick and scar on her tan arms and legs. "What's this from?" she asked in Korean. She had fostered 31 babies, but it was as if she'd known only Rae. Rae was half grossed out, half purring. Somebody had just rushed in with the missing four months of her life. The foster mother wept. We wept.

All of us, all six American families, sat in one room at a home for unwed mothers outside Seoul across from 25 unwed mothers, some who had just given up their babies, some soon to. They looked into their unmet children's futures. We looked into our unmet birth mothers' pasts. A 17-year-old Korean-American girl— roughly the same age as the distraught girls in front of her—rose and choked out, "I know it's hard for you now, but I want you to know I love my American family."

Another 17-year-old adoptee met not only her birth father but also her four elder birth sisters. They were still a family—had always been one—but they had given her up as one mouth too many to feed. Then they told her that her birth mother had died of an aneurysm two weeks earlier. So how was she supposed to feel now? Joy at finding her father and her sisters? Grief at 17 years without them? Anger at being given up? Gratitude for her American parents? Horror at coming so close to and then losing her birth mother? We heard her story that night on the tour bus, went to our hotel room and wept some more.

All these kids—even the three who never found their birth relatives—were piecing together the puzzle of their life at whiplash speed. This is where you were born. This is the woman who held you. This was the city, the food, the smells. For them, it was two parts home ("It's so nice," Rae said amid a throng of Koreans on a street. "For once, people are staring at Kel and Jake instead of me") and three parts I'm-never-coming-here-again (a teenage boy ate dinner at his foster parents' home only to discover in mid-bite that they raise dogs for meat).

When the day came for our visit with Rae's birth mother, we were told "It has to be handled very, very carefully." She had three children by a husband she had never told about Rae, and she was terribly afraid someone would see her. And that's how we found ourselves hiding in that van like Joe Friday, waiting for the woman of a lifetime to show up. It is a very odd feeling to be staring holes in every Korean woman walking down a Korean street, thinking that your daughter may have sprung from her womb. All we knew about her was that she 1) might have her newborn girl with her, 2) was tiny—the birth certificate said she was 4 ft. 10 in.—and 3) would look slightly more nervous than a cat burglar.

First came a youngish, chic woman pushing a stroller. "That might be her!" yelled Rae—until she strolled by. Then a short, fat woman with a baby tied at her stomach. "There she is!" yelled Rae—until she got on a bus. Then a pretty, petite woman in yellow with an infant in a baby carrier. "I know that's her!" yelled Rae—and lo and behold, the woman quick-stepped into the coffee shop across the street.

The only problem was, she didn't come out. She stayed in that coffee shop, talking to the interpreter for what seemed like six hours but was probably only 20 minutes. We stared at the dark windows of the shop. We stared at the cell phone. We stared at one another. What was this, Panmunjom? Finally, the interpreter called Kim: Drive down the alley and wait. We drove down the alley and waited. Nothing.

By this time, I could have been the centerfold for *Psychology Today*. Rae was still calm. I told her, "If she's not out here in five minutes, I want you to walk right in and introduce yourself." Rae swallowed. Suddenly, at the van window . . . and now, opening the van door . . . the woman in yellow with the baby. And just as suddenly, inside . . . sitting next to her daughter. Our daughter—all of ours. She was nervous. She wouldn't look at us, only at her baby and the interpreter. "We'll go somewhere," said the interpreter.

Where do you go with your deepest, darkest secret? We went to a park. Old Korean men looked up from their chess games in astonishment to see a gaggle of whites and redheads and Koreans sit down at the table next to them with cameras, gifts and notebooks. Rae presented her birth mother with a book she had made about her life—full of childhood pictures and purple-penned poems—but the woman showed no emotion as she looked at it. Rae presented her with a silver locket—a picture of herself inside—but again, no eye contact, no hugs, no touches. The woman was either guarding her heart now the way she'd done 11 years ago, or she simply didn't care anymore, maybe had never cared.

Months before, Rae had drawn up a list of 20 questions she wanted to ask at the big moment. Now, unruffled, she pulled it out of her little purse. Some of us forgot to breathe. "Why did you give me up?" Rae asked simply. All heads turned to the woman. The interpreted answer: Too young, only 19 then, no money, great shame. "Where is my birth dad?" The answer: No idea. Only knew him for two dates. Long gone. Still no emotion. I ached for Rae. How would she handle such iciness from the woman she had dreamed of, fantasized about, held on to? Finally, this one: "When I was born, did you get to hold me?" The woman's lips parted in a small gasp. She swallowed and stared at the grass. "No," she said slowly, "they took you from me." And that's when our caseworker, Kim, said, "Well, now you can."

That did it. That broke her. She lurched, tears running down her cheeks, reached for Rae and pulled her close, holding her as if they might take her again. "I told myself I wouldn't cry," she said. The interpreter wept. Linda wept. I wept. Right then, right that minute, the heavens opened up, and it poured a monsoon starter kit on us, just an all-out Noah. Yeah, even the sky wept.

Any sane group of people would have run for the van, but none of us wanted the moment to end. We had finally got her, and we would float to Pusan before we would give her up. We were all crying and laughing and trying to fit all of us under the birth mother's tiny pink umbrella. But the rain was so loud you couldn't talk. We ran for the van and sat in there, Rae holding her half sister and her birth mother holding the daughter she must have thought she would never see.

Time was so short. Little sentences contained whole lifetimes. She thanked us for raising her baby. "You are a very good family," she said, eyeing the giants around her. "Very strong and good." And how do you thank someone for giving you her daughter? Linda said, "Thank you for the gift you gave us." The birth mother smiled bittersweetly. She held Rae with one arm and the book and the locket tight with the other.

Then it was over. She said she had to get back. She asked the driver to pull over so she could get out. We started pleading for more time. Meet us for dinner? No. Breakfast tomorrow? No. Send you pictures? Please, no. The van stopped at a red light. Somebody opened the door. She kissed Rae on the head, stroked her hair one last time, stepped out, finally let go of her hand and closed the door. The light turned green. We drove off and watched her shrink away from us, dropped off on the corner of Nowhere and Forever.

I think I was still crying when I looked at Rae. She was beaming, of course, which must be how you feel when a hole in your heart finally gets filled.

CHAPTER FIVE: ROUGH

CHAPTER FIVE: ROUGH

Perfect Pard

JUNE 12, 1995—You are looking at a man whose Bubble Shaft was nearly wrestled to the ground by Secret Service agents. You are looking at a man who called the most powerful man on the planet "babe." You are looking at a man who has survived Bubba golf.

The idea was to tee it up with President Bill Clinton, golfing conundrum—an Oxford man with a publinx soul, a guy who looks as if he might putt with his glove on, swear over a game of Bingo Bango Bongo and pull a cold beer out of his bag at the 5th hole. I wanted to know if he really did carry 19 clubs in his bag, take more mulligans than the entire field of the Killarney Elks Invitational and would rather buy a $398 Monster Martha driver than spend $35 on a half-hour lesson from his local professional. In other words, I wanted to find out if he was like me.

So, after almost a year of asking, waiting, reasking, waiting, begging, waiting, scheduling and hoping, I reserved a room at a Washington-area hotel for Friday night, May 26, because the White House had said that possibly, perhaps, barring unforeseen schedule changes, I would play golf with the President the next morning. When I checked in that night, my little red light was on. Of all the little red lights I've had in all the hotels in all the world, the greatest of all was this one.

Be at the White House at 8 a.m.

White House deputy chief of staff Erskine Bowles and SPORTS ILLUSTRATED managing editor Mark Mulvoy would be in the foursome with us. Taking the motorcade there. To Congressional Country Club. Comped. Is that any good?

Golf is like bicycle shorts. It reveals a lot about people. And presidents. What would it reveal about Clinton?

Rain wasn't going to kill the day. Clinton has been known to play in high wind, rain and sleet. Once he supposedly finished 18 with ice on his irons. "He'll drag me out for nine, 10, 11 holes in the late afternoon," Bowles told me before the round, "make us play until it's dark. Until *after* it's dark. Then we go back to work." Clinton started playing golf at age 12 and caddied as a teenager in Hot Springs, Ark. He entered the White House as a 16 handicap, but I'd heard he was down to a 13 now, which would put him in a league with our finest golfing president, John Kennedy. I'd also heard that the 13 was phonier than Cheez Whiz and that he would probably go out and shoot himself a radio station—a Magic 102 or a Zoo 105.

I wanted to find out all of this for myself, as well as, I admit, tear off a swatch of the presidency. Ever since the second grade, I've loved the presidency. Didn't matter who was in office, it was royalty to me. I wanted to touch the spike marks Ike left in the Oval Office floor. I wanted to sit in front of FDR's fireplace in a cardigan. I wanted to rub up against Gerald Ford's toaster.

After ironing my shirt three times and my pants twice, laying my socks in my shoes two different ways, not sleeping, putting in the room at 3 a.m., ordering room service at 6:01 and then actually ironing my *sweater*, I finally arrived at the White House at quarter to eight. After the Secret Service had checked under our rental car with mirrors and in the trunk and in the golf bags, and after Mulvoy and I had each shown our driver's licenses three times, we were finally allowed up the South Lawn drive. A gaggle of agents waited for us.

"You didn't have to go to all that trouble," I said, trying to break the tension. "We could've just hopped the fence like everybody else." Exactly nobody laughed.

At 9:15 there was a rush of people into the Diplomatic Reception Room, where we were waiting—a valet named Lito, steely Secret Service types, a photographer, a press aide and a few others. Then somebody said, "The President is coming," and suddenly he was there, shaking our hands, much taller and sturdier than I expected, with pale blue eyes and a deluxe set of gray hair that was still a little wet from a morning workout and shower upstairs. This was not a guy who looks as if he IV's from a McDonald's fry vat. He looked more like the high school linebacker you kept secretly hoping would show up fat at class reunions but never did. The President wore khakis, loafers, white socks and a blue golf shirt that was maybe too tight for him, which old football players will do, with a Camp David logo and the presidential seal on the left breast.

He invited us to ride in the presidential limo, a Cadillac Fleetwood, for the 15-minute ride to Congressional, in Bethesda, Md. I got in the jump seat directly across from him, and our knees were jammed together. There was a large, black, nylon bag sitting between us, which I figured had the red phone or, at least, a retractable bazooka inside, but then he opened it and said, "Anybody like some hot tea or juice or, let's see, there's fruit in here." Not exactly John le Carré stuff.

We were the heart of a convoy of six police cars, six black Suburban vans, an ambulance and three motorcycle cops blocking traffic on the narrower streets, taking up the two right lanes on the highways, with our escorts' lights running but their sirens silent. I asked the President if he ever putts on the Oval Office rug. No, he said, but he and the USGA have restored the original Eisenhower putting green. It sits not 50 paces from his office door. He also sneaks out now and again and blasts drives from one end of the South Lawn to the other. "It's 300 yards," he said, beaming, "and one time my ball stopped eight yards from the fence."

When we arrived, Clinton swung his legs out, and somebody handed him his white Softspiked golf shoes. He put them on right there, which only shows that no matter how high up you get in this world, you still have to change your shoes in the parking lot. The course was not closed to other golfers because of the presidential outing. According to assistant pro Brian Kiger, the President is among the select group of dignitaries who have playing privileges at Congressional without being members or paying. "He'll probably only play out here four times this year," said Kiger. "If it was too much more than that, he might start hearing it from people."

We did not have a tee time. But somehow Congressional squeezed us in. The club did not stop foursomes from playing ahead of us, but with about eight Secret Service agents with us, I got the feeling playing through would be no problem.

I was wrong about Clinton playing with 19 clubs, but it looked like at least 18. Apparently he has vetoed the 14-club limit for life. He carries Henry-Griffitts custom-made irons, a bunch of Callaway metal woods, including the HeavenWood and the club he drives with, the $500 Great Big Bertha. He told me he just recently stopped carrying his juiced-up, oversized Master Blaster, which was two inches longer than most drivers and was hook-faced to correct his slice and apparently fell under the assault weapons ban. Yet, despite all the techie stuff, the President putts with an old Bullseye that looks like it was lifted from a Little Rock putt putt. "I must have 30 putters," he said, "but I like this one."

He has a serviceable swing, though maybe he's a little too upright and a little too much on his toes, which causes him to hit the ball high and right. But his iron game, even with his long irons, is terrific. Like most guys, he is driven by the hope that deep inside him lives a single digit who is just waiting for the shankless wedge to be invented. He is the kind of guy who looks in everybody else's bag and says, "Mind if I swing this?" He had already mentioned once or twice in the limo that the best score he'd ever had at Congressional was an 81. He said it again while we were on the practice range. He'd never broken 80.

And so we set out to the 1st tee, each of us with his hopes and 100-compression dreams. I have three major goals in life: 1) achieving world harmony, 2) winning a Nobel Prize and 3) having the President of the United States call me Pards. So I quickly suggested that Clinton and I team in a better ball against Bowles and Mulvoy, who both happened to be wearing khaki pants and green shirts and looked like the night shift at Denny's. Despite the fact that we were both 13s, they played Clinton as a 14 and reduced me to a 12, which proves that America does have a caste system. I put a serious sportswriter snap slice on the first ball, far out-of-bounds (F.O.B.), but the President said I could have a 1st-tee mulligan, which, as we all know, is provided for under the Constitution. He took a mulligan, too, but never another the rest of the day.

Do you know that feeling when you show up as a single at the course and you're praying you get thrown in with somebody fun, not Mr. and Mrs. Crumpacker and their delightful teenage boy, Cheddar? Well, Clinton is a guy you'd be happy to get thrown in with. He's the sort of guy who keeps a tee in his mouth as he walks and, yes, putts with his glove on and leans on your shoulder as you pencil in the scores, writhing or celebrating depending on how the match is going. "That's my pards!" he'd say when I hit a good shot and "I gotcha, Partner," when I didn't. He was charming and warm and amazingly normal.

He took the team part of the golf to heart and often stood close to me on shots. One time, I stepped back to take a practice swing and nearly brained him. He flinched and hopped back quickly, and the Secret Service guy gave me a little dirty look. That would be nice. Nuts turning the White House fence into a steeplechase, maniacs opening up with semiautomatic guns on Pennsylvania Avenue and people throwing Cessnas at him, and he doesn't get a bruise, and then I knock him cold with the dreaded TaylorMade Bubble Shaft driver.

Later, I asked him if he felt vulnerable out in the open like this. "No. I don't feel unsafe playing golf. I don't feel unsafe in the White House, either. They keep catching these guys. The system works."

Other than that, it was like playing with the assistant grocer down the block. He shanked a wedge once and turned to Bowles and Mulvoy (the single-digit handicappers) and moaned, "Now what'd I do there?" But he never invoked the Executive Privilege Redo or even the Presidential Override. He could have. Who was going to stop him? Lito?

Not that he was above taking a putt now and again when it didn't matter to the bet, but only after everybody from me to the caddies to the press aide had practically sprained a larynx trying to be the first to give it to him. A guy like Mulvoy does not normally give downhill, sidehill six-footers to an opponent, but I'm sure he wasn't eager to get audited for the next 20 years, either.

On about the 3rd hole Clinton was meandering along when I heard him say to Joe, his caddie, "I had an 81 here one day, but I wasn't thinking about things that day."

And so I stopped and said, "You thinking about something today?"

And he said, "I've got Bosnia about to blow up on me."

Oh, *that*.

Pards and I won the first nine, one up, and as the day progressed, I almost forgot about the Secret Service men with their backs to our drives, watching hole after hole for any suspicious robins. I also forgot about all the golf carts following us, some with telephones, some with Secret Service, some with aides-de-camp, one with the official White House photographer, one with the White House doctor and one with Lito, who would materialize magically now and again with refreshments.

On the 11th tee Lito appeared with five colorful and mysterious looking pills that looked a lot like George Jetson's dinner. The President looked at them as if they would have to be inserted somewhere other than orally. "Look at these," he groaned. "Honestly, now, do you feel any security in knowing that the leader of your country has to take this many pills?" We all laughed, except the doctor, who hollered, "Just take them!" He did. (The doctor said they were vitamins.)

President Taft called the White House "the lonesomest place in the world," but right then Clinton and his smile seemed a million miles from it. I could tell because he kept putting his arm on my shoulder and saying things like, "Some day, huh?" and, "This is terrific." I asked, "Mr. President, which keeps you from spending more time on the course, Hillary or the Secret Service?" And he said, "Oh, they don't mind. Hillary is actually very supportive of my golf. She thinks it makes me function better." I asked him how he had been able to take three strokes off his handicap and still find time to run the world. "It's all because I get to play with so many good players now," he said. "The best perks of this office are who you get to play golf with. I've played with Jack Nicklaus, Arnold Palmer, Raymond Floyd, Amy Alcott. Amy Alcott had a 33 on the front nine the day I played with her. Thirty-three!"

At one point I became so comfortable with him that he read a putt and said, "Right lip," or something like that, and I answered, "You got it, babe," before I realized I had just given presidential protocol a free drop. But he said nothing, and Bowles said nothing. Only the press aide seemed to blanch. Is this a great country or what?

I knew for sure that it was on about the 15th when Joe watched Clinton sky-fade another shot and grumbled at him, "Doggone it, stay off them toes! You ain't no *ballet* dancer!" There are countries where Joe and all his descendants would be hung from their tonsils for such an utterance. In America, Joe's president merely sighed, "I know. Sorry."

Actually, Mr. President played very well. He had a 41 on the front and had every chance to break 80 for the first time when he sank a 25-footer on the par-5 10th for a birdie. But he three-putted the next two holes and never quite pardoned himself. "Those two three-putts broke my spirit," he said forlornly. In the end he shot 82, hitting eight fairways and nine greens, with 32 putts and two sandies. It was good enough to beat me by two strokes, which I feel very patriotic about. I feel it's every citizen's duty to lose to his president by two shots.

Still, despite the fact that we were four shots under our handicap, we lost the back nine and the match to Mulvoy (77) and Bowles (76). I reached to pay up, and Bowles said, "We never actually play for anything. It's just fun."

Then the real world started to close in on us. As we walked, Bowles handed Clinton a legal-sized gray folder that seemed to appear out of nowhere and looked like something that got couriered around a lot in *Fail-Safe*. I guessed it was a dossier with political and intelligence material on Bosnia. Bowles became quite serious, commanding Clinton's attention, while all at once a few hundred Congressional members wanted to shake his hand and the Secret Service agent, who had walked next to us all day and been so friendly, suddenly threw a Dennis Rodman elbow in my gut to get next to the President. Clinton rode back to the White House in the limo with the dossier. We rode back in a Suburban.

We said a quick goodbye 15 minutes later in the Oval Office. He seemed to have enjoyed the round a helluva lot. "You guys made my day," he said. I knew he had to make calls in exactly two minutes to French president Jacques Chirac and British prime minister John Major about Bosnia, and I could see he didn't want to have me hanging around, going, "Tell them hi for me!" He was trying to find a nice way to tell us to get lost. "I'd love to have you guys stay, but I have to, you know. . . ," and he gestured toward the big phone on the Resolute desk.

So he put away his smile and he went back to his life, trying to decide whose lives are worth risking in a spiral staircase of a war 5,000 miles from home, and I went back to mine, trying to fix the wife's passenger-side power window. As I walked out of the White House, I looked back one last time through the thick bulletproof glass, where I saw him put the phone to his ear and his forehead in his hand, ready for a long night in the lonesomest place in the world.

Good luck, Pards.

POSTSCRIPT: *A week after this ran, I was working diligently in my office (read: napping), when the phone rang. I was a little groggy and the voice said, "Hold for the president." And I thought, "The president of what? The Kiwanis Club?" And then there was this southern voice going, "Rick, we're just all laughin' like hell over here!" And I still didn't know who it was. I think I said, "You are? What'd I do now?" And Bill Clinton said, "The piece. Funn-knee! Loved the line about the Denny's shirts!" And I said something really witty like, "Oh, well. . . ." And he said, "Well, gotta go!" And that was how I didn't get to be Ambassador to Switzerland.*

—•—

Mon Dieu! *Better Safe Than Sorry*

JULY 26, 1999—Do you realize you could be British Open champ?

You telling me you can't make a six on a par 4? A double bogey? You could make double bogey in flippers and a snorkel. You could hit a five-iron, an oar and a rigatoni noodle and make a double bogey. A well-trained chicken could make a freaking double bogey.

The only golfer on earth who *can't* make a double bogey when he has to is France's Jean Van de Velde, which is too bad, because he needed a simple double bogey on the 72nd hole on Sunday in Carnoustie, Scotland, to win the British Open.

The trophy was polished. The 10-year exemption was ready. The wife was lipsticked up. All he needed was a six. He made a seven.

The last hole at Carnoustie is a 480-yard par 4 with a wee burn that crosses the fairway three times. All you want to do to make double bogey is hit two little five-irons in front of each crossing, then a little wedge and *three-putt* for immortality.

Instead, Van de Velde hits a driver. A freaking driver! A driver brings the first crossing of the wee burn into play. A driver brings Carnastie's wrist-breaking botany into play. Van de Velde needs to hit a driver like Strom Thurmond needs a nipple chain.

Why doesn't his caddie stop him? "Well, zere was a lot of zee wind," says Van de Velde's odd caddie, Christopher (he wouldn't give his last name), a 30-year-old Parisian who wears a beatnik's tuft under his chin and a white beret over his bleached-blond hair.

Wind, Chris? *Wind?* You've got *three shots* to reach the green! If I'm Chris, I snap the driver in half and say, "Fine. Hit the driver."

O.K., Van de Velde hits the driver and pushes his shot a kilometer right, nearly onto the 17th tee box. Now he's got 240 yards to the green with nothing but burn and heartburn in between.

Any erect-walking mammal with an ant's nostril of sense hits a 120-yard wedge into the middle of the fairway, then another 120-

yard wedge onto the green, three-putts and orders up champagne.

Instead, Van de Velde hits a two-iron. A freaking two-iron! A two-iron is the worst idea since Lou Brock for Ernie Broglio!

Why, oh, why doesn't his caddie stop him? "Well, we talked about zis, but zee lie, it was just so *parfait*," says Christopher.

Zee lie, Chris? *Zee lie?* If I'm Chris, I say, "My, zat is a nice lie, iz eet not, Jean?" and throw everything but the wedge and the putter into the burn.

So *les misérables* hit a two-iron, and the ball sails *two* kilometers right, caroms off the grandstand and bounces back over the burn, into some heather high enough to lose Ian Woosnam in. Uh-oh.

"Jean was *peezed*," says Christopher. "He sayz to me, 'Why don't you make me hit wedge?' He says, '*On est trop gourmand!*' ['You are a glutton!'] I theenk that he and I, we want too much show."

Now Van de Melt has the worst lie since "I did not have sex with that woman." He can barely *see* the ball. He hits it right into the wee burn.

So, laying three, the ball is sitting mostly under water, with the six-foot-high creek wall right in front of it, and, obviously, he's going to have to drop and—*No!*

No, no, no! Please tell us Van de Velde *isn't* taking off his shoes and socks, rolling up the legs of his pants and climbing into the wee burn to *hit* it. He *is*! He's going to play it out of the burn!

Why, oh, why doesn't his caddie stop him? "Well," says Christopher. "He wants to do zees, but zee wall, it iz very tall."

Van de Velde finally has a sudden growth spurt of brain cells and decides to drop instead—back into the haggis. This time, he easily hits it over the wee burn and straight into zee beach.

Now he's got to get it up and down out of a greenside bunker just to make the playoff, which he does. Of course, by then he needs a whisky, a massage and emergency psychoanalysis and proceeds to lose to someone named Paul Lawrie, who is as shocked as anybody to even *be* in the playoff, seeing as he might as well be a vacationing upholsterer from Glasgow.

"For a time," decides Christopher, "thees was zee best day of my life. Now, it iz zee worst."

Van de Velde put on a brave face for the fans, but once in the scoring trailer, he sobbed into his hands. "Next time," he said, bittersweetly, "I'll hit zee wedge. You'll say I'm a coward, but I'll hit zee wedge."

No, next time, give Christopher the wrong dates.

POSTSCRIPT: You can't imagine what a godsend Jean Van de Velde was to us poor golf scribes, standing there, with one hole to play, in blustery, dreadful Carnoustie, wondering how the hell we were going to make a Frenchman beating an unheard of Scot by three shots in the British Open interesting. And then this wonderful, nutty man started rolling up his pants! It was like setting a 24-ounce steak in front of a man who hadn't eaten in a week! Don't tell me there's no guardian angel for sports columnists.

Day of Glory for a Golden Oldie

APRIL 21, 1986—That arm. Who could forget that arm? In the roar of roars at the 18th green, from behind a Masters scoreboard glittering with the names of golf's power brokers—BALLESTEROS and WATSON and LANGER and KITE—under the sign that said No. 18, beside the huge black letters that read NICKLAUS, next to a red 9, came the arm that had put that number there, the arm that seconds before had placed a red 8 next to NORMAN, and that arm was pumping furiously.

No head, no body, no shoulder, just an arm belonging to the leader-board man, pumping and pumping for pure, wallowing joy. To hell with employee objectivity. Jack Nicklaus had just won the Masters, once again, and that arm just couldn't help itself. If it was Old St. Nick who had delivered the goodies; if it was the Ancient One who had posted that birdie at 17, then parred 18, while Greg Norman had taken out his Fore!-iron and mailed the gallery a souvenir on the same hole; if it was the Olden Bear who had mystically come from five shots and a couple of decades back to hijack the Masters golf tournament, then it was that arm behind the scoreboard that was telling us what it meant.

Can't you see? That red 9 set off an avalanche of history. Jack Nicklaus, a 46-year-old antique, had won his 20th major golf championship, his first green jacket in 11 years, his sixth over three decades and all in this, the 50th, and arguably the best, Masters.

How complete, how whole this was for Nicklaus. Hadn't he been duped out of that 20th long ago? Hadn't Tom Watson's chip taken the U.S. Open from him at Pebble Beach in 1982 and broken his spirit? How many times had he led a major only to have his pocket picked at the end? Now the spikes were on the other foot. Here was Nicklaus, in one swell swoop, reaching down from another era and snatching a major championship from the reigning czars of this one. It is a trick no other golf god has pulled, not Palmer or Hogan or Snead or Sarazen. Nicklaus had beaten young men at a young man's game on young men's greens and beaten them when they were at their youthful best. As Tom Kite, destiny's orphan, put it, "I hit nearly every shot the way I dreamed about it today. But that's the strange thing about golf. You don't have any control about what your opponent does."

And just in the Nicklaus of time, too. Who else but Jack could save us from the woeful, doleful bowl full of American Express (do-you-know-me?) golf winners of late? And who else could play John Wayne, riding in to rescue the Yanks from golf's rampaging foreign legion: the dashingly handsome Seve Ballesteros of Spain; the stone-faced Bernhard Langer of West Germany; Australia's Norman, he of the colossal swing and larger-still reputation, more unfulfilled now than ever; and Zimbabwean–South African–Floridian Nick Price, who on Saturday broke the course record that had gone unsurpassed for 46 years, then on Sunday recoiled in the giant shadow of what he had done.

Here had come Nicklaus, an American legend still under warranty, armed with a putter the size of a Hoover attachment, denting the back of Augusta's holes with 25-foot putts at an age when most guys are afraid to take the putter back. Here had come Nicklaus, sending such a deluge of decibels into the Georgia air that lakes rippled and azaleas blushed; starting such a ruckus that grown men climbed trees, children rode on shoulders, concession-stand operators abandoned their posts, all just to tear off a swatch of history. Was that Jack in the checked pants and yellow shirt? Hmmmm. Yellow goes nice with green, doesn't it, Jack? You devil.

Maybe that was it. Maybe Nicklaus had drawn up a contract with Lucifer for one last major, for that slippery 20th that had eluded him since 1980, for a sixth green blazer. In exchange, Nicklaus would do pro-ams in Hades the rest of his days.

What else could explain it? How else to explain the guy in 160th place on the money list, just one spot behind Don Halldorson, winning the Masters? How else to explain a man who hadn't won in two years charging back the last day, going seven under for the final 10 holes, sculpting a 30 that tied the Masters record for the back nine—winding up with a sporty 65 as he roared past eight players and won? This is a guy who missed the cut at the Honda, for the love of Hogan. In fact, Nicklaus missed the cut in three of seven tournaments this year and withdrew from a fourth. Of the ones he finished, his most impressive showing was a tie for 39th at the Hawaiian Open, which didn't exactly throw a scare into Corey Pavin, who won. The $144,000 for winning the Masters means he's up to $148,404 for the year. Nicklaus goes through more than that in limo tips.

The man is older than Pete Rose, for crying out loud. He has played in more Masters (28) than Pavin has lived years (26). When Nicklaus won his first Masters, in 1963, Norman was eight years old, Ballesteros and Langer five. Nicklaus either signed his soul away or is angling for an endorsement contract with Efferdent.

"I read in the Atlanta paper this week that 46-year-olds don't win Masters," said Nicklaus. "I kind of agreed. I got to thinking. Hmmm. Done, through, washed up. And I sizzled for a while. But I said to myself, I'm not going to quit now, playing the way I'm playing. I've played too well, too long to let a shorter period of bad golf be my last."

More remarkable in all this comeback talk was the fact that rumors were flying that Nicklaus had been missing some serious greens, and not just the kind you take a Toro to. "My company was a mess," Nicklaus says.

In an effort to improve the fortunes of his own company, Golden Bear International, Nicklaus let the contract of his chief executive officer, Chuck Perry, lapse seven months ago and assumed day-to-day control of the business himself. "Chuck worked very hard for me," says Nicklaus, "but he wanted to build an empire. He was sending out p.r. releases talking about a $300 million empire and all that stuff. But I don't want an empire. What am I going to do with an empire? I've got five kids, a beautiful wife and I'm hoping on some grandkids. That's what I care about."

Nicklaus admits that he has been distracted by business worries, in particular about a couple of his many golf-course and real-estate deals. But he says he is not in a financial crunch, which makes it just a coincidence that he recently signed as a spokesman for Nabisco Brands and is in negotiation with ABC-TV to appear on golf specials for five years. "The ABC contract is with the lawyers right now," Nicklaus says.

With his business dealings weighing heavily on his shoulders, to say nothing of his checkbook, it was no wonder he was floundering on the golf course. His irons and woods were still Jack Be Nimble, but his putter had been pure Tip O'Neill. Take Thursday's opening round, for instance. He had 11 putts inside 15 feet and made one. On Sunday's front nine he missed two four-footers. "If I could just putt," he said Friday, "I might just scare somebody. Maybe me."

But that seemed fanciful, and it wasn't just newspaper writers typing him off. CBS analyst Ken Venturi told *USA Today,* "Jack's got to start thinking about when it is time to retire."

After all, who could take Nicklaus seriously after his opening rounds of 74 and 71? Besides, by Saturday, the leader board was doubly stocked with people you had actually heard of. One was a certain swashbuckling Spaniard who has been out of work much of this year, what with his father's recent death and his sword-fighting with PGA Tour commissioner Deane Beman. Coming into the Masters, Ballesteros had played only nine competitive rounds in all and had made precious little money. "Ninety dollars," he joked. "All on practice-round bets with [Ben] Crenshaw and [Gary] Player."

Still, Ballesteros's rapier hardly looked rusty, and when he opened with a convincing 71–68 and a one-shot lead, nobody could make him less than the favorite for his third coat. "They ought to name this place after him," said Price. "He hits it so long and so high and draws it so well and is so imaginative around the greens that I don't think he'll ever finish out of the top five here."

Price's game isn't all that ill-fitting, either. On a windless Saturday that Watson said left the course as "defenseless as I've ever seen it," Price's 63 was a course record, a Jackson Pollock splash of birdies—nine in a series of 12 holes—that broke the course record of 64, set in 1940 by Lloyd Mangrum and equaled by Nicklaus and four others. That left him at five under. And when Seve got heavy on Saturday, turning a one-shot lead at 17 into a one-shot deficit by the time he hit the clubhouse, Price found himself tied with Ballesteros, Langer and Donnie Hammond, one shot behind Norman.

Everybody genuflect. It's Sunday morning in the cathedral of golf, and the high priests are all here. Norman leading, with Price, Langer, Ballesteros, Watson, Tommy Nakajima of Japan and Kite all within two shots, not to mention an altar boy, Hammond. Nicklaus, with a Saturday 69 ("The first time I've broken 70 since I can't remember when," he said), was looking surprised but quite harmless at four back.

"My son Steve called me at the house we're renting this morning," Nicklaus said, "and he asked me, 'Well, Pop, what's it going to take?' And I said, 'Sixty-six will tie and 65 will win.' And he said, 'Well, go ahead and do it.'"

But as Sunday's round began, Nicklaus looked as if he was going to keep on doing what he had been doing, which was knocking the ball tight and putting loose. He missed four-footers at the 4th and the 6th, and when he got to the 9th tee, he was right where he started—two under. He was also five shots behind Norman.

Then, suddenly, all heaven broke loose.

Playing two groups ahead of Ballesteros and Kite, four ahead of Price and Norman, Nicklaus finally got a birdie putt to drop, an 11-footer. Four shots back.

At the 10th, he birdied from 25 feet, which should have put him three back, except for an odd set of goings-on at No. 8, where both Kite and Ballesteros had left the hole without ever pulling their putters. Kite had holed a wedge from 81 yards for an eagle, followed by Ballesteros from 40 for another eagle. Not only did that speed up play considerably, but it also kept Nicklaus four back of the leader, now Ballesteros.

But when Ballesteros bogeyed No. 9 and Nicklaus answered with a birdie at the portal to Amen Corner, No. 11, Augusta National began to overheat like a $99 Impala. Two back.

Then Nicklaus did something that got him cooking. He made a bogey 4 at the 12th hole. Three back.

"I don't know why, but it really got me going," he said. "I knew I couldn't play defensive with the rest of the course. I knew I needed to be aggressive coming in."

On to the par-5 13th, the Curtis Strange Memorial Hole, where the Masters is often lost and rarely won and where Nicklaus bent a three-wood so precariously close to the woods that his part-time caddie and full-time son, Jackie, thought he had put it in the creek on the left-hand side. "Shots like that are a little too much for a 24-year-old heart, Dad," he told him. Dad hit a 210-yard three-iron over Rae's Creek and to within 30 feet, then two-putted for birdie. Two back.

Now it was Ballesteros's turn at 13, only he did it better, letting a six-iron drift lazily in left to right and sinking an eight-footer, his second eagle of the day and third of the tournament. At this rate, with the par-5 15th still to come, the Spaniard looked as if he could radio ahead with his sleeve length. Nicklaus was four behind him, two back of Kite. See you at the awards stand, Seve.

Desperate, at the 15th, Nicklaus let loose a mammoth drive, 298 yards, so big it surprised even him. He had changed his swing (less hands) and his diet (more food). He had gone on the Eat to Win Diet and lost. "I was down to 170 pounds and I realized I couldn't play golf at 170," he said. He's up to 190 and hitting it farther than ever. Fat Jack is truly back.

With 202 yards to go at 15 and the tournament in the balance, Nicklaus turned to Jackie and said, "You think a three would go very far here?" To which Jackie said, "let's see it."

Obligingly, Nicklaus hit his four-iron to 12 feet and made the eagle putt for exactly that—a three. The crowd's yelp was downright frightening. Two back.

As Nicklaus walked from the 15th green to the 16th tee, one had the odd feeling of being indoors at, say, an overtime Kentucky basketball game, yet all the while being outdoors. That's loud.

And wild. Six-figure executives were slapping high fives. Women in $400 dresses were sprinting ahead to get a vantage point. "He's hot! He's hot! He's hot!" one man kept shrieking, perhaps about to ignite himself.

"The noise was deafening," said Nicklaus. "I couldn't hear anything. I mean, nothing! I wasn't trying to think about the leader board. All I knew was that I was putting the ball on the green and making birdies and I was going to keep doing it."

As Ballesteros was walking up the 15th fairway after a King Kong–like drive, Nicklaus was pulling out a five-iron at the par-3 16th. "I nailed it," he said. But he couldn't see it. "I could hear the gallery at the green starting to rumble and I said, 'Oops, I've hit it close.'"

Oops, he had come within inches of a hole in one, the ball skittering three feet by the pin. The eruption from the gallery may have been the most resounding in Masters history, next to, of course, the one that greeted the putt that came next. One back.

What does one feel like when all around you, a golf course, a state, a country, are coming unglued and you are the only person keeping them from imploding entirely? Ballesteros surely found out as he stood over his four-iron, 200 yards from the 15th green, his ears ringing. What he felt like when he hit it is unknown since he was off the Augusta property within minutes of the finish of his round. But to watch your Masters chances go kerplunk in green-dyed water as his did cannot be good for your est training.

"He had an awkward lie up on a knob, but he hit his last few iron shots heavy," Kite said. "It was a tough situation: the lie, the circumstances, what Nicklaus was doing, the noise. It was so noisy you couldn't even hear each other."

"I wasn't under pressure," Ballesteros said on Monday. "It's just that I hit too easy a swing with a four-iron. I should have hit a hard five. I played very good. Just one bad shot, that's all."

Now Nicklaus had reeled in Ballesteros but not Kite, who would birdie 15. That made it a three-way tie at eight under par. Meanwhile, Norman had quickly recovered from a double bogey at 10 and was sitting two back.

Nicklaus tried to get ready to drive at the par-4 17th but had a small problem. "I kept getting tears in my eyes," he said. "It happened to me once at Baltusrol. But here, it happened four or five times. I had to say to myself, Hey, you've got some golf left to play."

After driving into the left rough he hit a 125-yard pitching wedge to 11 feet. He drained the putt. "Dead center." Nicklaus leads. One up over Ballesteros and Kite.

Moments later, Ballesteros, shaken, three-putted at 17 for bogey, but Kite made par from the back of the green and Norman was stormin', too, making birdies at 15 and 16. Still one up, now over Kite and Norman.

Eighteen surrendered without incident for Nicklaus. He hit onto the front of the tiered green, almost precisely where the pin traditionally has been set for the final round. This year, the green had been redesigned, and the pin was now set on the back level. He nearly holed out from 40 feet, dropped it in for the par, then hugged Jackie.

"I was getting choked up with all the people cheering on every hole. I was so proud of him," Jackie said. "Finally, when he putted out on 18 I told him, 'Dad, I loved seeing you play today. It was the thrill of my lifetime. I mean, that was awesome.'"

Father and son walked arm in arm to the scorer's tent and then to the Bob Jones cabin to wait and see.

What they saw first was Kite at 18 lining up a 12-foot putt for birdie and a tie. Would Kite, so long denied, finally have a chance at a major?

"I made that putt," said Kite. "It just didn't go in. Honest to God . . . I made it so many times in the practice rounds—seven or eight times—and it never broke left once." It broke left. Still one up.

Now the only obstacle between Nicklaus and perhaps his most remarkable major of all was Norman.

"We heard the roar [for Nicklaus] on 15 and then another roar and another," Norman recalled. "By that time, Nicky [Price] and I were back there with about 50 people following us. So I said to Nicky, 'Let's do something to wake these people up.'"

Out of an impossible divot lie on 17, Norman somehow made a pitch-and-run shot over a hill that stopped 12 feet from the hole, then sank the putt. Tie. Nine under par.

With pandemonium all around him, Norman chose to hit a three-wood from the 18th tee. The shot was fine and straight, except that it left him holding his four-iron, which in Norman's hands lately works about like a waffle iron. It was the four-iron he had hit into the gallery at 10 to set up the double bogey.

He sliced it this time into the gallery ringing the 18th green, and couldn't get up and down for par, his 16-footer missing left. "I just basically spun out and pushed it to the right," Norman explained. "I was trying to hit it too hard and too high. . . . I was going for the flag. I was going for the birdie and the win. It was the first time all week I let my ego get the best of me."

Your usual, Jack, 42 regular?

"This," said Nicklaus in triumph, "was maybe as fine a round of golf as I've ever played."

He drove down Magnolia Lane and out the iron gates in green for a preposterous sixth time. He had won at Augusta in 1963, when Sam Snead finished two strokes back, and '65, '66, '72, '75 and now, '86. That's a 23-year span between his first and last fitting. His original jacket was a 44 long. "It fits me like a tent," he said. "I wore [New York Governor] Tom Dewey's jacket for years, and finally I had my own jacket made."

His record of longevity and dominance is unequaled. And that includes his victories in five PGA Championships (1963, '71, '73, '75, '80), four U.S. Opens ('62, '67, '72, '80), three British Opens ('66, '70, '78) and two U.S. Amateurs ('59 and '61). He has now won three majors in his 40s, which is another first.

All of which says, truly, once and for all, that if there ever was a better golfer than Jack William Nicklaus, then Woody Allen can dunk.

"I finally found that guy I used to know on the golf course," Nicklaus told his wife, Barbara. "It was me."

So welcome back.

POSTSCRIPT: His is still the greatest sports moment I was ever lucky enough to witness. I remember, after Nicklaus left the old press quonset hut at Augusta National that night following one of the most amazing one-hour press conferences I'd ever heard, guys started gagging. One old columnist, who must've seen everything twice, just kept staring at his keyboard, muttering, "It's too big!" Another well-known writer started his column off that day with, "My fingers won't type." I followed Jimmy Breslin's advice that night: The bigger the story, the smaller your focus. When John Kennedy died, Breslin interviewed the gravedigger. So I went with that arm. I wrote clean through to 7 a.m. and never looked at my watch until the sun hit me in the eyes.

Need a Fourth?

MARCH 31, 1997—You would not believe the looks on some of the faces. Three players will be waiting for the fairway to clear, waiting to hit their first drives of the day at the public Rancho Park Golf Course in Los Angeles, when the starter will crackle over the public-address system, "Sending a single to join you." And the threesome will turn to greet the stranger, only to find that he is O.J. Simpson, wearing a single black glove. "You get some pretty funny reactions," Simpson said during a one-hour interview at Rancho Park on March 19. "But nobody's walked away yet. Not once."

Of course, even Simpson, acquitted of double-murder charges but still guilty in the minds of countless Americans, including the 12 members of a civil jury that found him liable for the deaths, knows that given the choice between playing and not playing, golfers would tee it up with Mussolini if they had to.

So this is how Simpson will play out his life. Effectively banished from the posh Riviera Country Club (his status is "inactive"), where he has been a member for almost a decade, and not exactly somebody you'd like to sponsor at any club anywhere else in the world—*You want us to consider whom?*—the 1968 Heisman Trophy winner and NFL Hall of Fame running back is confined to a world of shaggy greens, divot-ravaged tee boxes and $1.95 fried-egg sandwiches: a minimum-security facility known as public golf. He has no choice. He's a golf addict.

"Some days my mom and my sister [who live with him, along with his two youngest kids and his brother-in-law] notice how tense I am, and they say, 'Why don't you go play golf?' and I'll say, 'I played this morning!'" says Simpson, who also talked with me for 30 minutes by telephone last week. "For five hours a day golf takes all my concentration, and nobody bugs me. People are good about it. It's like a golf course is kind of sacred. If I didn't have golf, I'd be in Bellevue."

A lot of the regulars at Rancho Park, where Simpson plays two to three times a week—"two to three times a week too many," grumbles assistant pro Paul Hopps—wish he were in Bellevue or Leavenworth or anywhere else. He is a kind of human unplayable lie. "If he ever gets in my group," says two-time Rancho Park club champion Nicolas Beauvy, "I'll walk away. Just having him around here makes my skin crawl."

Simpson gets no preferential treatment at Rancho Park. Just to get a weekend tee time, he must call the computerized reservation line at 5 a.m. a week before and hold for at least an hour, until the system starts assigning times. Failing that, he shows up on the day he wants to play and puts his name on the singles list.

Simpson on a golf course is like having a wolf on the loose. Most people will look, but they won't get close. There are few autograph requests after he putts out on 18 and passes the golfers who are practicing at Rancho's dusty two-tiered driving range. There's whispering, there's pointing, but when he looks toward the range, there are suddenly a lot of heads snapping back to check foot alignment. And when he and his three playing partners that day take a table in the dim and bare Rancho bar to play the 19th hole, you can't help but notice that they are soon isolated from other groups. Not that it's anything new. You'd be amazed how many half-empty restaurants Simpson walks into that have an hour wait. "Hey, I'm not naive," he says in the Rancho bar. "I know that, looking around in this room, a lot of people think I'm an a------. I mean, it's easy to be anti-me. But nobody can say I wasn't nice to them and polite and cordial to them through this whole thing [his criminal and civil trials]."

One twentysomething Rancho regular, who begged anonymity, says Simpson flirts with her, adding, "He asked me one day, 'Do you believe in love at seventh sight?' And I said, 'O.J., if I went out with you, my parents would kill me. And my girlfriend would kill me. And then *you'd* kill me. Then where would I be?'"

Simpson actually laughed at that one. He even has a favorite O.J. joke. "O.K.," he says. "O.J. and A.C. [Al Cowlings] are in the Bronco. And O.J. is pissed. He goes, 'I said Costa *Rica*, mother------! Not Costa *Mesa!*'"

It is a curious situation. A guy who used to frolic at country clubs with movie stars while the valets washed his car now hits striped balls off sickly green driving-range mats while waiting for his turn on one of the most-played courses in America. "He gets the freeze out here," says Beauvy. Of course, some freezes thaw quicker than others. One night Simpson finished his second Heineken and left. The barmaid, who had cold-shouldered him, watched him go and then rushed to his table. She grabbed his signed scorecard and tucked it in the pocket of her apron. "A signed O.J. card?" she shrieked. "That's 300 bucks!"

"I don't feel unwelcome," Simpson says. "Usually when I come out alone, I'll be on the putting green, and people will yell over, 'Juice, you need a game? Play with us.' I get that all the time."

A lot of his golfmates are people he has met since he was acquitted of the criminal charges, like ad salesman Ken Smitley. They met in the bar after a round at Woodley Lakes Golf Course in Van Nuys. "He's one of the kindest, warmest, gentlest people I've played golf with in 30 years," says Smitley. "And absolutely the most etiquette-minded player I've ever been around." And what does Smitley's wife think of his new golf buddy? "Well," Smitley says after a long pause, "let's put it this way: Your wife isn't going to like every friend you have." And does he think Simpson committed the murders? "No. No way. From what I've seen of him, I don't think he could take the mother of his children."

If you invite Simpson to join your group, you will be surprised at his size and presence. He will be 49 in July, but his face is smooth. His hair is speckled with gray, but his eyes are young and his demeanor is nervy and loose and lively. His chest is still barreled, and his arms and hands are as thick and as gnarled as those of a mason. His waist is trim. He walks like anybody else, though maybe slower, and his left knee is turned out.

Simpson's handicap is about a 10, and he plays out of a huge black tour bag. ("Ito kept my Big Bertha oversize [irons]," he says.) He swings like a mover of pianos—powerfully and awkwardly and all upper body—but he has the touch of a Van Cliburn. On March 19 he says he toured Rancho's front nine in even par and the back in five over, for a 76. (Note to civil-suit plaintiffs' attorneys John Kelly and Daniel Petrocelli: He won about $20.) "*Acchh*," says a ponytailed man named Robert sitting at Rancho's bar. "I played behind him all day. No way the guy shoots 76. He cheats!"

In Simpson you get a talker without speed bumps, a conversation dominator, the kind of guy who is always finishing the stories of his friends. He is twice as animated on the course, yelping and moaning and exulting at nearly every shot. On the day he shot the 76, I joined his group as an uninvited observer at the 11th hole, whereupon he rope-pulled one into the trees. He spun on his spikes, pointed his Big Bertha driver at me and roared, "*You* did this to me!" My heart arrested until he broke into a cackle. On the 17th he smashed his drive into a palm tree. "Oh, I *killed* that one!" he bellowed. Nobody smirked.

He doesn't have much else to do with his time. He can't get a job. Can't get endorsements. Can't get a book deal. He would like to do some public speaking but offers aren't exactly vibrating the beeper off his belt. "I have no net worth," he says. "I make just enough to play relatively new golf balls. My relatives give them to me." He does not miss a day. On Feb. 10 he had just finished a round and was heading into the clubhouse bar when the announcement was made that the civil jury had found him liable for $25 million in punitive damages. "I'm standing there [watching the live television report]," he says, "and they go to this reporter who is standing outside my house. And he's going, 'O.J. has been holed up inside here all day. He came out for just a short time, looking confused, saw the cameras and went back in.' And I'm standing in the bar watching!"

Having a man who most Americans think murdered his wife, Nicole, and Ron Goldman, an acquaintance of Nicole's who worked as a waiter, mixing among wives and waiters has been a little sticky. Lately it's worked out to about an incident a week. At Balboa Encino Golf Course in Burbank, an *Inside Edition* cameraman said Simpson attacked him. (Simpson says he never touched the guy.) At the Camarillo Springs Golf Course in Cheviot Hills, a group of women said Simpson's foursome delayed the start of a women's tournament by 40 minutes because the foursome wanted to play at the last minute. (A course spokesman said Simpson was not to blame; a seniors tournament that went off earlier in the day caused the holdup.) And news reports said that when a twin-engine plane crashed at Rancho Park, Simpson was on the next fairway and refused to help those onboard. (Witnesses and Rancho officials said he was in the bar at the time.) "Hell, I figure I'm going to get blamed for everything," Simpson says.

And what does it feel like to be the most unwelcome man in America? "I can take people's shots," he says. "The Bible says I'm going to get it back seven times. The deeper they get into me, the more I get back down the line."

That's funny, because some of his golfing brethren think just the opposite. A rugged man in a big straw hat who identified himself only as Naylor watched Simpson leave the Rancho bar one evening and said, "I'd never play a hole with him. There are 400 other people out here I can play with who don't happen to be murderers." Of the handful of Rancho players I talked to who hadn't played with

Simpson, only one said he would. "I'd get in his group," the man said, "and then I'd mess with his mind."

Does Simpson ever worry about his safety? "When God wants me," he says, "he'll take me."

You wonder how long Simpson can last out here, rubbing wedges with a public that sees him so emotionally, one way or the other. "We try to give him the hint," says Hopps. "He's not welcome here. But he keeps showing up."

Simpson would like to move to Florida, where, he says, "I believe you can't have your home attached in judgments." But, of course, he is about as welcome in most neighborhoods as termites. Whenever a report of Simpson's moving to a city surfaces, the townspeople trot out the biggest unwelcome wagon they can find. Some folks in Vero Beach, Fla., who mistakenly thought he was ready to buy a $2.2 million place there, buried the town council in protests. Meanwhile, a mortgage company started foreclosure procedures on Simpson's house in Brentwood last week, so the house will probably be sold to satisfy that loan and to start paying for a) his appeal of the $33.5 million judgment and/or b) the judgment itself. He's stuck between a Rockingham and no place.

Yet where most notorious figures might squirrel themselves away in some Swiss hamlet, Simpson will spend his days among a lot of plumbers with loops in their backswings and Pabst Blue Ribbons in their golf bags, where anybody can get an eyeful of the most infamous American murder suspect since Bruno Hauptmann, free of charge.

"It's my life now," he says. A pause. "Could be worse."

From the pro shop, Hopps watches Simpson swing away and mutters, "Gonna find a helluva lot of clues out there. Yessir."

POSTSCRIPT: *I have to say, I found O.J. Simpson very pleasant and congenial. The next day, he called me at my hotel and asked if we were going to run pictures of him in the story. "I'm sure," I said, because I'd arranged for a photographer to shoot his round that day. "Will you make sure they show the Callaway logo on my shirt and hat?" "Well, I suppose," I said, "Why?" "Well, ever since the incident, I haven't been getting anything from Callaway in the mail. I used to be on their comp list and I'd like to get back on." After I hung up, I thought about it. Can you imagine the Callaway board of directors meeting? And some executive gets up and says, "Gentlemen, why aren't there more murderers on our comp list? We lost John Wayne Gacy to Mizuno! Richard Speck went to Titleist! Dammit, somebody call O.J. back!"*

———•———

Southern Discomfort

OCTOBER 12, 1998—Take an e-mail, Poindexter. Address it to bill-gates@richerthangod.net.worth.

Dear Bill,

So you can't get into Augusta National Golf Club. You've been hanging around the place, playing golf with fellow billionaire Warren Buffett, bunking at the cabins. You've let on that you'd love to be a member. You've even given a new building at your company headquarters the code name Augusta.

Yet you've gone and double-bogeyed this thing. The notification letters will be going out to new members in a few weeks, but you're not gonna get one. Crazy world, ain't it? The initiation fee is only about $40,000. Hell, you've got that in your couch cushions. Yet you're still waiting down at the Magnolia Lane guard shack. You're worth $58 billion. You could buy the club. You could buy Georgia. Yet you can't buy a membership. Even you gotta admit it, Bill, this is *rich.*

Problem is, you don't understand the place.

First off, your name. It's gotta go. This is Augusta, son. The chairman of the club is named Hootie. Everybody else is either Cletis or Stump. They're all worth half of downtown Etlanna, but it don't make no never mind. You need to tack on something friendly, something homespun. How 'bout Gitalong? Gitalong Gates. Smile a lot, and we'll call you Pearly. Hell, at least give 'em Billy Jim.

Come to think of it, maybe you oughtta do something about the name of your company, too. This is an all-male club. Most of the members voted against Lincoln. In the locker room they dispense Viagra right next to the witch hazel. They're not gonna be real excited about hearing the words *micro* and *soft* over and over.

Now, for that mug. You look like the equipment manager for the junior high chess team. You're 42 years old trying to get into a club where the average age is coma. Add 30 pounds. Lose some hair. Grow some dandruff. Put your glasses on a chain around your neck and then constantly search the top of your head for them. Stick one of those little suction cups on the end of your putter so you don't have to bend over to get the ball out of the hole.

Another thing. Don't go down there ordering lobster and arugula. Think blue plate, not silver. Fried chicken, macaroni and cheese, collard greens. Everything's Chez Aunt Bee. Learn to stick a supper of *bobbycue,* fried *oakree* and a mess of cobbler down your neck, shove back from the table and say, "Well, that'll push a turd."

That's the other thing. You gotta speak fluent Augusta. It's *goff,* not golf, and *guff,* not gulf, as in the sentence, *Ahm fixin' on playin' me some goff with that ol' boy from Guff Earl.* When thirsty at the turn, say, *Lordy, ah show could use a Sebmup.* And if you play awful, say, *Ah hit it everwhichaways,* and then add humbly, *Ah prolly orta quit ratcheer.*

Now, about your game. You've only played about five years. Your handicap is 26. Get yourself some lessons. Join Pine Valley and Cypress Point and the R&A. Drop sentences like, "Sandy and I had a helluva good match at Machrihanish." Develop a reverence for the loose-impediment rule and make sure a ratty copy of *Down the Fairway* falls out of your ball pocket in front of the members.

The most important thing is, you gotta want it less. Remember going on dates in high school? O.K., not a good question for you, but for a lot of us, the more anxious you seemed in high school, the less chance you had. Same deal at Augusta. Some of the members didn't like the way your candidacy became so public. You're not even supposed to know you're up for membership. They all think of it as the world's plushest tree house. They like to put an arm on you, drag you up and rub bloody thumbs together. Act surprised.

You do have a few things going for you. You're in a nasty rassle with the U.S. gubmint. The boys'll like that. You play fast. Bad, but fast. That's good, too. I figure you'll be in by the time you're 50. They encourage all members to help out with the Masters. So first thing you do is sign up for the concessions committee. No reason in particular, except I just love the idea of you sticking little $1 price tags on pimento cheese sandwiches.

All I ask is that, when you do get in, have me down. After this column, you're my only shot.

Give Casey Martin a Lift

FEBRUARY 9, 1998—Casey Martin has a right leg two sizes too small and a heart three sizes too big. His doctors say chances are good he'll lose that leg, maybe someday soon. He'll step in a gopher hole or he won't see a tee marker, and his balsa tibia will snap. When it snaps, the leg will probably have to come off. "I only have so many steps left in it," Martin says.

Won't that be a proud moment for Arnold Palmer and Jack Nicklaus and PGA Tour commissioner Tim Finchem? And won't all the others who've tried to stop the kid from using a cart—to preserve the "purity" of the game—be feeling awfully noble then? Maybe they'll stand on their two strong legs in their mahogany trophy rooms and drink to their integrity.

Shame on them. Shame on their lawyers. Shame on every self-important and greedy Tour pro who won't budge an inch of tradition to fit in a spoonful of compassion.

Of course Martin should get a cart. Anybody with a bus token for a heart knows that. Golf fans want to see golfers play golf. I've never heard anybody yet say, "Hey, let's get over to 9 and watch Seve walk!" Fans don't care if a pro walks, rides or pogo-sticks to the next shot—they just want to see him hit it.

The 25-year-old Martin isn't asking for any help playing the game. He's only asking for a lift to his ball. Golf isn't an obstacle course. Any blimp can walk 18 holes. Exhibit A: Fat Jack, who ate up every tournament he entered, including the buffet tables. Hey, who leads the Tour stats in Holes Walked, anyway?

Look, I've heard all the arguments against Martin's using a cart, and I wouldn't give you a warm pitcher of spit for any of them. PGA Tour officials say they're trying to protect the "tradition" of the game. If that sounds familiar, it's the word they trotted out in the 1950s to keep blacks off the Tour. Here's golf busy celebrating Tiger Woods and the game's new *diversity*, but, yo, fellas, diversity isn't just about color. Diversity is a guy wearing a leg-long bandage whose knee aches every minute he's on it, trying to prove something to himself and, by the way, to the world.

Martin is suing the PGA Tour for a cart, citing the Americans with Disabilities Act. But the PGA Tour says carts would tilt the level playing field. Then why are carts allowed during the Tour qualifying stages? And on the Senior tour? Arnie himself, the one who testified against Martin in a deposition two weeks ago, rode one on the Senior tour last year. Please.

The PGA Tour says it's a slippery slope. If Martin gets a cart, does Fred Couples get one for his back? José María Olazábal for his feet? No problem. The rule will be simple: If you qualify for disabled parking, we'll give you a cart.

The people who invoke that "purity" argument are the same ones who whined about yardage markers, gallery ropes, metal drivers, the "hot" ball, cavity-backed irons, the long putter and soft spikes. They've all arrived, and, last I checked, golf is more popular than ever.

I hear old guys wheezing on about Ben Hogan's having to walk during his comeback after crashing into a bus. Do you think what Martin has done is any less brave? He suffers from a rare circulatory disorder, and doctors say his condition is "worsening." The minute he takes the two support stockings off his right leg, it swells up like a bagpipe. He's in pain 24 hours a day, so now he has trouble sleeping too. During his swing he turns on a leg as skinny as a Little Leaguer's bat. Yet he *won* the Lakeland Classic on the Nike tour last month. What, only Hogan gets to be a legend?

"Casey Martin has a window here," says his surgeon, Don Jones, "and the window gets smaller every day."

Listen, a brawler like this comes along once in a lifetime. Martin says if he loses the trial, which started on Monday, he's going to try to walk. This kid is willing to trade a leg for his dream. They both get more brittle every day. This is no slippery slope. This is the Eiger, and Martin has damn near climbed it. If all these purists in their plaid pants and self-important frowns would step back a foot, he could get there while there's still time.

Nicklaus has said that if Martin is allowed to ride a cart, we'll "lose the game of golf forever the way we know it."

Well, thank god.

POSTSCRIPT: *In 2000, Casey Martin finally got his tour card and was allowed to play with a cart. Near as I could tell, golf was not overrun by players in EZ-Go's. In fact, the only other person in a golf cart was Nicklaus himself, who used one for a senior tournament while he recovered from a hip operation.*

———•———

S.O.S. from the AT&T

FEBRUARY 15, 1993—You make me sick.

You have no idea what it's like, do you? You sportswriters are all alike. You sit in your press tent and eat your catered lobster bisque and look up at the scoreboard and cackle. *He's bogeyed three holes in a row! What's he playing with, gardening implements?* If Greg Norman isn't leading the tournament, you file an official grievance. *Who cares? This guy will be running the Topeka Putt-Putt inside of six months.* You howl about how any pro could make a 7. *For chrissakes, I could do better than that!*

No. You *couldn't* do better than that. I know. I know because that's exactly what I used to howl in the press tent over my catered lobster bisque. But now that I'm out of the press tent and actually *playing* on the PGA Tour regularly . . . well, now that I've played in one Tour event, last week's AT&T Pebble Beach National Pro-Am . . . I have only one thing to say to the whole lot of you do-nothing, late-sleeping, easy-living media swine:

Can I come back now?

It is difficult to tell exactly *when* I realized that playing in the AT&T was a mistake on the order of, say, New Coke, but it was probably at some point between the sight of 1) my first shot of the tournament still rising as it sailed over the first crested waves of Carmel Bay on its way into the vast Pacific and 2) Charles Schulz, the harmless 70-year-old creator of "Peanuts," beating my butt by seven shots—gross—last Thursday.

No. I take that back. I probably knew it the day before, during a rainstorm at the putting green at Spyglass Hill, when I noticed all the other caddies holding umbrellas over their players. I hollered over to my friend and caddie, "Two-Down" O'Connor, the world's most avid golf gambler, that maybe now was a good time to start thinking about getting out the umbrella. "Good idea," yelled Two-Down, who pulled out the umbrella and held it over his head. "Gettin' kinda wet there for a while."

Like the 1970s, this all seemed like a good idea at the time. This is how it happened: Boss throws out his back. Boss already shelled out $3,500 to play in the AT&T Pro-Am. Boss has no choice but to send freeloading 15-handicap writer in his place. Writer nearly pulls groin yanking invitation from mailbox. Writer immediately regrips ball retriever, buys 11 new sweaters and steam-cleans head covers. Tournament still three months away.

If you didn't have a bad back before coming to this tournament, you might get one from hauling home the loot. For the $3,500, an amateur player gets an AT&T answering machine–phone, a Waterford crystal clock, an ugly decanter with golf tees in it, invitations to three celebrity-stuffed parties and a framed picture of his foursome, which in my case included my pro, Dennis Trixler, and Schulz and his pro, Jeff McMillen. Of course, since I paid exactly nothing for this tournament—and since it wasn't really *me* who was invited in the first place—I realized it wasn't fair that I get to keep all these expensive gifts. I am sending my boss the ugly decanter.

The phone was nice. It made me think it would be a smart thing to go up to Robert Allen, the chairman of AT&T, one of the most powerful and busiest businessmen in the world, and say, "Hey, thanks for the phone." As though he'd actually packed it himself. As though he might say, *Did you like it? I wasn't sure if brown was O.K. or what. I've got the receipt if it doesn't work out.*

What I really wanted, of course, was what every Pebble Beach amateur wants: to play on Sunday. At every party and lunch and practice putting green you hear it:

"You gonna play Sunday?"

"Let's get serious and play on Sunday for once, huh?"

If you play on Sunday, it means that of the 180 teams entered, yours is one of the 25 to make the Saturday-night cut. Jack Lemmon has not made it to a Sunday for 20 straight years. At one tournament party Bill Murray, Clint Eastwood, Dan Quayle and Donald Trump went unnoticed by the poor saps who were trying to figure out the key to making Sunday. "It took me five years to learn this," one man told me. "Forget your total score. Just make 10 pars." I asked him how many Sundays he had ever played. "None."

Trixler, 35, my partner for the week, was a touring pro from San Mateo, Calif. Oh, I know, some people might want Curtis or Payne or Fred, but there are a lot of us out on the Tour like Trixler, guys who have to arm-wrestle the marshals for every birdie they get, guys who have lost their cards more often than their keys. Guys who know what a rigged game golf is. Ask yourself this: Does Michael Jordan get to shoot his free throws from eight feet? Does Kirby Puckett take his pitches from second base? Why then do golf stars get the best tee times and the "c" category players, like Trixler, get the worst? Why should a Trixler have to putt greens that look like they just hosted an Arthur Murray class?

It is such a disadvantage to be a "c" category player that this year one of the penalties the Tour will hand out for slow play is a "c" category tee time. What did guys like Trixler do to get penalized?

"Do you know how many times I've had some guy on a Toro lawnmower on my butt as the sun is going down and I'm trying to make a six-footer to make the cut?" says Trixler. "The marshals? When Greg Norman comes through, they're wide-eyed and alert, all ready to watch *exactly* where his ball goes. But by the time I come through at six o'clock, they're snoozing, sunburned, tired. They've had nothing to eat or drink. And you say, 'You didn't happen to see where my ball went, did you?' And they say, 'Get bent.'"

Trixler is also the funniest thing in pants. When he is playing horribly, he will say, "God, I'm playing well. I'm hitting it *sooooo* good. I've got tickets for the doubleheader Saturday." Once he hit a perfect shot that flew the green. Later he described it to a friend this way: "I'm pumped. I flag a four-iron. I'm posing. Every shutter in the place is releasing on me. The world at my feet. Then, goodbye, gone, see ya. Does the word *alcoholism* mean anything to you?"

Great guy, Trix. Besides, I *tried* to get Fred, Curtis or Payne. They were taken.

As tough as it is for us out here on the Tour, I have to say we are treated with a modicum of human decency. Most players get courtesy cars, usually brand-new Buicks. There is a nutritious breakfast waiting for us at the driving range. And, best of all, there are hordes of fully grown men waiting to give us free things when we come out to play. The balls, clothes and clubs are free. A man from Titleist gave me two dozen balls free, someone from U.S.T. shafts offered to reshaft me, and some guy from Founders metal woods gave me a very fresh three-wood—all at absolutely no cost. I really considered pitching a tent on the range and leaving it at that. Two-Down was agog at all this.

It quickly became apparent that choosing an old pal as my cad-die was perhaps not a wise move. Two-Down does not do bibs well. He had never caddied before in his life. The gambling jones is incurable in him. For instance, here's what he carried in his so-called rain-delay kit: five sets of dice, three minibottles of Scotch, a juggling book, moonwalking instructions, Sam Snead's guide to golf hustling, a bottle of Brain Pep and a miniroulette wheel. The man is a walking pigeon trap.

Before he even arrived in Monterey, he was talking about "subletting" the job, which would keep him fresh for the evening card games.

"Why not?" he said. "I'll just walk along with you, and when you say, 'Five-iron,' I'll turn to the kid holding the bag and say, 'Five-iron.'" In our first practice round, on Tuesday, I hit a ball out-of-bounds, then hit one down the middle. Two-Down walked with me to the fairway ball. "Aren't you going to look for the first one?" I asked.

"What for?" he said, incredulously. "The guy just gave you two dozen free ones!"

Trix gave me some pointers about 1st-tee jitters before our open-ing round at the Pebble Beach Golf Links on Thursday. "Just think about this," he said. "In 15 minutes not one person standing here will remember how your shot went. Actually, even right now they don't really give a rat's ass. So screw 'em and have fun."

I also thought of James Garner's secret to playing televised golf tournaments. "Set up to the ball," he advises. "Squint into the sun. Take your swing. And no matter what happens, no matter how bad you've hit it, start walking right down the middle of the fairway." Unfortunately, Garner admits, there was one time when it didn't work: "The time my ball hit the camera lens."

With all this in mind, I went out Thursday and hit two over the cliff at 10. Trixler hit one over the cliff there himself. Then I hit another one over the famous cliff at 18, and Trixler hit one off the majestic cliff at 8. By the end of the day we had searched more cliffs than the heroine in *Wuthering Heights*. After one hole we were two over par as a team, which meant that we were only 44 shots behind last year's pro-am team winner.

When we finally putted out on that first hole, Schulz, the creator of Charlie Brown, actually said, "Good grief."

Still, the day was not a total loss. At one point Trixler advised Two-Down and me that we could take a ball out of play as long as it was "out of round." We both found it a fascinating phrase and decided it would be quite useful in other situations in life.

Hey, Fred, I heard you're getting a divorce.

Yeah, Bob, I am. Gladys got a little out of round.

By the end of the first day, Trixler had shot a four-over 76. Our team shot 68, six behind the leaders. I say this with all honesty and candor: Linus and Lucy could've beaten us.

We Tour players sleep fitfully if we end the day on a bogey or, in my case, six bogeys in eight holes. That is why Tour players practice after their round, often until dusk. In fact, Tour players feel the need to practice after their round even if they've shot 66. I asked Trixler why. "Mostly guilt," he said. "Most of the time it doesn't help anyway. You're just out there doing penance. You see another guy out there putting, and you don't want to get passed, so you do it yourself. If Catholicism had an official sport, it would be golf."

The truly devoted keep practicing long after the sun punches out. They say Billy Casper putted so much at home that he had to change the carpet in his house every few years. Nowadays Andrew Magee may be the Tour's best hotel/motel practicer. I asked for a few tips.

"First thing you have to do is get a room with blackout curtains," Magee said. Apparently you shut those big, thick drapes and, voilà, instant golf range. "Start with full wedge shots," he said. "The window won't break. You can pretty much go through all your short irons and not break the window." I had only one question: Wouldn't you break a lot of windows until you found just the right thickness of curtain? "Well," he said, "one night I'd had a few beers, and I was ticked off because I missed the cut, and I went back and started hitting full wedge shots into the curtain. I guess I didn't care if the window broke or not, but it didn't."

Magee also recommended getting a cheap hotel room whenever possible. The cheaper the hotel, the thinner the carpet pad, which means the faster and truer the putts roll. Anything over $69 a night isn't going to help your putting a damn.

On Friday, Trix and I went out to Poppy Hills and didn't knock it into the Pacific Ocean once. Instead we hit it into and off of every tree in the Del Monte Forest. I had to chip out of the trees on holes 4, 5, 9, 10, 12, 14, 15, 16 and 17. It was my personal Arbor Day.

O.K., so Trix was not at his best this week, either. He threw a little six-over 78 at the field on Friday, which left him only 15 shots behind the leader. He was really playing great. Hitting it long. Putting well. He has brunch reservations Sunday.

And yet, somehow, we shot a team score of 65 on Friday. The AT&T Pro-Am is a best-ball tournament. Since my handicap is 15, I got a free shot on each round's 15 hardest holes. Pros, of course, get no free shots. So if Trix made a 4 and I made a 4 on one of my free-shot holes, then our team score for that hole was 3. Things just seemed to work out on Friday. Every time I was stuck chipping out from behind a Georgia-Pacific crew, Trix was making par. And every time Trix was finding new and inventive ways to make a 6, I was banking one off two blue spruces, a pine tree and Bambi for par. After two days we were only two shots off the cut. I could just *feel* Sunday morning coming down.

Schulz and his pro were still three shots ahead of us, though. Schulz not only has a great sense of humor and more money than Saudi Arabia, he also has a helluva golf game. On Friday he knocked the ball four feet from the hole on a par-5—*in two*. I loathe that man.

During a wait I asked Trix what he would do if he won a tournament. He talked as if he'd had his answer ready for years. "First of all, I'd cry," he said. "Then I'd hug my wife. Then I'd rent the Golden Gate Bridge and throw the largest party in the history of San Francisco. The best wines and abalone for everybody. Spend $50,000 on it. Limos. The works. And everybody would go home knowing the greatest feeling in the history of life."

There was a long pause.

"Orrrr . . . I'll just continue to miss cuts by 28 shots, play myself off the Tour and become the prep cook at the Des Moines Denny's."

I asked Charles Schulz if, in 42 years, Charlie Brown has ever worn anything but that yellow sweater with the red zigzag stripe. "Yes," he said. "For the first two weeks of the strip, he wore a plain white T-shirt. But then I realized the strip needed more color, so I drew the sweater." Great trivia question.

I decided on Saturday that if Two-Down got any more out of round, I was going to have to put him to sleep. First, he started hinting that if we won, he was going to be "very upset" if there was no caddie crystal. Then he began complaining about the weight of the bag. I think he purposely tried to leave my two- and three-irons behind on the range, but Andy Bean yelled, "You forgot something." I gave Two-Down a dirty look.

"Wouldn't have mattered," Two-Down said with a shrug. "You haven't used them all week."

Did I mention that the driving range for the AT&T is quite possibly the coolest place on earth? There is only one for all three courses, and so all the stars and players meet there before and after their rounds. It's like when you were kids and met at the tree house before school. It's maybe the only place in the world where, in 100 yards, you can see Joe Pesci hitting next to Davis Love hitting next to Dan Quayle hitting next to John Daly hitting next to a 15-handicap schlump like me. This can only happen in golf. I have yet to see Pesci down punting with the Raiders before one of *their* games.

The problem is, as you stand there on the sixth day, having already played five rounds and scaled five-story hills, you realize that if you set up over one more five-iron, your aching legs and back might decide to spasm you to death.

"The average amateur," says pro Roger Maltbie, "gets a look at these beautiful free Titleists on the range and hits 5,000 balls the first day and then walks 18. Then, the second day, he overhears some pro talking about a swing change, and he picks that up and tries it and hits 5,000 more balls and walks 18 more. Then, the third day, some Tour rep handing out drivers gives him one, and he decides he's going to use that. So by the time the tournament starts, he has hit 15,000 balls, walked 54 holes, got a new grip, a new swing and new equipment, and he's exhausted. And he wonders why he can shoot 85 at home with the boys and never break 100 here."

Sounds exactly like me.

Our final day, Saturday, was at the toughest of the three courses, Spyglass. But Team Trix felt Sunday in its bloodstream. Why not? We had it right in front of us. We were at 11 under. Most people figured 18 under would make the cut, so all we needed was seven net birdies. We had averaged that the two previous days. Besides, Trix hadn't made a birdie since Thursday. "I got seven in me today," he said. He looked like he meant it, too.

But Trix got his glove on correctly, and that was about it. He crossed up the field and threw a little 82 at them. For the week, that was 76-78-82—236, just 31 shots off the pro pace. He couldn't get a break. At the 8th hole he hit a shot just off the green, on a little hill. No problem. But as we were walking to the green, the ball suddenly decided to roll back down the hill into an impossible bunker lie. His face got all purple, and I thought he might just bite the rake in half. At one point, as he was crouched behind me reading my putt, I said, "What do you think?"

"I am quitting the game," he said with teeth clenched. "Put that in your [expletive] article." I really felt miserable for him. He was trying so hard. The thing was, we still had a chance. I came within one foot of a hole in one on the 12th hole, and we were 14 under at the turn. We had guessed that if we could make five net birdies on the back nine, we would be at Pebble on Sunday. Posing. Shutters releasing. Autograph sessions.

Instead we played like diseased yaks. We not only failed to make four more net birdies, we hardly made any more net pars. Our tournament ended on the 14th hole at Spyglass, an easy par-5. We both had 100-yard wedges over a pond to an uphill green. Trix went first and spun it back into the pond. So, naturally, I skulled mine down a 40-foot ravine to the right. We both made seven. Two-Down pulled something out of the bag and showed it to me. The bottle of Brain Pep.

Trix never did make another birdie. However, on our 16th hole of the day, he missed a five-footer for birdie, walked over to a nearby pond and very calmly deposited his putter within. Good move. His putting improved. He made a nice four-footer with his driver on the last hole for par. We finished at 12 under, seven shots from making the cut, 15 shots behind Magee's team, the pro-am leaders.

I never did make 10 pars in one day for my pro. I'm not sure my pro made 10 pars for my pro. We were so bad, we tied with Jack Lemmon. Make it *21 years* in a row. More bad news: Schulz missed the cut by one lousy little shot. Good grief.

There would be no Sunday services at St. Pebble for Team Trix. Still, I want to mention that we defeated Joe Montana, Orel Hershiser, Johnny Bench and Bobby Rahal, every one of 'em a Hall of Famer. Why don't you media types write *that*?

Next time, I've got to have 18 shots.

And Trix needs at least six.

CHAPTER SIX: WRECKS

CHAPTER SIX: WRECKS

———◆———

On a Wing and a Prayer

SEPTEMBER 20, 1999—Now this message for America's most famous athletes: Someday you may be invited to fly in the backseat of one of your country's most powerful fighter jets. Many of you already have—John Elway, John Stockton, Tiger Woods to name a few. If you get this opportunity, let me urge you, with the greatest sincerity. . . .

Move to Guam. Change your name. Fake your own death. Whatever you do, do *not* go. I know. The U.S. Navy invited me to try it. I was thrilled. I was pumped. I was toast.

I should've known when they told me my pilot would be Chip (Biff) King of Fighter Squadron 213 at Naval Air Station Oceana in Virginia Beach. Whatever you're thinking a Top Gun named Chip (Biff) King looks like, triple it. He's about six-foot, tan, ice-blue eyes, wavy surfer hair, finger-crippling handshake—the kind of man who wrestles dyspeptic alligators in his leisure time. If you see this man, run the other way. Fast.

Biff King was born to fly. His father, Jack King, was for years the voice of NASA missions. ("T-minus 15 seconds and counting. . . ." Remember?) Chip would charge neighborhood kids a quarter each to hear his dad. Jack would wake up from naps surrounded by nine-year-olds waiting for him to say, "We have a liftoff."

Biff was to fly me in an F-14D Tomcat, a ridiculously powerful $60 million weapon with nearly as much thrust as weight, not unlike Colin Montgomerie. I was worried about getting airsick, so the night before the flight I asked Biff if there was something I should eat the next morning.

"Bananas," he said.

"For the potassium?" I asked.

"No," Biff said, "because they taste about the same coming up as they do going down."

The next morning, out on the tarmac, I had on my flight suit with my name sewn over the left breast. (No call sign—like Crash or Sticky or Leadfoot—but, still, very cool.) I carried my helmet in the crook of my arm, as Biff had instructed. If ever in my life I had a chance to nail Nicole Kidman, that was it.

A fighter pilot named Psycho gave me a safety briefing and then fastened me into my ejection seat, which, when employed, would "egress" me out of the plane at such a velocity that I would be immediately knocked unconscious.

Just as I was thinking about aborting the flight, the canopy closed over me, and Biff gave the ground crew a thumbs-up. In minutes we were firing nose up at 600 mph. We leveled out and then canopy-rolled *over* another F-14. Those 20 minutes were the rush of my life. Unfortunately, the ride lasted 80.

It was like being on the roller coaster at Six Flags Over Hell. Only without rails. We did barrel rolls, sap rolls, loops, yanks and banks. We dived, rose and dived again, sometimes with a vertical velocity of 10,000 feet per minute. We chased another F-14, and it chased us. We broke the speed of sound. Sea was sky and sky was sea. Flying at 200 feet we did 90-degree turns at 550 mph, creating a G force of 6.5, which is to say I felt as if 6.5 times my body weight was smashing against me, thereby approximating life as Mrs. Colin Montgomerie.

And I egressed the bananas. I egressed the pizza from the night before. And the lunch before that. I egressed a box of Milk Duds from the sixth grade. I made Linda Blair look polite. Because of the G's, I was egressing stuff that did not even *want* to be egressed. I went through not one airsick bag, but two. Biff said I passed out. Twice.

I was coated in sweat. At one point, as we were coming in upside down in a banked curve on a mock bombing target and the G's were flattening me like a tortilla and I was in and out of consciousness, I realized I was the first person in history to throw *down*.

I used to know cool. Cool was Elway throwing a touchdown pass, or Norman making a five-iron bite. But now I *really* know cool. Cool is guys like Biff, men with cast-iron stomachs and Freon nerves. I wouldn't go up there again for Derek Jeter's black book, but I'm glad Biff does every day, and for less a year than a rookie reliever makes in a home stand.

A week later, when the spins finally stopped, Biff called. He said he and the fighters had the perfect call sign for me. Said he'd send it on a patch for my flight suit.

What is it? I asked.

"Two Bags."

Don't you *dare* tell Nicole.

POSTSCRIPT: *I've been told by other pilots Chip (Biff) King would've suffered untold ridicule if he hadn't made me throw up that day. It's the Top Gun's code of honor. Still, there are tradeoffs. Like when it's late and the kids are asleep and my wife says, "Put on the flight suit."*

Next Time, Stop the Freaking Race

AUGUST 17, 1998—There's a man buried in your kitchen.

He's right in that stack of newspapers there, about three weeks down, a headline one day, a one-graph follow-up the next, a nobody since.

His name is Ken Fox. He went to a race at Michigan Speedway on July 26 and was torn in half by a tire that flew into the stands, and they didn't even stop the freaking race. Now he's just part of a stat that sportswriters will fish out the next time a racing fan dies because he sat in the wrong seat—*four fan deaths in the last 11 years*, they can write now. So the CART circuit moved on to the all-important Miller Lite 200 in Lexington, Ohio, last week, where . . .

But wait just a second.

Ken Fox deserves one minute before we forget him. Ken Fox was somebody. He was 38, with a seven-year-old son, Christopher, who walked by his casket and left a little note with big sloppy letters. *I love you, Daddy.*

Ken Fox had a best friend, Steve Dawson, who can't eat now and can't sleep and can't forget about the day he went to a car race and everybody sitting around him left in body bags. Ken and Steve, from Lansing, Mich., worked together as drill instructors at a boot camp for first-time felons. They commuted to work together, bowled together, hashed out their divorces together. And they went to car races together. Steve had four tickets to the U.S. 500, and Steve's dad was too tired from working all night and Ken's brother had to study and Steve's fiancee couldn't go, either, and thank god. But Steve and Ken went, and they were damn good seats, too, ninth row, fourth turn. *Damn good seats.*

They were having a blast. Ken was whooping for Michael Andretti to win, and it was a gorgeous day. Then, on Lap 175, Steve thought he saw something black out of the corner of his eye, and he ducked. When he turned back around, he saw that Ken was dead, and the woman just in front of Steve, Sheryl Laster, was dead, and, within the minute, the friend she was with, Mike Tautkus, was dead. "I don't know why I'm alive," Steve says. "I don't know if it was luck or fate or what. I've thought, Did Ken save my life? And I don't know that either. I don't know anything."

They build these race cars to explode on impact because it takes G forces away from the driver, makes it safer for him. But how many engineers are worrying about making guys like Ken Fox safer?

And they didn't even stop the freaking race. Race officials yellow-flagged it as a safety crew cleared the fourth-turn stands, but they left Ken and Sheryl and Mike lying there, covered by blankets, as the cheers started up again and the drivers went flying by again at 200 mph. Congratulations, Greg Moore, you just won the world's fastest funeral procession.

Steve hasn't been able to go back to work, and he's in crisis therapy, and there's a replay in his head that won't shut off. But he's figured out one thing. "Everybody wants to ask me about the blood and how the bodies were twisted, but all I want to do is tell them about Ken," he says. "I just want people to know that Ken was a great guy, a fun-loving, moral, stand-up guy. Everybody seems to be going on like none of this makes a difference. Well, I think it should."

You wonder if it does for Adrian Fernandez. The CART publicity sheets say he's having the best year of his life, ranked fourth in the points standings. But the sheets don't mention how he lost control of his car on the fourth turn that day and smashed the wall, sending his right front tire spinning up and over the 15-foot-high fence and through Christopher Fox's dad.

Three people are dead, and all Fernandez has done is send flowers. He hasn't visited or spoken with the victims' families, and all he has said since the day of the race is, "No comment." The CART people say he was a brave guy to climb back behind the wheel and win on Sunday in Ohio, but he hasn't had the guts yet to look into the eyes of the mothers and the kids.

Yeah, racing and sports and the world spin on at 9,000 rpm. Someday maybe Adrian Fernandez will figure he owes somebody a call. And someday maybe Steve Dawson will be fine, except for an empty seat next to him in the car and a chill that won't go away and the memory of the number of the seat Ken Fox took just ahead of him that gorgeous summer day.

Thirteen.

Heaven Help Marge Schott

MAY 20, 1996—Alone in her bedroom, alone in a 40-room mansion, alone on a 70-acre estate, Marge Schott finishes off a vodka-and-water (no lime, no lemon), stubs out another Carlton 120, takes to her two aching knees and prays to the Men. To Charlie, the husband who made her life and then ruined it. He taught her never to trust. To Daddy, the unsmiling father who turned her into his only son. He taught her never to be soft. To Dad Schott, the calculating father-in-law, whom she may have loved most of all. He taught her never to let herself be cheated.

"I pray to them every night, honey," she says. "How many owners do that, huh? Hit their knees every night?"

Hard to say. For that matter, how many baseball owners keep in their kitchen drawer plastic bags containing hair from a dog that died five years ago? Or are worth millions but haven't shopped for clothes in nine years? Schott just wears the stuff people send her. "If it fits, honey," she says in her No. 4 sandpaper voice, "I wear it."

Honey is what Schott calls everybody, unless you're *baby* or *sweetheart*. It's what she does instead of remembering your name. "This guy is from SportsChannel, honey. He's here doing a big story on me."

"Sports Illustrated, Mrs. Schott."

"Right, honey."

Schott does not really have to remember anyone's name, because she's 67 years old, as rich as Oman, and she answers to nobody. She owns 43% of the Cincinnati Reds, but she hasn't had time to actually learn the game yet. After all, it has only been 12 years since that Christmas when she "saved the team for Cincinnati," as she has said over the years. (Why ruin the story by mentioning that the previous owners insisted that they never would have sold the Reds to anyone but a Cincinnatian, and there were no offers on the table from any other city. None of the men in Cincinnati were stepping up to buy the team, she says now.)

It is not unusual, for instance, for Schott not to know the names of her players. Oh, she knows a few—Eric Davis, Barry Larkin, Chris Sabo—but the rest are just uniforms that she steers her current St. Bernard, Schottzie 02, around before games, hoping to spy a familiar face.

"Who's that, honey?"

"George Grande, Mrs. Schott."

"Oh."

Grande has been the Reds' TV broadcaster for four years.

Marge sees Sabo. "Hi, honey."

"Hi, Mrs. Schott."

"Tell Schottzie you're going to win for her tonight."

Sabo looks around uncomfortably, then mutters at the ground, "Uh, we're going to win for you tonight . . . Schottzie."

In a recent game against the Philadelphia Phillies, there was a hot smash to Reds first baseman Hal Morris, who shouldn't have meant anything to Schott except that he has played on her team since 1990 and was leading the club in hitting at the time. Morris bobbled the ball. "Oh, you stupid guy!" Schott screamed.

Morris recovered and flipped the ball to the pitcher, who covered first.

"Who was that, honey?"

"Who was who?"

"Who ran over?"

"The pitcher?"

"Oh, good."

Schott is not big on baseball history, either. There is not a single banner commemorating the Big Red Machine years in Riverfront Stadium, not a single retired number on display to honor Pete Rose, Johnny Bench, Joe Morgan or Tony Perez. Not a single reminder of Rose's record 4,192 hits. That kind of thing sounds expensive, and Schott is much bigger on saving money than memories. Besides, who can remember all that stuff? During a rain delay in the game against Philadelphia, the Jumbotron was showing highlights of the classic 1970 World Series between the Reds and the Baltimore Orioles, in which Orioles third baseman Brooks Robinson was merely Superman.

"Who's that, baby?"

"Brooks Robinson."

"Brooks Robinson? I thought he was one of the first black players."

"That was Jackie Robinson."

"No. . . ."

Of course, having Aunt Bee as your team's owner has its advantages. For instance, Schott doesn't raise her ticket prices every season, as a lot of other owners do. You don't do that to family members, which is what Reds fans are to her. Riverfront's most expensive seat is $11.50, cheapest in the majors. Schott still charges only $1 for a hot dog. (A jumbo frank costs three times as much at Shea Stadium in New York.) She does not often meddle in player deals, mostly because she has no real interest in baseball. Night after night she sits alone in her vast luxury box with just her telephone and Schottzie, not paying much attention to the game, waiting for some high-ranking employee to show up at the door and take Schottzie for a walk. Afterward there's always a report.

"Tinkle or poo?" she will ask.

"Just tinkle," the director of marketing or some other front-office-type will answer sheepishly.

In the sixth inning Schott moves down to her box seats behind the Reds' dugout to chain-sign autographs, hardly looking up except after loud cracks of the bat. She hates it when the bats break, but she does not lose money on them. She has an employee take them to the gift shop at a downtown Cincinnati hotel and sell them. (To show their undying love for her, some Cincinnati players smash their cracked bats into two pieces so they're in no condition to be sold.)

After the game Schott drives the 20 minutes to her mansion in suburban Indian Hill, where she is even more alone: no husband, no kids, no grandchildren, no live-in help, precious few friends, a tiny television sitting cold in the kitchen, the newspaper lying unread, books untouched. She doesn't sleep much at night, despite all the Unisom she takes, not to mention the vodkas (Kamchatka, the cheap stuff). She sits in bed making picture frames to match her furniture and falls asleep, only to wake up in half an hour to smoke another cigarette. Finally she rises, fresh from a good night's nicotining, ready to seize the day.

Because she's set apart from the world like that, it's no wonder Schott's political and social views have not really changed since the Edsel. Over the years she has insulted homosexuals ("Only fruits wear earrings"), blacks ("Dave is my million-dollar nigger," she said of Dave Parker, a Reds outfielder from 1984 to '87) and Jews ("He's a beady-eyed Jew," she said of Cincinnati marketing director Cal Levy, according to *Unleashed*, the exhaustive biography of Schott written by Mike Bass in 1993). As for Adolf Hitler, she takes a compassionate view. "He was O.K. at the beginning," she says. "He rebuilt all the roads, honey. You know that, right? He just went too far." Two weeks ago she repeated that opinion in an interview with ESPN, setting off a storm of protest, including outrage from the Anti-Defamation League and other Jewish organizations, and casting baseball in an embarrassing light yet again. Two days later she issued a written apology, which was accepted by the Jewish Community Relations Council of Cincinnati.

Schott is a proud third-generation German-American. Her mother's sister had five sons who fought for Germany in World War II. "She used to send us little Nazi soldier dolls with the swastikas and everything, honey. We used to play with them," says Schott. She even has a Nazi armband she keeps in a bureau drawer in the hallway leading to her living room. She forgot about the armband until a Christmas party in 1987, when Levy happened to find it and asked her about it. "Figures a Jewish guy would find it, huh, honey?" Schott whispers, which she does when a matter under discussion is a little sticky. "What's a Jewish guy looking through my drawers for anyway? Right, honey?" (Levy, who is no longer with the club, says Schott had sent him in search of a dinner bell.)

She says she's not really a Nazi sympathizer, although she once told ABC's Diane Sawyer that the armband "is not a symbol of evil to me." Mostly it's a case of Schott not throwing anything away. If a bag lady had a trust fund, her house might look like Schott's: crammed with junk. There's a room full of stuff she received on two baseball goodwill visits to Japan. There are closets full of mementos and stuffed Saint Bernards and clocks with miniature baseball bats for hands, most of which were given to her. Charlie's suits still hang in his closet, right where he left them, and he has been dead, what, 28 years?

MargeVision is set on the 1950s, and she sees it clear as a bell. She often feels like speaking out for what she believes, and it hasn't hurt her much. While Al Campanis, Jimmy the Greek and Ben Wright lost their jobs for saying one fiftieth of what Schott has said, she got only a one-year suspension from baseball in 1993 for making racial and ethnic slurs. A sensitivity-training course was thrown in for good measure. The course didn't really take. Sending Schott to sensitivity training is like sending a pickpocket to a Rolex convention.

Take a recent night, when Schott was leaving the Montgomery Inn restaurant in suburban Cincinnati after actually tearing up over the all-American vitality and clean-cut looks of a girl who had asked her for an autograph. As Schott was piling into her junk-strewn Riviera, she saw a group of high school-aged Asian-Americans walking down the street, laughing and talking.

"Look at that," she said.

"What?"

"That's not right, honey."

"What isn't?"

"Those Asian kids."

"It's not?"

(Whisper) "Well, I don't like when they come here, honey, and stay so long and then outdo our kids. That's not right."

If you were her public relations adviser, you would have her followed by six men in flame-retardant suits with a fire hose. In 1989 at Riverfront Stadium, as *60 Minutes* cameras rolled on her and Bart Giamatti, who was then the baseball commissioner, Schott saw something she didn't like.

Schott: "Is this a girl batboy or a boy that needs a goddamn haircut?"

Giamatti: "Well, Marge, that's a question you ought to take up with the young person after the game."

Schott: "Is that a boy or a girl?"

Giamatti: "It's a young man with a modern haircut."

Schott: "Well, he'll never be out here again with long hair like that. . . ."

Giamatti: "Marge, you're killing me here!"

Even in trying to say something nice about someone, Schott gets it all wrong. In boasting recently of her meeting with Japanese prime minister Kiichi Miyazawa on one of her baseball goodwill visits, in 1991, she recalled what he had said to her, using a cartoonish Japanese accent: "He says to me, honey, he says, 'No want Cadirrac, no want Rincoln, want Mosh Shott Boo-ick.'"

In the first six weeks of the 1996 season, Schott rewrote the book on loafer-in-mouth disease.

Chapter 1: When umpire John McSherry died of a heart attack after collapsing at home plate on Opening Day at Riverfront, Schott objected to the cancellation of the game and complained about how McSherry's death put *her* out: "I don't believe it. First it snows, and now *this*!"

Chapter 2: The next day Schott took flowers somebody else had sent her, ripped off the card, wrote a new one with heartfelt condolences and sent the flowers to the umpires' room at Riverfront.

Chapter 3: At the start of the season the Reds weren't providing fans with scores from other games on the Riverfront scoreboard. "Why do they care about one game when they're watching another?" argued Schott, who had stopped paying her bill for the service (it costs $350 a month) during last season.

Chapter 4: Following the sixth home game, after being raked over the coals by the media for her stinginess, she reversed her scoreboard decision and blamed it on her employees, saying in front of a roomful of reporters, "I've got to have the worst public relations staff in America!" Now those employees have to track the scores by calling to other ballparks and listening to the radio.

Chapter 5: On April 14 she tried to apologize for her McSherry gaffe minutes before the first pitch against the Houston Astros by approaching the umpires working the game—none of whom were at Riverfront on Opening Day and all of whom resented her publicity-minded opportunism. One, Harry Wendelstedt, turned his back on her.

Not that sheer Jell-O-headedness is always behind Schott's troubles. Many of her idiocies are clearly thought out in advance. For years she has made it known that she would prefer that the Reds not hire women of childbearing age. Women in the workplace is not a cause Schott champions, despite the fact that she is one herself. (Besides the Reds, she owns two car dealerships, at least three vehicle-leasing firms, a concrete company and several other businesses in various states, not to mention a large chunk of General Motors stock, most of it under the control of her Cincinnati-based holding company, Schottco.) "I'll tell you something, honey," she says. "Some of the biggest problems in this city come from women wanting to leave the home to work." And: "Why do these girl reporters have to come into the locker room? Why can't they wait outside?" And: "I don't really think baseball is a woman's place, honey. I really don't. I think it should be left to the boys."

She despises the city ordinance that prohibits smoking at Riverfront, the one that keeps her sitting alone in her 20-chair luxury box instead of behind the dugout with the fans, whom she loves. Besides, MargeVision doesn't see cigarettes as being all that bad. "I'll tell you something, honey," she says in her smoker's rasp. "They had a jazz festival here awhile ago, and we walked around, and they were doing nothing but crack!"

Schott detests facial hair, too, and forbids it on any player or employee. The close, comfortable shave, she feels, is her lasting contribution to the game, even though it was a long-standing club policy that Cincinnati players not grow facial hair when she bought the team. "If nothing else, the thing I'm most proud of [about the Reds] is the no-facial hair and earrings," she said recently to Chip Baker, her one-man marketing department (by comparison, the Atlanta Braves' marketing department has 10 employees), even as she looked at a photo of the 1896 Reds, all of them bewhiskered.

"Don't you think, Chip?"

"Yes, ma'am."

"Did Jesus have a beard, Chip?"

"I think so, Mrs. Schott."

"Oh." Pause. "Have you met our friend from Sports America here, honey?"

"Sports Illustrated, Mrs. Schott."

"Right, honey."

It is not just baseball Schott is a little behind on. She seems to have been on Neptune for much of the 20th century. Once, she showed up very early for a meeting in a Chicago hotel and then was overheard growling into a pay phone, "Hey, why didn't you tell me there was an hour difference between Cincinnati and Chicago?"

Schott and computers don't see eye to eye, either. At her car dealerships and other local businesses, which she usually visits in the mornings before going to the ballpark, some employees have taped signs to their computers begging her not to turn them off. She does that to save electricity, even though, she admits, it makes a computer "lose all those thingies on the screen."

Schott doesn't read much anymore, either. "I don't like the words so much, honey. I like the pictures. Pictures mean so much more to me than words, honey."

She is always ready with her stack of photos. Here's a shot of Marge as a baby, one of five daughters of Edward Unnewehr, who made a fortune in the lumber business (mostly from plywood and veneer). Five daughters, and all Daddy ever wanted was a boy.

"Well, what'd you have, Ed?" people would ask him.

"A baby," he would snarl.

Daddy was strict. "Very *achtung!*" as Schott says. When Daddy wanted Mother, he would ring a bell. Daddy did not eat meals with his children until they were over the messy age—about four. And you had better be tough. "You didn't get sick in Daddy's family, honey," Schott says. "We coughed into our pillows."

Since Daddy couldn't have a boy, he treated Marge like one. He called her Butch. She grew up the wisecracking girl Daddy took to work whenever he could, the circle-skirted jokester who would bring cigars to slumber parties and smoke them. She was less comfortable around women than men, whom she was learning to love and hate all at once.

And here's a photo of Butch marrying Charles Schott, son of a wealthy society family in Cincinnati. Here's Daddy, sulking throughout the wedding. "He wanted me to run his business, honey," she says, "and now he was losing me." Here's Marge with Charlie's father, Walter, who took her on the road with him, took her to make the boys in the board meetings laugh at all her one-liners. Once the meeting started, though, she had better stay quiet.

Still Marge learned a lot at the feet of Dad Schott, who in 1938 had become the largest auto dealer in Ohio. Today she knows where every penny goes, how every tax shelter works, how wide every loophole can be made. Schott may come off as having sniffed too much epoxy, but she knows her way around a financial statement and the county courthouse. "I hate lawyers, honey," she often says, "but I keep 'em busy."

The Men ran her life, enriched it and, ultimately, ruined it. According to *Unleashed*, Charles was a hopeless alcoholic, who left her alone on their wedding night to play cards and left her alone hundreds of nights after that.

Yeah, she learned lots about men. Like when she found out years after the fact that it had been two male members of her family who, shortly after she was married in 1952, had sneaked one of her Saint Bernards out and had it killed because they didn't like it. You don't think that hurt? Men, honey.

Here's one last picture of her with the chubby, grinning Charlie. When he died in 1968 of a heart attack, he was rumored to have been found in the bathtub of his mistress, Lois Kenning. It is a subject Schott does not like to discuss but has not quite figured a way to lie about.

"Where did your husband die, Mrs. Schott?"

"I don't know, honey."

Since then she has waged a one-woman war for fidelity. Her goal is to rid baseball of "cutesy-poos," as she calls them: the groupies who end up in ballplayers' hotel rooms. She says she has hired private investigators to videotape her players getting on and off buses and going in and out of hotels, to make sure there is no cutesy-pooing going on. Reds general manager Jim Bowden confirms only a little of this. "A couple of years ago we videotaped our players getting off a couple of charter flights, just to make sure our rules and regulations were being followed," he says. "At no time were rules being violated."

The last two seasons Reds players have complained that their mail has been opened and taped shut again. "Ray [Knight, the team's rookie manager] thought some of the boxes that came in the mail looked like they'd been opened," says Bowden. "He told Mrs. Schott, and she said she would look into it." Some of the players suspect Schott did the opening. Schott says she doesn't know a thing about it.

Then there are the phone calls. "I tape every call in and out of the clubhouse," Schott boasts. "These players are not going to pull any cutesy-poo stuff on me."

"But isn't that illegal, Mrs. Schott?"

"Oh. Oh, no. Not tape, honey. I just mean I have the operator log every call to the clubhouse. That's all, honey."

Schott is tighter than shrink-wrap, but whatever price she has to pay to protect the Great American Family, she will pay it. This is because she never had children herself. It is her single greatest sorrow. "I just don't think I did my job," she lamented recently in her Riverfront office. "In my day girls were raised to raise kids, and I didn't do it. My life would've been completely different with kids. I wouldn't be here, honey, I can tell you that."

It did not help that her sister Lottie had 10 kids, the way Marge thinks good Catholic girls should. And it was not because Marge didn't try. She hired the best doctors, up to and including one who she says had treated the shah of Iran. "And he about killed me, honey, giving me all these drugs," she says. "About killed me." She says she tried to adopt twins once, "but the nuns wouldn't let us, honey. Wouldn't let us." She whispers: "'They're interbreds,' they told us. 'They'd only be a frustration to you.' I told 'em, 'No, we'll educate 'em,' but they wouldn't let us have 'em." In *Unleashed*, Bass reported that Charlie's mother attempted to arrange adoptions, but Marge and Charlie refused to follow through because they didn't know the children's backgrounds.

When Charlie died, Marge was only 39. She could have tried for kids again, but all the men who seemed attracted to her were already married. "I never knew so many guys' wives didn't under-stand them, honey," she cracks. She was going to marry Harold Schott, Charlie's uncle. She says he called her six times one day to tell her he was flying back from Florida to ask for her hand, but he died that same day. "First the family said it was a heart attack," Marge explains. "Then they said he drowned. The best swimmer in the family. Something funny going on there."

And so she was left alone to raise other things: 22 Saint Bernards, a baseball team and even cattle, though she refused to let anybody slaughter the calves. She let them live. She looks out on the calves in the distance from her yard and grabs your elbow and says, "Look at them. Isn't it beautiful seeing the families out in the field?"

Adults, especially ballplayers and newspaper people, she's not so big on, but she is nuts for animals and children. Once a week or so she will get to the ballpark early, gather up 20 or so small kids and let them run out to the rightfield wall and back before a game. Once she went to the opening day of a little league for disabled children and spent most of an hour crying like a baby.

On April 3, Reds second baseman Bret Boone flew to Birming-ham to have elbow surgery just hours after his wife, Suzi, gave birth in Cincinnati to their first child, Savannah. Immediately after the operation he flew home to be with her and their hours-old baby. Schott went to the hospital that night to check on them. She took gifts and stayed with Suzi for a couple of hours while Bret, still groggy from his surgery, slept on a couch. "It was weird," says one former marketing employee. "She was great to our families. Absolutely terrific. But she treated us like s---."

Whatever generous spirit there is inside Schott flickers out when she sits behind that owner's desk. "I think she is the single worst person I've ever known," says one longtime Reds employee. "Spiteful, mean-spirited and evil."

Says a former top-level employee, "She's the most cold, calculat-ing person I've ever known. To feel sorry for her is ridiculous."

Schott believes she must be bottom-line tough, like the Men, coughing into her pillow all the way. Drink hard, work hard, feel hard. And this is how you get the dimly lit discount hell that is the Reds today. There is not a drop of sweetness left in the organization, possibly because Schott watches even the candy. In a stadium store-room there are boxes and boxes of leftover donations from a Leaf candy promotion tied to the Celebrity Bat Girl and Bat Boy nights at Riverfront. But Schott did not hand it out. She did not give it away to charities. She hoarded it for special occasions. One was last January, when she indicated to her shrinking, pitifully paid front-office staff (Exhibit A: Former public relations assistant Joe Kelley more than doubled his salary by taking a similar job with the city's minor league hockey franchise) that there would be no holiday bonus again by throwing some Leaf candy on each person's desk. How old was it? On the outside of some of the wrappers was an ad for a contest. It said, "Win a trip to the 1991 Grammy Awards!"

Schott has a front-office staff of only 41 people, fewest in the league. Almost every other team has twice as many employees. The New York Mets have 120, the Colorado Rockies 111, the San Diego Padres 104. This does not include scouts, on whom Schott has never been big. "All they do is sit around and watch ball games," she once said. The Reds have 25 scouts. The Los Angeles Dodgers have 57.

Schott is paranoid about being cheated. Reds policy is that she must sign any check over $50, and any purchase over that amount requires three bids before she'll agree to it. "That means even if you're reordering paper clips," says a former publicity employee, "you have to call around and get two more bids, even though you know exactly what you want already."

During the 1994–95 baseball strike Schott stopped having the Reds office bathrooms professionally cleaned, so some employees did the job themselves. She has been known to rummage through the trash barrels to make sure scrap paper is written on both sides. She eliminated free tissues for employees. She keeps the lights off whenever possible, extinguishing them when you leave your office just to walk down the hall. The hallway carpeting is so old and tat-tered that the seams are held together with duct tape. Schott wants the heat turned down to 55° at five o'clock, so some employees have been known to bring in their own space heaters. She does all of this at every place she owns.

No wonder, according to Bass, that male employees of Schott's occasionally ask her to sign a publicity shot for a "niece," then take it into the men's room, place it in the urinal and fire away.

Schott has eliminated the Reds' customer-service and community relations departments. Her private secretary became fed up with Schott and quit last spring, and for a year Schott answered her own calls rather than hire a replacement. The *New York Post* called last season to request head shots of the Reds' players, and after the playoffs Schott had a member of her staff call the newspaper and ask for them back.

"It's so crazy," she says. "You're spending millions and millions out on the field for these players, honey, and you find yourself arguing about envelopes and paper clips in the office. You try to cut on silly stuff. It's like Disneyland on the field and the real world in here."

"No," says one employee. "It's like Disneyland on the field and Bosnia in here."

Schott does have one of the major leagues' highest player payrolls—"They [Bowden and her other baseball advisers] con me into spending money on the players, honey," she says—though she has cut back this year and plans to make serious cuts next year. But just because she has had to purchase a Rolls-Royce doesn't mean she won't use the drive-thru window. Schott won't pop for video equipment to let players check past performances against certain pitchers and hitters. She won't pop for Cybex machines. She won't even pop for extra hats or sweatshirts. "Anything extra," says outfielder Davis, "we pay for ourselves."

Even when the glory comes, Schott does not seem to be able to pry open her pocketbook. When the Reds won the World Series in 1990, she didn't throw a party for them. Some of the players finally went out and brought back hamburgers.

To Schott, most of the players are just empty uniforms into which she pours money, and it sticks in her craw. One game in April, Cincinnati pitcher Mark Portugal gave up a line drive base hit. Watching from her front-row seat in the stands, Schott shook her head. "Three million dollars," she grumbled, apparently unaware that Portugal is earning $4.33 million this year, "and he's just not worth a damn."

Then there was this exchange during the same home stand in April, as she sat looking at the program in her luxury box, waiting for the coat-and-tied security director to come back from his walk with Schottzie.

"There's what's-his-name, honey."

"Who?"

"The guy I'm paying $3 million a year to sit on his butt."

"Jose Rijo?"

"Yeah. Three million, sweetheart. For crying out loud."

Rijo, the 1990 World Series MVP, who actually is making $6.15 million this season, hasn't pitched for the Reds since July 18, 1995, because of a serious elbow injury.

"It's kind of a circus atmosphere, but you do your job," says Larkin, the 1995 National League MVP. "The only thing I don't like is when the dog takes a crap at shortstop, because I might have to dive into that s---."

Even though Cincinnati won the 1990 World Series and was the NL Central champion last year, anybody in baseball will tell you privately that the Reds are leaking oil three lanes wide. They routinely lose their best scouts to better-paying clubs. Attendance is down for the second straight year. In the playoffs last year there were more than 12,000 unsold seats for one game at Riverfront and more than 8,000 for another. For some reason, aside from Bowden, who is considered one of the best young executives in the game, top-notch baseball minds aren't inclined to come to work in an office chilled to 55° for substantially less than what other teams are paying, bringing their own tissues to the office and wondering who else is listening to their phone messages.

The Reds don't often bid for high-priced free agents, which is fine with Schott, who prefers to bring in players from her farm teams. But Cincinnati's minor league system is unraveling. *Baseball America* recently listed the top 100 teenage prospects, and no one in the Reds' organization was listed in the top 50. No problem. One day recently Schott returned from seeing a thrilling trapeze act and had a great idea. "We need to start checking that circus for ballplayers," she reportedly told a member of her staff. "There are some real athletes there."

Another of her ideas is to have a woman playing on her team. "I've got my scouts looking for a great girl," Schott says. "Wouldn't that be something? Her coming in and striking all these boys out, honey?"

Incredibly, the county plans to build new stadiums for both the Reds and the NFL Bengals, and town leaders are petrified about the influence Schott might have over the new ballpark. Pay toilets? Bugging devices in every showerhead? A dog run in left center? "I just wish she'd get out," says one source high in the Reds' ownership structure. "We all wish she'd get out. She's a despicable person."

Baseball would not miss her, to say the least. She is on none of the owners' committees and has shown no interest in helping to resolve the issues that plague the game. Wouldn't baseball be better off without her? "There is no appropriate answer to that question," says Bud Selig, acting baseball commissioner and owner of the Milwaukee Brewers. But one owner did say that Schott is "truly embarrassing. Worse than embarrassing."

Wait your turn. People want Schott out of more than baseball. General Motors has tried twice over the last eight years to take her Chevrolet dealership from her. The reason, says Chevrolet, is the franchise's poor sales performance. Schott twice hauled Chevrolet before the Ohio Motor Vehicle Dealers Board, which regulates auto manufacturers and dealers throughout the state, and on both occasions she managed to retain her franchise. But there may be questions still. According to documents obtained by SI, a former Reds employee has received ownership notices and a service reminder for a 1996 vehicle he does not own and says he has never seen. In fact, last weekend the car the former employee supposedly bought was on one of Schott's lots. Schott says that if these facts are correct, they are the result of an innocent mix-up, and she denies that her dealership is falsifying records to inflate sales figures in order to meet quotas set by Chevrolet. Chevrolet says it will look into the matter.

So, you've got to ask, why doesn't Schott just take the $30 million profit she stands to make if she cashes in her stake in the Reds, go ahead with her plans to build a new elephant wing for the Cincinnati Zoo ("Elephants never ask you for any raises, honey," she says), sell the car dealerships, the concrete company and the holding company and just find a good canasta game somewhere?

"I don't know, honey," she says, sitting all alone in that luxury box, the lights off, the thick windows keeping her from the cheers and the sun and the joy of the baseball game that is being mimed below. "As long as the little guy out there still thinks I'm doing a good job, that's all that matters. I don't give a damn what the stupid press thinks."

Actually, the little guy may have had it up to here. Schott has fallen drastically in popularity polls in Cincinnati. Last summer a *Cincinnati Post*-WCPO-TV poll found that approximately 47% of the public had a positive impression of Schott, compared to only 34% for Cincinnati Bengals owner Mike Brown. The most recent poll, though, gave Brown a 49% favorable rating, compared to only 37% for Schott. But she has an explanation: "I think somebody's trying to get me out, honey, somebody that wants to buy the team. It's a kind of vendetta against me, honey. It's kind of like a woman thing." She asks herself all the time, would the Men have given up?

"Nah," she says, "I don't wanna cave, baby. I've been through bad times before. Besides, I'm always best when I'm battling."

Right about then, an employee in a full-length dress and pearls comes back from walking Schottzie.

"Poo or tinkle?"

"Tinkle."

"Hey, have you met this guy from Sports Thingy?"

POSTSCRIPT: *You may know the rest. When Chevrolet investigated our findings that Schott was hiding cars to earn sales bonuses, she was penalized and reprimanded. When Major League Baseball read about the remarks about Hitler, working women, and Asians, they suspended her from baseball for two years. She's never been back.*

Saturday Night Fever

FEBRUARY 8, 1999—Play pinochle. Catch up on your thumb-twid-dling. Guess the number of cashews in the hotel room minibar. Knit. Scratch. Levitate. Any of these are fine things to do the night before a Super Bowl.

An example of what's *not* a fine thing to do: Leave your wife, two kids, father, uncles, aunts and teammates, jump in your rental car, drive to the fishnet part of town and attempt to purchase $40 worth of oral sex from a female cop posing as a street-corner trollop.

Honey, I'm just going out for a quart of milk. Would you have two twenties?

Atlanta Falcons free safety Eugene Robinson was charged by Miami police with doing exactly that last Saturday night, thereby putting the XXX in Super Bowl XXXIII. Not that it was a *distraction* or anything. He just had to be bailed out at 11 p.m. by Atlanta's general manager, try to explain the episode to his wife and family *(See, I've got this superstition)*, not sleep the entire night, keep his teammates up stewing about the incident and keep his sore-hearted coach up for hours fretting about it.

But a *distraction*? Nah. Robinson was able to go right out and con-tribute all he could to the Denver Broncos' easy 34–19 win. He missed more tackles than the extras in *The Galloping Ghost*, twice was faked out of his shorts (O.K., bad example) by Terrell Davis and got burned in the crushing play of the game, an 80-yard sting operation from John Elway to Rod Smith that gave the Broncos a 17–3 lead. As one Denver fan's sign read: EUGENE ROBINSON FOR PRESIDENT.

Why this guy wasn't benched, I'll never know. Because he was innocent? In a bit of fluent Clintonese, Robinson said after the game that he thought he was "innocent in this deal, not righteous in this deal." Say what? Then he spent the next 15 minutes begging forgiveness from Jesus Christ, his wife, his family, his teammates and his coaches. "I will have to make amends with everyone that knows me," he said. Does that sound like an innocent man to you?

Denver coach Mike Shanahan wouldn't have benched him. He'd have killed him.

No, I take that back. Robinson wouldn't have been in jail on Saturday night because he never would've gotten out of Broncos lockup. Here was Denver's Saturday night: dinner at 7, meeting at 8, meeting at 8:30, mandatory snack at 9, curfew at 11. "Mike treats us like men," Elway said earlier in the week. *Exactly.* If the fire marshal would let him, Shanahan would chain his players in their rooms the night before a game. Now, here was Atlanta's Saturday night: no team dinner, no team meetings, no restrictions except a midnight curfew. The Falcons coaches might as well have said, "Gentlemen, Miami is one of the most dangerous, hypersexed, drug-riddled cities in all of North America. Have fun out there!"

Robinson's idea of fun allegedly centered around the good-time intersection of N.E. 22nd Street and Biscayne Boulevard, which is about a hundred yards from the Miami Police Edgewater Mini Station. Some sneaky undercover work by Miami vice, no? Makes you wonder what other warning signals Robinson might have missed that night.

Hey, big boy, can I see your . . . license and registration?

On one corner is a vacant lot. Someday the NFL Historical Society might put up a plaque: ON THIS SPOT EUGENE ROBINSON BLEW THE SUPER BOWL. The hookers could point to it with pride.

Atlanta coach Dan Reeves probably would've rather had his sutures ripped out with a fire ax than not have Robinson in this game. Robinson was his team motivator, the player who has intercepted more passes than anybody in the game today, the man who's played about as many games against Elway as any other defensive back. "Anybody but Eugene," Atlanta linebacker Henri Crockett said Sunday before the game.

You'd think so. Robinson, 35, is model handsome and active in charitable affairs. "It's my personality to reach out to the community," he says. In fact, earlier in the day of his arrest for reaching out to one too many members of the community, Robinson's "high moral character" won him the Bart Starr Award from Athletes in

Action. Next week he's scheduled to accept the James Worthy Award from Athletes Looking for Action.

The whole thing is sad, really. It's sad when a man arrives at his big night, determined to fulfill his ultimate quest, only to be denied.

Then, to lose a football game the *next* night, well . . .

Locked In *with NBA Players*

DECEMBER 21, 1998—I'll take a few questions now. Yes?

Q: Is it true that last week you conned your way into a pickup game with Shaquille O'Neal, Antonio McDyess and other NBA stars?

A: Yes.

Q: Which did it involve, cash payments or incriminating photographs?

A: Neither. It was just me and some of my homies—Shaq, Dice, the Wizards' Otis Thorpe, the 76ers' Mark Davis, former NBA standout Rodney McCray, guys like that.

Q: Is it true that you wore your geeky Ivy League glasses and test-pattern shorts? And your watch, for god's sake?

A: Only so the paramedics would be able to affix time of death.

Q: Why in the name of all that is good and decent in the world did they let you play?

A: Because I asked.

Q: You asked?

A: Sure. Because of the NBA lockout, I had heard, a lot of stars were hangin' at the Westside Tennis Club in Houston, where the Rockets usually practice. So I asked the club president if I could play, and he said, "O.K., but only for the first 10 minutes when the pros are still kind of warming up. That way there's a chance you might not get killed."

Q: Did you?

A: Well, I admit, on the first trip down I did an unwise thing: I tried to set a pick for Shaq on the 6' 9", 250-pound McDyess. But I was only without breath for maybe 75 to 90 seconds, tops.

Q: *Whom did you guard?*

A: I didn't know him, but I assumed he was either a lottery pick or a college star from the area.

Q: *You got smoked by a complete nobody, didn't you?*

A: Like a trout. He turned out to be 27-year-old Ramone Veal, who, while never having been in the NBA, did play in the pro leagues of Colombia, where I'm guessing that he was a living legend.

Q: *What's this about you gagging a wide-open 15-foot jumper?*

A: Does anyone else have a question?

Q: *I'm the only one here.*

A: Yes, it's true, but, philosophically, can any jumper truly be considered "wide open" when you're being guarded by a Colombian living legend?

Q: *I heard you blew an alley-oop pass, too.*

A: O.K., Shaq made this great block and fired an outlet to me. Out of the corner of my eye, I saw a teammate streaking toward the hoop. Now, in my usual game at the Y, we do not get a lot of chances to throw alley-oops. Dr. Manny Glickstein, the urologist, generally can't get that high, and certainly not Father Casey. So, I thought, why not? I lofted a perfect pass only to find that the streaking player was the Jazz's Chris Morris, who, while a wonderful shooter, would not be considered a leaper in a herd of elephants. He couldn't quite reach my pass and instead only batted it off the glass with his fingertips.

Q: *You airmailed the poor guy.*

A: Yes. So now the ball is loose, right? What do I do? I swoop in, rebound it, blow past Timberwolves guard Stephon Marbury like he's a YIELD sign and kiss it sweetly off the glass for two.

Q: *You blew past Stephon Marbury.*

A: Yes, in the sense that he was sitting in a chair under the basket support. Still, the fact remains, my career NBA lockout line reads: 10 minutes played, .500 shooting percentage and one rebound. Plus, I outscored Shaq, who had zero points during my stint.

Q: *I'm not surprised, with you as his point guard. Did you guys talk?*

A: I did tell him once, "Next time down, gimme the pill and run an iso for me." He did not laugh.

Q: So, did you win?

A: Well, we were behind 8–4 when I was taken out, but it does not go down as a loss, officially.

Q: So, just to recap, you had Shaquille O'Neal and three other NBA stars as teammates in a pickup game, but you lost to a team led by a man named Ramone Veal. Would you agree this ranks as the lowest moment in this godforsaken NBA year?

A: Absolutely, but afterward, Shaq paid me the ultimate compliment, saying, "Well, at least you're better than Elden Campbell."

Q: I'm outta here.

A: I'm not sure he was kidding.

And the Band Fought On

OCTOBER 5, 1998—Look at college football. Players tearing each other's uniforms off. Squads crushing each other bloody. Fights that send people to hospitals.

And that's just between the bands.

Take, for instance, Prairie View A&M versus Southern on Sept. 19. Halftime. Packed house. Nobody cared about the game. Are you serious? Prairie View hadn't won a football game in nine years. No, everybody was there to see the bands, two of the nation's slickest. High steppers. Wicked formations. Crisp cuts. Fliers that were circulated before the game even hyped it as THE BATTLE OF THE BANDS.

They got that right.

Southern was coming off the field after eight boffo minutes. Prairie View was waiting to go on. The tension was high. Prairie View's band had just been ranked No. 1 in a Web site poll on the Internet, over, uh-huh, No. 2 Southern. There was some trash-talking. "I don't want to go into what was said," says Prairie View's band director, George Edwards.

Band smack?

Yo, John Philip Sousa called. He wants his uniform back.

Southern's band director, Isaac Greggs, says members of the Prairie View band blocked Southern's exit march to the sideline. Prairie View band members say Southern came high-kneeing through them in a flying wedge, sabotaging their formation.

For whatever reason, Southern says its drum major, Terrell Jackson, got whacked with a pair of brass instruments, twice in the side of the head and once in the nose. As a music man he knows all about bridges, and he says his is still a little swollen.

Right about then the two bands started dotting each other's eyes. Drumsticks started flying. Trombones started sliding. Everybody was doing the big-band swing. A woman from Prairie View went to the hospital after she took some kind of wind instrument to the face. I hope it wasn't a flugelhorn. Guarantee you what, you don't want to catch the business end of a flugelhorn.

It was musical mayhem, the spats spat of all time. We're talking 370 marchers total. Guys got beat up in three-quarter time. People got good and drummed. It was the kind of day when you hoped your band had a really good concussion section. "It was like a big firecracker went off," says Chris Gulstad, a sportswriter for the *Beaumont* (Texas) *Enterprise*, who saw it all at Lamar's Cardinal Stadium, the neutral corner for the game. "It was a full-on, 100-percent street brawl."

All these years mothers have made their sons go out for band because it's safe. Pah! Everybody went postal—except the light wind instruments. They backed off. I've always said this: I love the piccolo, and I want you to love the piccolo, too.

The fracas went on for almost 20 minutes. It was like a scene from *Stomp*, with each side grabbing the other's instruments, throwing them down and jumping on them. Three Prairie View sousaphones were ruined at $6,500 each. That's almost $20,000, blown.

Greggs says he has never seen anything like it in 30 years as Southern's band director. "I got some F-horns all bent up," he said, looking over the F-carnage. "I got some trombones dinged, some baritones [instruments, not singers] dinged up. We lost some hats and capes, too. I know because one of their guys was showing it off in the stands afterward, wearing it."

The ultimate indignity: another man wearing your cape.

But out of all this, something amazing happened. Maybe the Prairie View football team figured that pretty soon its band was going to beat the spit valve out of it. Or maybe the Panthers' coach, Greg Johnson, signed a few guys from the horn section, but guess what? Prairie View went out and won its next game!

After 80 straight losses, the longest losing streak this side of Wile E. Coyote's, Prairie View beat Langston 14–12 last Saturday in Oklahoma City. Unfortunately, the Prairie View band didn't get to see it. Both fighting bands were banned from appearing anywhere for two weeks, and the commissioner of the Southwestern Athletic Conference is demanding a full report from each school to see who might be to blame.

Oh, and the Stanford band wants a piece of the winner.

<hr />

A Chauvinist Pig in a Poke

APRIL 24, 2000—Someday somebody may whisper in your ear, "Hey, buddy, how'd you like to spend an entire day rubbing bodies with 107 fit, glistening young women?" Resist! If you don't, you'll end up like me, a semifunctioning blood clot, a man with more scratch marks than Ricky Martin, a boy toy used and discarded by ruthless females.

That isn't what I expected when I agreed to be the only man to compete in last week's WNBA predraft camp in Chicago. What I expected was a) a good roomie; b) some partial nudity; and c) to have my way with these girls, basketball-wise.

See, I had never attended, watched or given two bobby pins

about a WNBA game. I figured it was women in comfortable heels shooting two-hand set shots and running to the bench to check their Maybelline.

Right away there were signs that maybe I was wrong. For example, at the player physicals the day before the camp, Dr. John Heffrin shook my hand and said, "We're going to have the defibrillator at the gym, just in case." He wasn't smiling.

Then, in my complimentary WNBA player's bag—which included, yes, sports bras—some wise gal had slipped in a listing of Chicago funeral homes. Then I got a look at the schedule for the next day: 9:15 a.m.–12:15 p.m., half-court games; 2–8 p.m., full-court games. And I thought, 8:03, defibrillator.

Now, I may not be Billy Blanks, but I'm not Tyra Banks, either. I'm 6' 1", 180 pounds, sturdy in a 42-year-old kind of way. But when I went to my power-forward spot and a woman named Frankie Boyd, 6' 4" and 180 pounds, senior, Ole Miss, got the ball in the post, yo-yoed it, slammed her butt into my intestines and her elbow into my teeth (sending me skidding back on my shorts), and laid in the uncontested bunny, I wished very much that I had stayed home and rotated the tires.

Why must women be so violent? They grabbed me. They shoved me. They pinched me. They held their ground. They were *huge*. At one point I was guarding 6' 4", 250-pound UCLA center Janae Hubbard, a woman who on the court didn't seem to care in the least about Maybelline. I came out, and my coach, Greg Williams, an assistant with the Detroit Shock, said, "Son, you couldn't play dead in a cowboy movie."

I tightened my sports bra. I bruised, pinched and elbowed the women back. For me, chivalry was dead. In one skirmish with Boyd, I held her, she slapped my hands away, she hooked her arm around my back, I grunted, we leaned hard into each other, both bathed in sweat, thus re-creating most of my high school dates.

I started making shots. A baby hook. A three-pointer. A thumping putback. I returned to the bench. "I bet you scored 10 points out there," Williams said, "and gave up 20."

But you don't understand! I had to guard 6' 8" Rhonda Smith, who had fingernails like RuPaul! I had to stay with Michelle (Spin-derella) Marciniak, the 1996 Final Four MVP! I had to stop women who would humiliate the tall white geeks at the end of every NBA bench. "Did you play basketball when you were young?" a well-meaning teammate asked me on the sideline. Uh, ouch. *Oh, yes,* I wanted to say. *I was in charge of getting the ball out of the peach basket.*

Then came the full-court games. Refs. Stat crews. At one point, gassed, I looked over to Williams and pulled on my shirt, the universal sign that a player needs to come out. Williams just looked blankly at me. I did it the next time down. Nothing. A third. Zilch. I grew woozy. There was a timeout. "Didn't you *[pant]* see me *[gulp]* tug on my *[spit]* shirt?" I asked.

"Oh," Williams said. "I thought your jersey was sticky."

God, it was fun. My teammates took me in, slapping me on the rear and never laughing at my air balls. I love the WNBA now. There's more teamwork than in the NBA, better fundamentals and far fewer paternity suits. I have a new definition of femininity. What I look for now in a beautiful woman is big hands, scabby knees and a nice box-out butt.

As I was leaving, I saw Nancy Lieberman-Cline, one of the greatest woman basketball players ever, who's now G.M. and coach of the Shock. I asked her what she thought of my game. "I honestly think," she said, "you'd be a very good fifth-round pick."

That soothed my aching pride until that night, in the tub, I read something that sort of took the glow off: Tuesday's draft has only four rounds.

POSTSCRIPT: *There was only one downside to this one: Coming back from a weekend with 107 fit, glistening college co-eds and explaining to your wife the long scratch marks down your back.*

CHAPTER SEVEN: ROYALTY

CHAPTER SEVEN: ROYALTY

A Paragon Rising above the Madness

MARCH 20, 2000—On Tuesday the best man I know will do what he always does on the 21st of the month. He'll sit down and pen a love letter to his best girl. He'll say how much he misses her and loves her and can't wait to see her again. Then he'll fold it once, slide it in a little envelope and walk into his bedroom. He'll go to the stack of love letters sitting there on her pillow, untie the yellow ribbon, place the new one on top and tie the ribbon again.

The stack will be 180 letters high then, because Tuesday is 15 years to the day since Nellie, his beloved wife of 53 years, died. In her memory, he sleeps only on his half of the bed, only on his pillow, only on top of the sheets, never between, with just the old bedspread they shared to keep him warm.

There's never been a finer man in American sports than John Wooden, or a finer coach. He won 10 NCAA basketball championships at UCLA, the last in 1975. Nobody has ever come within six of him. He won 88 straight games between Jan. 30, 1971, and Jan. 17, 1974. Nobody has come within 42 since.

So, sometimes, when the Madness of March gets to be too much—too many players trying to make *SportsCenter*, too few players trying to make assists, too many coaches trying to be homeys, too few coaches willing to be mentors, too many freshmen with out-of-wedlock kids, too few freshmen who will stay in school long enough to become men—I like to go see Coach Wooden. I visit him in his little condo in Encino, 20 minutes northwest of L.A., and hear him say things like "Gracious sakes alive!" and tell stories about teaching "Lewis" the hook shot. Lewis Alcindor, that is. Kareem Abdul-Jabbar.

There has never been another coach like Wooden, quiet as an April snow and square as a game of checkers; loyal to one woman, one school, one way; walking around campus in his sensible shoes and Jimmy Stewart morals. He'd spend a half hour the first day of practice teaching his men how to put on a sock. "Wrinkles can lead to blisters," he'd warn. These huge players would sneak looks at one another and roll their eyes. Eventually, they'd do it right. "Good," he'd say. "And now for the other foot."

Of the 180 players who played for him, Wooden knows the whereabouts of 172. Of course, it's not hard when most of them call, checking on his health, secretly hoping to hear some of his simple life lessons so that they can write them on the lunch bags of their kids, who will roll their eyes. "Discipline yourself, and others won't need to," Coach would say. "Never lie, never cheat, never steal," Coach would say. "*Earn* the right to be proud and confident."

You played for him, you played by his rules: Never score without acknowledging a teammate. One word of profanity, and you're done for the day. Treat your opponent with respect.

He believed in hopelessly out-of-date stuff that never did anything but win championships. No dribbling behind the back or through the legs. "There's no need," he'd say. No UCLA basketball number was retired under his watch. "What about the fellows who wore that number before? Didn't they contribute to the team?" he'd say. No long hair, no facial hair. "They take too long to dry, and you could catch cold leaving the gym," he'd say.

That one drove his players bonkers. One day, All-America center Bill Walton showed up with a full beard. "It's my right," he insisted. Wooden asked if he believed that strongly. Walton said he did. "That's good, Bill," Coach said. "I admire people who have strong beliefs and stick by them, I really do. We're going to miss

242

you." Walton shaved it right then and there. Now Walton calls once a week to tell Coach he loves him.

It's always too soon when you have to leave the condo and go back out into the real world, where the rules are so much grayer and the teams so much worse. As Wooden shows you to the door, you take one last look around. The framed report cards of the great-grandkids. The boxes of jelly beans peeking out from under the favorite wooden chair. The dozens of pictures of Nellie.

He's almost 90 now, you think. A little more hunched over than last time. Steps a little smaller. You hope it's not the last time you see him. He smiles. "I'm not afraid to die," he says. "Death is my only chance to be with her again."

Problem is, we still need him here.

———————

This Girl Gets Her Kicks

OCTOBER 19, 1998—Q: How come nobody said a word last week after the Chatfield (Colo.) High homecoming queen accepted a single white rose at halftime of the football game, locked arms with the king and then ripped off her satin sash and sprinted into the players' locker room?

A: She still had two quarters to play.

Katie Hnida (pronounced NYE-duh) is 17, with long blond hair, melt-your-heart blue eyes, and legs that won't quit kicking. This season she's perfect: 23 for 23 on extra points, 3 for 3 on field goals and 1 for 1 in homecoming queen elections.

Among the best sports moments of the 1990s, this one has to be in the top 10: Katie tearing off her helmet at the end of the first half, taking her place among other members of the homecoming court in their dresses and high heels, being announced as queen, wriggling the sash on over her shoulder pads, waving thanks to everybody, smiling for the photographers and sprinting to the dressing room. "I only had a minute," she says of her coronation.

Is this a great time or what? We're past the 1970s, when girls had two options in sports: cheerleader or pep squad. We're past the '80s, when girls had two options in life: to be a jock or a girl. Now we're into the Katie Era, when a young lady can kick the winning field goal on Saturday afternoon and look drop-dead in her spaghetti-strap number on Saturday night. "I know I looked gross at half-time," Katie says. "No makeup or anything. But I'm a football player. How else am I going to look?"

Actually, the only way anyone on the other team can guess that the 5' 9", 135-pound Katie is a girl is by the ponytail that runs out from beneath her helmet and down her back. One time, as a fresh-man, she got flattened after a PAT by a massive nosetackle, who ended up on top of her. They both opened their eyes at the same time, only it was the nosetackle who screamed, "You're a girl!"

Not that the guys on the Chatfield High team seem to notice much. "I don't mind when they burp, fart and spit around me," she says. "It lets me know they think of me as their teammate."

Another first: players *thanked* for impersonating water buffalo.

Katie's life can be strange. After one game last year the Chatfield players and their opponents were exchanging postgame handshakes when a hulk on the other team stopped Katie and asked, "Do you have another number besides 40 I could possibly have?" She didn't bite, but it still goes down as the single best pickup line in high school football history.

The only downside of the whole thing is that Katie has to shower and dress in the girls' locker room, away from the rest of the team. "Sometimes we'll win a big game and I can hear all the guys whooping it up," she says, "and I want to get in there with them."

Other than that, Katie "gets to be who she wants to be," says her mother, Anne, who never had that chance in high school. "I kept stats for the boys' basketball team," she says. Katie, meanwhile, has a 3.2 grade point average, writes and edits for the school newspaper, plays soccer in the spring, doesn't drink, won't smoke, can take a lick and kicks like a mule.

"Wearing a little skirt and jumping around after touchdowns isn't quite the same," she says. "I want the competition. I want to be part of the team. Girls ask me all the time, 'What's it like to be around all these gorgeous guys all the time?' They have no idea. I've seen these guys break down and cry in the huddle, and I've seen them so incredibly happy after a big win. I wouldn't trade anything for what I've had, being part of this team."

Yeah, she'd even trade the sash. "Ten years from now, nobody's going to be impressed that I was homecoming queen," she says, "but they might think it was cool I could kick a 40-yard field goal."

Katie, who has already booted a 35-yarder, has this crazy dream that would make things even cooler. She wants to become the only Division I woman football player next season. Colorado coach Rick Neuheisel already has asked her to walk on. Me, I'd bet my last pair of hose on her.

One thing, no guy's ever going to have to give Katie his letter jacket. She's got her own, thanks. "I guess what I want to show is that it's O.K. to be athletic *and* feminine."

Hey, tell it to Carl Lewis.

If nothing else, Katie Hnida gave us a rare moment, in which the homecoming queen walked off the field after the game and had little girls come up to her, saying, "Chin strap?"

POSTSCRIPT: *Not only was Katie named one of* Teen People's *top 25 teens in America, she made the University of Colorado football team as a walk-on and has a chance to become the first woman in history to score in a Division I game.*

No Fuss Necessary in Wayne's World

APRIL 26, 1999—I've dug ditches, lubed jackhammers and manned the graveyard shift at a 7-Eleven. But the worst job I ever had was writing Wayne Gretzky's autobiography.

It was like trying to draw personal revelations out of a 1970 Plymouth Duster. The only thing Gretzky hates worse than going into the corners is going on about himself. Humility's O.K., I guess, but it tends to give ghostwriters facial tics.

"Gretz, seriously, you've got to go into a little more detail about yourself," I'd moan.

"All right, all right," he'd say. "What year are we up to now?"

"Nineteen eighty-four."

"I didn't do much that year, did I?"

"Oh, no, not really, except you led the freaking league in goals and assists! Won the Hart Trophy! Won the damn Cup!"

"Good. Go with that. Now, what happened in '85?"

Last week everybody up to and including the prime minister of Canada begged Gretzky to play one more season, give the world one last chance to ticker-tape the greatest team athlete in history.

Gretzky would rather spend a year flossing rhinos than do that. The man hates a fuss, and farewell tours are fuss times 99. Throughout his career, any time games would be delayed so Gretzky could accept giant crystal bowls or get handed keys to Rolls-Royces, he'd feel bad for his teammates. "They're ready to play a game," he'd groan. "They're athletes, and they have to just *sit* there, waiting."

If Gretzky was about anything, it was team. Do you realize Gretzky had more assists than Bobby Orr, Frank Mahovlich and Mike Bossy *combined*? He broke Gordie Howe's alltime assist record in 1,086 fewer games than Howe took to set it. That's 13 seasons! Do you know that Gretzky has the first, second, third, fourth, fifth, sixth, seventh, eighth, 10th, 11th and 12th greatest assists seasons in NHL history?

On Sunday, as Gretzky played his last game, I heard people say he was the Michael Jordan of hockey. Horsepuck. Jordan was the Gretzky of basketball. In 1983–84 Gretzky could've stopped playing on Jan. 7 and *still* won the scoring title. That's almost three months before the end of the season. How's this? Gretzky took the single-season points record from 152 to 215, an increase of 41%. Jordan would've had to average 71 points a game to do that!

Did anybody do more for his sport than Gretzky did for hockey? He snatched it from the bullies. He showed how ugly violence could be when set next to grace. He gave the game an imagination, passing off nets and skates and Gatorade bottles. One night in St. Louis, he flipped in a goal from behind the net off the back of goalie Mike Liut and scored not once but *twice* on face-offs. Liut is still in therapy.

Yet to sit next to Gretzky on a plane, you were sure he ran a small life-insurance agency in Keokuk, Iowa. For one thing, he didn't have to click in his teeth before the meal. For another, he was 5' 11" tops, 175 pounds including headphones, and he benched a whopping 140. For a third, he was usually imbedding his fingernails into the armrests, white as snow, sweating like a Dubai dry cleaner.

The plane would hit a patch of rough air, and before you could get him calmed down, he'd be sitting up with the pilots, making sure they had all the needles and levers in the right position. When the plane would finally level out, he'd come back, smile and say, "Just flicked a couple switches." That's another reason to be happy for Gretzky. He never has to go wheels-up the rest of his life.

For a legend, he desperately needed a couple years at Ego School. He'd ask tongue-tied kids if they wanted anything signed. He'd screw up something and say, with a grin, "Hey, that's why they call me the Great One." We'd want to go to dinner at Morton's or Spago, and the place would be booked. "Do it, Wayne," his wife, Janet, would say. "Just give them your name." He'd pick up the phone, puff out his chest and then chicken out. Another night ordering in.

Be happy for Gretzky. He's finally free. He's been a celebrity since he was six. He's been in national magazines since he was 11. Been a pro since high school. After 32 years, the pressure is finally off.

Starting this week, Gretzky never has to be Great again.

—•—

The Appeal of O'Neal

JUNE 5, 2000—Nobody ever sends Goliath a thank you note, so . . .

Thank you, Shaquille O'Neal, win or lose, for everything you do and everything you don't.

Thanks for never showing up in the sports section my kids read with a bowl of cocaine, three "freelance models" and a Glock 17.

Thanks for never getting stopped for weaving down the middle of the San Diego Freeway at 3 a.m. with the blood-alcohol level of Boris Yeltsin.

Thanks for not throwing your dates through windows or down staircases or out of limousines. A lot of us have daughters who admire you.

Thanks for busting your rather enormous butt. How a guy 7' 1", 320 pounds making $18 million a year stays hungry I have no idea, but you do. You played more minutes this season than ever before. You can't sleep after losses. You have your own key to the Mira Costa High girls' gym just so you can go and shoot free throws for an hour—sometimes even after *wins*.

Thanks for not sticking a big stogie in your mouth after every win or conducting your postgame interviews with two bimbos under each arm. You're kind enough to let your owner do that.

Thanks for being big-time generous. You gave $1 million to the Boys and Girls Clubs of America, which inspired Bill Gates to pony up enough for 30 new clubs, which sparked AOL chairman Steve Case to provide 30,000 computers and 30,000 Internet accounts for Boys and Girls Clubs around the country. And they say one person can't make a difference.

Thanks for being small-time generous, too. You make the payments on your trainer's truck. You dress up in ridiculous costumes, Shaq-a-bunny at Easter and Shaq-a-Claus at Christmas, to take the embarrassment out of folks having to take a handout. That's decency. People don't forget that. Kareem Abdul-Jabbar is hanging around the Los Angeles Clippers now and nobody seems to mind, but Lakers fans will have you bronzed 10 minutes after you retire.

Thanks for wanting to get better. Some young stars level off. Penny Hardaway, for instance. But you've ratcheted up everything about your game this season. You blocked more shots, scored more points, had more assists and cleared more rebounds than ever before. You even improved your free throw percentage. Hey, as the midget in elevator heels said, "Every little bit helps."

Thanks for smiling. You fall on your keister skateboarding and laugh. You ride your motor scooter around, looking like an elephant on a roller skate, and laugh. You cruise the Hollywood Hills on your custom Titan motorcycle and laugh. Kareem used to schedule one smile a year whether he thought he needed to or not.

Thanks for being the kind of superhero we think we'd be. During a day off in Phoenix you showed up at the house of the Suns' team photographer because you knew it was his 10-year-old son's birthday. You had ice cream and cake, played video games and then went to the boy's hockey game. You even gave his team a pregame speech. *Uh, fellas, I don't know much about hockey, but the fourth quarter is OURS!*

Thanks for having the self-control of a Chuck E. Cheese manager. What opponents do to you three nights a week would fill a season on ER. Nobody gets more welts, lumps and contusions than you do—and they're league-sanctioned! There's even a term for abusing you, Hack-a-Shaq, as though it were something in the playbook, like double-down or box-and-one. If I were you, a half-dozen Portland Trail Blazers would've left on gurneys by now.

Thank your dad for us, too—Sarge, your stepfather, Phil Harrison. Yeah, he was tough on you—making you copy pages out of the dictionary, making you crouch against the wall, knees bent, thighs parallel to the floor, holding an encyclopedia in outstretched arms—but he gave you something every kid needs: somebody you didn't want to disappoint. "I could never act a punk," you say. "He'd let me have it." But when you called him to tell him you'd won the MVP award, he wept. It's true: Good men raise good men.

You quoted Aristotle the other day when you said, "You are what you repeatedly do." Well, win or lose, in front of millions of kids every day, you repeatedly do the right thing, which makes you the right guy.

So, just thought somebody ought to say thanks.

POSTSCRIPT: *I like Shaq, but I will never again travel in a motorized vehicle with him. The 4,000-watt car stereo he installed in his Ford Expedition is so loud my Mountain Dew danced the rhumba in my cup holder. My hair actually blew from the movement of the woofers. I could feel my inner organs moving. And that was at "3" out of 10. When he cranks it to 4 is when he grins hugely and mouths the words, "OK, what'd you want to talk about?"*

The Goal-Goal Girls!

JULY 5, 1999—Admit it. You were thinking, *Joe Torre in heels.*

You figured when a U.S. women's team finally broke through, one that made even the truck drivers care, it would be a bunch of women with Bronko Nagurski shoulders and five o'clock shadows.

Well, the revolution is here, and it has bright-red toenails. And it shops. And it carries diaper bags. The U.S. women's soccer team is towing the country around by the heart in this Women's World Cup, and just *look* at the players. They've got ponytails! They've got kids! They've got (gulp) curves!

Captain Carla Overbeck crawls across a magazine page in a leopard-skin dress. Midfielder Julie Foudy calls the team "booters with hooters." Lethal scorer Mia Hamm makes PEOPLE's 50 Most Beautiful. Midfielder Brandi Chastain shows up in the pages of *Gear* wearing only a soccer ball, which gets her on *Letterman*, who sends *Late Night* shirts to the whole team, which snaps a picture of the players apparently wearing only the shirts and cleats, which causes Letterman to refer to them forevermore as "Babe City."

"Hey, I ran my ass off for this body," says Chastain. "I'm proud of it."

This team is a wonderful combination of Amazonian ambush and after-prom party. "We're women who like to knock people's heads off and then put on a skirt and go dance," says Chastain.

In fact, they're one of the first American women's teams with their own groupies. Very dumb groupies, but groupies nonetheless. The other night, for instance, one came up to defender Kate Sobrero in a bar and said, "You're on the U.S. soccer team, right?"

"Right," said Sobrero.

"Sooo," he said, pawing the floor with his boot, "uhh, well, are you a lesbian?"

Just to mess with him, Sobrero said, "I'm not, but my girlfriend is."

Whoever they are, they're absolutely impossible not to watch. They were 3–0 through Sunday, and every win was decisive. Every game is a happening, a Thrillith Fair packed with girls and moms. The U.S. women play technically perfect and emotionally riveting soccer. Not only that, but they *try* to score, as opposed to most men's teams, who try to get up 1–nil and then pack 11 guys in their own box for 85 minutes. Nobody except the Pope put more fannies in the seats at Giants Stadium than the women's team did two weeks ago. They sold out Soldier Field last Thursday, and had more than 50,000 at Foxboro Stadium on Sunday. Are the boneheads who planned NBC's Olympic broadcast from Atlanta listening?

Look at what our American men's international teams have done lately. Ryder Cup: humiliated. Presidents Cup: humiliated. USA Hockey: dead humiliated. World Cup: dead last.

The women's soccer team is a machine. It's a juggernaut. But most important, it's a floating slumber party. Before games lately, they've been gathering in the hotel hallway for their crucial pregame preparation: putting a dance CD on the boom box, singing at the top of their lungs and painting each other's nails. You figure the Knicks do that?

Hamm calls her teammates "a buncha goofballs," but every one of them has a college degree or is a full-time student. In Japan the minute a player gets married, she quits the game; not the U.S. women. Even when these women give birth, they only pause at 10 centimeters. Overbeck lifted weights on the day she delivered her only child. Mother of two Joy Fawcett, probably the best defender in the world, used to breast-feed in the back of huddles during breaks in practice.

Actually, they're not only fully functioning females, they're fully functioning human beings, too. This off-season, a kid knocked on the door of legendary American midfielder Michelle Akers's home outside Orlando and said, "Can you come out and kick the ball with us?"

Now, if this were the door of most American male professional athletes, the kid would've been: 1) escorted away by security, 2) rolled away by paramedics or 3) simply trying to make contact with her biological father.

What did Akers do? She went out and kicked with her, but only after bringing out an armful of pictures, books and pins. Ain't it great? Ten-year-old girls all over the country are taking down their Backstreet Boys posters and putting up the Goal-Goal Girls.

That ad is right, of course. Clinton would be crazy not to come to the World Cup final on July 10 in Pasadena.

Who else would you want presiding over Babe City?

POSTSCRIPT: I took vats of crap for this column, much of it from women who found it sexist. But it wasn't me who decided to market the team partly around their sex appeal. It wasn't me who sent David Letterman a photo of the team dressed in nothing but T-shirts and cleats. It wasn't me who appeared nude in Gear *magazine. And I didn't rip off my jersey upon winning the Cup. Not that I'm against ripping off your jersey after winning. I just hope it doesn't spread to the Senior Golf Tour.*

The Mourning Anchor

SEPTEMBER 26, 1988—What is it the poet said? Like muffled drums, our hearts beat a funeral march to the grave. And so it is that Bryant Gumbel, a man who is nothing if not prepared, keeps a list of his pallbearers.

Who has been true? Who has transgressed? Though only 39, he has done it many times. Gumbel hates surprises. The list changes every few months or so. He keeps track.

"I don't want to wait until something happens to see who my friends are," says Gumbel. "Or maybe I just don't want to be the guy who, when he dies, they can't find six guys to carry his coffin. Maybe this is a way to be sure I have six."

There have been days when he has wondered. Gumbel has a couple of thousand acquaintances but very few friends. Not that he couldn't have more. It's his choice. "If I'm in a room with 100 people, will I be able to find one person I'd like to have dinner with?" he asks. "Probably not," he answers.

Forget that. There are times when friends visit the Gumbels and Bryant won't come out of the den. "I've long since stopped apologizing to company for his grumpiness and aloofness," says June, his wife of almost 15 years. "Sometimes he doesn't feel compelled to entertain. It doesn't bother me anymore."

Strange man. Stubborn man. A man who might have best described himself when he said, "It's not that I dislike many people. It's just that I don't like many people."

The problem with people is that they just aren't as good as a certain Chicago probate judge who has been dead for more than 16 years—Gumbel's father, Richard. People don't try as hard as he did; they don't work as hard, achieve as much, carry themselves as tall. And who could be as heroic? Once, in the Philippines during World War II, Richard continued to march despite being obviously ill. The medic finally pulled him aside, sat him on a rock and took out his tonsils, then and there. And what did Sergeant Gumbel do? He got up and marched on. The man never let up. When he returned from the war, he put himself through Xavier University in New Orleans while working full-time to keep his family eating. He was senior-class president and yearbook editor. Then he put himself through Georgetown law school while working two jobs. He graduated second in his class.

Let's face it. Compared to Richard Gumbel, most people come off like Lumpy Rutherford. So Bryant finds it hard to be impressed; he finds himself getting let down a lot. He has more feuds than some people have friends: David Letterman, Connie Chung, Linda Ellerbee, Steve Garvey. It's not his fault. People aren't good enough. People aren't professional enough. People aren't true enough. And so he sits alone in the den of his 14-room home in Waccabuc, N.Y., making a list that weighs heavy on his mind. Who can be trusted to hold up one-sixth of his memory?

If you happen to be among the listed, consider yourself lucky. In Gumbel, you have a man of wit, style and grace. You have a man who, as anchor of NBC's *Today* show, is the only TV interviewer who might make Ted Koppel look over his shoulder. When the situation gets tense, Gumbel is a lock as the silkiest talent strapping on an earpiece.

You also have a friend you can take to any party, for there is no subject on which he is not conversant. You have the world's best Trivial Pursuit partner, a *Jeopardy!* fiend, one of the last of the Renaissance men. You also have the Beau Brummell of this age, an impeccable dresser, a man with more than 100 suits (18 of them made specially for the Olympics by award-winning designer Joseph Abboud), some with the tags still uncut, a man who wouldn't think of leaving the house without color-coordinated tie, cuff-links, underwear and socks.

You have a whiz in the kitchen, a connoisseur of champagne, a global citizen, a 12-handicap golfer, a father of two (daughter Jillian, 5, and son Bradley, 9) and a multimillionaire by virtue of a contract with NBC that pays him some $7 million over the next three years, enough to keep him up to his thorax in cuff links.

And that doesn't include the biggest prize of all: his job as host of the most expensive TV undertaking ever—NBC's coverage of the Seoul Olympics. Over the 16 days of the Games, Gumbel's image will be projected by more prime-time cathode rays than any network anchor's in history. The assignment is the fattest enchilada ever handed out by NBC, and the ultimate testament to Gumbel's talent is that no one has yet mentioned that it went to a black man.

It's 98° in Chicago, and Rhea Gumbel, 68, has all the windows open in her seventh-floor apartment. She has an air-conditioner in the bedroom, but it's not enough to cool the whole apartment. She would go somewhere cooler if she had the energy or a car, but she has neither. Sold the car. Too much trouble. So five mornings a week, she takes the bus to her job as a city clerk. Plenty are the days when she wishes she could afford to retire.

"Did you see what Oprah Winfrey bought her mother the other day?" one of the other clerks asked Rhea recently. "A brand-new beautiful mansion, that's what." Rhea knows what that woman would *loooove* to say next: *And your son, the big-shot NBC man, host of the "Today" show, what does he give you? You live in a lousy apartment. You won't go out at night and get milk because you're afraid of walking in the streets. What kind of fancy son is this you have?*

Still, she would never ask him for money. For one thing, she's too proud. For another, "It would hurt me like a knife if he said no. Besides, if he wanted to do something for me, he'd go ahead and do it on his own, wouldn't he?"

She knows what the trouble is. She has this one glaring fault. She's not his father.

Judge Richard Gumbel was a big man, 6' 1", four inches taller than his younger son, Bryant. Richard, the child of a New Orleans gambler, was "one of the most amazing men I've ever met," says Dr. Norman Francis, president of Xavier.

As a student, Richard was nearly straight A. As a leader, he was the first black to hold office in a national Catholic student organization. As a father, he was both strict and kind. While rearing his four children in the racially mixed neighborhood of Hyde Park, near the University of Chicago, he not only wouldn't let them get away with bad grammar, but he also wouldn't let their friends get away with it. "He was very hard to impress," says Bryant's brother, Greg, 42, a sportscaster with the Madison Square Garden Network and, starting with football season, with CBS. "A C should have been a B, and a B should have been an A, and if it *was* an A, why wasn't it an A before this?"

Yet when the family went on a picnic, Richard would play pepper with his boys for two hours. Or they would go to the sandlot and work on grounders for three. On summer days Bryant rarely missed a Cub game at Wrigley Field and also saw plenty of the

White Sox at night at Comiskey Park. What a life. In his day, he not only caught more than 100 batting practice balls and fouls, he wore them all out, too.

Greg lost that boyhood idolization of his father in high school, but Bryant never did. Greg was handsome and popular in high school; Bryant wasn't. Because racial attitudes then favored lighter skin, and his skin was the darkest of any in his family, including his cousins, Bryant felt ugly. Lacking social confidence, he stayed away from the dances and the back row at the Bijou, and held close to his hero. "I don't think I'll ever see a man as good," Bryant once said of his father.

When Gumbel set out for Bates College in Lewiston, Maine, in 1966, he was still not very sure of himself. After a small success in his social life during his freshman year at Bates, he wrote home: "For the first time since I've been here, I don't feel like a complete failure to myself or to you."

Gumbel may have even married to please his father. June Baranco, a student at LSU who would later become a Delta stewardess, came through Chicago to visit a friend for a few days in 1968. On one of those days, Gumbel's dad ended up taking June on a tour of Chicago. Richard liked her. In fact, Bryant told *McCall's*, ". . . at the very beginning he thought more of her than I did. But that fact was very important to me." They were married in 1973.

His first job after graduating from Bates, where he majored in Russian history and had a 2.6 average, was as a salesman for an industrial paper manufacturer in Manhattan. Those were lonely times. He didn't like the job, and he wasn't much good at it, so he quit without telling his dad.

The last Christmas Eve his father was alive, in 1971, Bryant looked around his New York apartment and took stock: He had a mattress, an eight-inch black-and-white TV and a light bulb. Total. He went out, bought a Blimpie sandwich and called his parents, collect. Deck the Halls.

He finally took a job writing for a small monthly, *Black Sports*, and that was what he was doing on April 10, 1972, when a friend of the family called to tell Bryant his father had collapsed in his courtroom and died of a heart attack. Richard never saw Bryant on TV.

How long did it take him to get over that death? "You're assuming I am," says Gumbel.

And the truth is, he's not. As Greg has said, "Without sounding as if I don't miss [my father], I think it's fair to say Bryant misses him more. He suffers more. He gravitated tremendously to Dad. It's certainly nothing we've ever talked about, but I would say Bryant was probably my father's favorite."

This summer Bryant recalled the last time he saw his father. He was saying goodbye, and he had wanted to kiss him, but thought, "Nah, you're a man, now," and shook his dad's hand instead.

Ironically, a week after Richard's funeral, Bryant's career began to bloom. An acquaintance at KNBC in Los Angeles asked him to try out for the weekend sports anchor job. Gumbel flew in and was so good that the producer assumed Gumbel had memorized the audition script. Within a year, he was doing the weekday sports.

The world discovered Zero-Stumble Gumbel during the 1974 Oakland Los Angeles World Series. He was doing a wrap-up for his own affiliate, using NBC cameras, and the network people watching were so impressed that they called him in. "Here comes this chubby guy with hair down to his shoulders," remembers the associate producer that day, Michael Weisman, now executive producer of NBC Sports. "He stands up and rolls it through in one take. *O.K., guys, see ya later.* We were dumbfounded. We had experienced network guys who would've taken two hours to do what he did in two minutes." In the truck, NBC Sports VP Chet Simmons was yelping, "Will someone please tell me: Who in the hell *is* that kid?"

The next year that kid was hired as cohost of NBC's wraparound show, *Grandstand*, paired first with Jack Buck and then with Lee Leonard, both of whom were phased out over the next few years. It wasn't their fault. Next to Gumbel, everybody else clunked like a dryer full of tennis shoes. When the show folded, Gumbel joined the first wave of ubiquitous sports anchors.

Before long, Gumbel was the rock of 30 Rock. Once, he was supposed to do an opener from the floor at an NCAA title game. What the producers didn't know was that the empty seats behind Gumbel at rehearsal would be filled that night by a very loud band.

When the show went on, there was a trombone threatening to turn Gumbel's tympanum to Malt-O-Meal. He not only couldn't hear what his producers were saying from the truck, but he also couldn't hear what *he* was saying. Unruffled, he spun through his segment as though he were chatting over a backyard fence, finishing at the correct second, cueless. "He saved the telecast for us," says Weisman.

Today called in 1980, and Gumbel began doing three sport slots a week for the morning show, a role that escalated sharply in '82 when he beat out Phil Donahue and various others for one of the cohost jobs. *Today* was another triple-host circus, Gumbel along with Jane Pauley and Chris Wallace, but before long, those two were playing the Supremes to Gumbel's Diana Ross. Later that year Wallace was reassigned to Washington, Pauley became host 1A, and that kid was suddenly The Man.

The early years on *Today* were dicey—the show was still running a distant second in the ratings in the summer of 1983—but by '85 it had tied *Good Morning America* in the Neilsens, and last winter it held a comfortable lead. One big reason, says *Today* writer Merle Rubine, is that "Bryant just improved every day, absorbed new material every day, got better, smarter, wiser and more sophisticated as he went along." Says rival Harry Smith, co-anchor of *CBS This Morning*, "As a sports guy and a black guy, he came into all this guilty until proven innocent. Yet he sits there and proves himself day after day."

Gumbel will turn 40 during the Olympics, the Carnegie Hall of his career. He will be dissected daily by every newspaper critic with a TV in his den. What, him worry? "Look, if Michael the Archangel hosted these games, he'd be lucky to satisfy 50 percent of the people," Gumbel says.

Anti-Gumbelers say his microchip perfection will wear out its welcome the first week. *Hey Gladys, does this Gumbo guy ever screw up?* Is he ever at a loss for words? Can a man who knows everything ever be surprised? Jim McKay, the perennial Olympic host for ABC, may have slipped a bit, but he at least seems human; he at least seems thrilled.

Gumbel-maniacs think he'll be golden. Bob Costas, who will follow Gumbel each night as NBC's late night Olympic anchor, says picking Gumbel was "a no-brainer. They needed somebody who had stature, who was tremendously facile and glib, who had supreme confidence in himself and wasn't likely to be rattled by anything. That's Gumbel."

What some people don't like about Gumbel is that he seems to *know* how good he is. Jim Lampley, the former ABC sportscaster now with KCBS in L.A., is impressed with Gumbel's ego, and Lampley is no wallflower himself. "Bryant makes me look humble," he says. "In Seoul, he'll make us all look humble."

Egocentric? O.K., so Gumbel once said that Pauley, *Today* movie critic Gene Shalit and weatherman Willard Scott "never looked better" than with him on the show. And, O.K., Gumbel doesn't read his mail or look at tapes of his performances or those of his competition. And, O.K., Gumbel always has to have the last line and the last laugh. Even he admits, "I've always got a comeback." But what's he supposed to do, take dull pills? Does Paulina Porizkova walk around without makeup?

Says *Washington Post* TV critic Tom Shales, "To me, calling Gumbel 'cocky' sounds too much like 'uppity.' It sounds almost racist." And if there's one thing you can say about Gumbel, it's that he's so good, the question of race almost never comes up. In fact, the only racism he encounters comes from other blacks. "You're not black enough," they write. Gumbel doesn't listen. "It's like [Georgetown and Olympic basketball coach] John Thompson said to me once: He wanted to be free not only from what the whites expected of him but what the blacks expected of him as well."

Only one problem: How do you get free of what you expect of yourself?

"My mom sees her sons as baby boys," says Gumbel. "Well, I stopped being her baby boy a long time ago."

Rhea has noticed. When Bryant is in town, he stays at a hotel and takes her out for dinner. Greg was on hand for his younger sister Renée's wedding. Bryant? He was at Fergie's wedding in London. "Renée is still hurting from that," says Rhea. And his sister Rhonda? Her birthday is the same day as June's. "You'd think he couldn't help remember that birthday," Rhea says. "But he never does."

But all that is side hurt. The real hurt is Rhea's. She reads of Bryant speaking eloquently about her husband, but never about her. She was so "heartbroken" after one article that she wrote a letter to Bryant that was almost unreadable from the tear stains.

"O.K., so I'm not a big shot," she says, reciting the letter from bitter memory. "I'm not a big person in the social life, not a cultural leader. But I brought you into this life, not him."

Bryant wrote back, "I'm not going to dignify some of your remarks. You wrote it when you were hurting."

Greg: "I think my father is probably bigger in death to Bryant than he was in life. With that constant, every-day comparison, there's no way she can measure up."

Bryant: "She probably doesn't think I'm as proud of her as I am. I just don't show it. I'm not good at showing a lot of things. . . . Besides, you've got to understand where most relationships are with me. If it's halfway decent, it's way up there with me. I guess she sees it as much less."

He's got that right.

Rhea: "I'm just trying to forget I have him."

Gumbel has a spare dark suit and tie hanging in his office in case the news is tragic and the suit he's wearing is too light for the occasion. He brings six golf shirts on a three-day golf trip just to make sure he looks perfect. Gumbel *never* loosens his tie or takes off his jacket, even in summer.

"Bryant is a perfectionist squared," says *Today* writer-producer Paul Brubaker. The reason is simple. If he knows that he "will never see someone as good" as his father, he knows that includes himself. Guilty as charged.

"In his best year, my dad didn't make what I do in a month," says Gumbel. "There's something profoundly wrong with that. My father did what he did better than I do what I do. What my father did required a lot more intelligence than what I do. He was smarter. He was more important to society. He had more worth." It is a constant process, Gumbel has said, "measuring myself against my father and always coming up short."

And so, to alleviate the guilt, to prove his worth, Gumbel works obsessively. He didn't become a lawyer as his father had hoped, so he'll be 10 times as good in television. His goal is to go into every interview unsurprisable. No answer can shock him because he knows all the answers. Gumbel sometimes stays over at his Manhattan town house, but when he sleeps at home in Westchester, he's up at 3:45 a.m., catches the limo at 4:30, arrives at Rockefeller Plaza at 5:30, studies notes for the day's show in his office until 6:15, goes to the studio to do his "sunrise tease" for *Today*, does the show until 9:00, tapes interviews and Olympic voice-overs or studies research on forthcoming guests until about noon, almost never breaks for lunch, studies and goes to meetings until about 4:00, reads research material for the show in the limousine on the way home, eats a quick dinner, then heads back to the den to finish studying from 7:30 to 11:00 and goes to bed by midnight. Gumbel might know more about Dan Quayle than Dan Quayle does. *Are you watching, Dad?*

Take the Olympics. He went on a coach-hopping tour, meeting with Olympic coaches from coast to coast. He personally edited scripts for more than 50 Olympic features and did the voice-overs himself. He took six weeks off to absorb eight network-prepared Olympic guides, each thicker than the Dallas Cowboys' playbook.

The remarkable thing is that he retains it all. He has a mind that would turn an IBM mainframe green. Without notice, Gumbel can tick off, to the day, how long he has been married, who started in 1963 on both sides of the line for the Chicago Bears, and the last five Speakers of the House.

It borders on the supernatural. Once, Gumbel was doing highlights on *NFL '81* when he was handed the news that the New York Yankees had just fired Gene Michael. He broke the story and then proceeded to reel off the last seven managers fired before Michael, with the year of each pink slip. "You will hear people say he's a son of a bitch," says *Today* writer/producer Allison Davis, "but you won't hear anybody say he's not a smart son of a bitch."

The only problem with perfection is that when you get there, there's nobody to talk to. "I have high expectations of people," he says. "When they achieve something, I say, 'So what?'"

People aren't good enough.

One morning, a presidential speech at the U.N. ended five minutes early. Connie Chung, the NBC newswoman, was anchoring the network desk with Gumbel. Producer Steve Friedman asked her off the air to remain on camera and help Gumbel kill time. She refused, saying she wasn't prepared. Gumbel killed the time himself, but he hasn't spoken to Chung since. "She acted in an unprofessional manner, so I disassociated myself from her," Gumbel says. "If it was an isolated incident, I'd forget about it. But it's not." Chung says she doesn't want to talk about it.

People aren't professional enough.

Once, during the taping of a prime-time *Today* special in Rockefeller Center's Channel Gardens, NBC late-night talk-show host David Letterman leaned out the seventh-story window and yelled through a bullhorn, "I am Larry Grossman, president of NBC News. And I'm not wearing pants!" While the *Today* show continued uninterrupted (Letterman was too far away for the microphones to pick up his voice), Gumbel was so angry that he has since refused to appear on Letterman's show—this despite the fact that *Today* show producer Friedman and Letterman's producer had discussed staging some kind of stunt. Doesn't matter. A professional wouldn't have done it, says Gumbel. Letterman says he doesn't want to talk about it. Gumbel says he doesn't want Letterman to grovel. "I just want him to pick up the phone," he says.

What? And ruin a good shtick? The Gumbel feud is an eephus pitch right in Letterman's wheelhouse. One night on his show, Letterman said Gumbel was the kind of guy who would spend a weekend "alphabetizing his colognes." Then there was the night a huge marquee appeared behind Letterman's desk with the billing BRYANT! THE MUSICAL.

Gumbel, who refers to Letterman as "the — —," isn't laughing. "It's this hip-sick-I'm-cool-you're-not kind of humor, a kind of mocking humor that I don't think is particularly funny," he says of Letterman's show. "He's insecure and it shows. But since he's competing against test patterns, he looks terrific." So forget the nightly coast-to-coast bashing Gumbel is taking from Letterman; he'll hold out. "Bryant can hold a grudge for a long time," says Brubaker. "He doesn't worry about p.r."

People aren't true enough.

Gumbel is godfather to Steve Garvey's daughter Whitney, as Garvey is to Bradley Gumbel, yet now the relationship has chilled. Gumbel won't say what happened, only that "You're seeing the new Steve Garvey now . . . the one who had too much pressure to become STEVE in capital letters."

People don't try enough.

If there's one thing Gumbel can't stand it's somebody "mailing it in," giving a half-hearted effort. This includes everybody from interviewees ("If somebody wants to sit there and look like an — — , I'll let him look like an — —," Gumbel says) to interviewers ("Nancy Reagan is a wonderful interview as long as you stick to wonderful subjects," he says. "But get to something else and she's monosyllabic. So when I interview her, I come out looking like an — —. But when David Hartman interviewed her, writers said he was 'warm and endearing.' Give me a break.").

Sometimes, women aren't good enough.

Gumbel has a grudge against New York *Daily News* TV critic Kay Gardella. He once promised that if they ever showed up at the same press conference, he would walk out. Nor is he fond of former *Today* contributor Ellerbee, who claims he refused to introduce her *TGIF* pieces on the show. "He's never liked me," says Ellerbee. "He has a locker-room mentality when it comes to women. . . . I think I was too strong a woman for him."

Says Gumbel, who denies, by the way, that he refused to introduce her *TGIF* pieces: "It's nothing personal against her. She just thinks everything is done better by a woman."

Hmmmm. Sounds a little like Gumbel in heels. Pauley once called Gumbel's attitudes toward women "Neanderthal." Truth is, Gumbel seems to be the anti-Alda. He likes all-male social clubs and eight-inch Cuban cigars. Like all good men, he believes that if talking won't settle an argument, a good punch will, which is exactly what he once threatened to do to Simmons during a contract negotiation. He hates "sensitive" movies—"You'll never get me to see *On Golden Pond* or *Julia* or

Tess," he says—and Woody Allen's films, but he loves Schwarzenegger's. One emotional movie he says he likes is a man's flick, *Islands in the Stream*, Hemingway's story of a doomed artist. Every day, a march to the grave.

That's Gumbel. A Hemingway man. A man's man. Grace under pressure. Men being valiant to other men. "I'm the kind of guy who cries when guys truly hug after a very important touchdown," he says. He can be sheer ice in a tender moment—during their courtship he signed letters to his wife with "best wishes"—but when the team is at stake, when competition is at stake, he gets emotional. In 1980, when he was wrapping up a 90-minute special on the Moscow Olympics—the Games he was supposed to host for NBC but didn't because of the U.S. boycott—Gumbel became so choked up he almost couldn't finish. Talking about it still brings tears to his eyes. "It was just so very emotional because of what we missed," he says.

True sports between men on the field, he cherishes. For instance, he is reverential about golf, partly because it is "a control game"—you control your fate, your opponent doesn't—and partly because it is primarily a man's game.

"Playing golf with somebody is such a pure thing," he says. "Sex is a pure thing too, but the closest thing you do with a guy is play golf with him. Your emotions are exposed when you play golf: humility, pride, anger, it all comes out with each swing. You lay it all on the line."

He belongs to two country clubs, Burning Tree, the political heavyweight's course in Bethesda, Md., and Whippoorwill in Armonk, N.Y. He assumes that both clubs have the same number of black members: one. And by the way, one member who helped Gumbel become a member at Burning Tree was a certain gentleman, name of Bush—George, that is.

Can you imagine if his father could be with him now, just for one weekend? Gumbel does, all the time. They would catch a game from the box seats. Take him to the club, have breakfast, get a couple of caddies and play a Nassau with the VP.

"He never sat in box seats in his life. Or had a caddie or played at a private club," says Bryant. "It's just not fair. The only reason I have what I do now is because of what he did back then. You're supposed to work hard so you can enjoy it, but he never got to enjoy it."

And so, whenever Gumbel plays with a buddy and the buddy invites his father along, Bryant aches. "It's such a beautiful thing." Pause. "Maybe I elevate golf too much."

Or is it fathers?

Rhea Gumbel has folded her hands in her lap and is about to cry. "He's distanced himself not only from me, but from the whole family," she says. "You love him and raise him, but you'd never dream this would happen."

She stares at the television, the box where her son lives, and then rolls her eyes to the ceiling: "If his father were alive, this would never happen. If he, for one minute, thought that they weren't looking out for me. . . ."

After a long pause, her visitor gets up to go. "What time is it?" she asks.

"Two o'clock."

"Good," she says.

"Why good?"

"Only eight more hours until I go to bed."

March to the grave. High above a checkerboard landscape, Gumbel reaches into the pocket of his first-class seat, pulls out his Filofax and draws out a yellowed piece of paper. The creases are so deep that the paper threatens to rip at the touch.

It is the eulogy from his father's funeral, the one Gumbel wrote and delivered that spring day in 1972. He keeps it with him always. It ends: *I say goodbye for those who knew him as "Your Honor." . . . I say goodbye for those who knew him as Dick or Richard and thereby shared in the joys which come of fine and rare friendship. I say goodbye for those who knew him as family. . . . I say goodbye for my dear mother who knew him as husband. . . . I say goodbye for Gregory, Rhonda, Renée and myself, who were lucky enough to call him father. . . . Goodbye, Daddy. We love you so very much. God has taken from us and unto himself, the finest man we'll ever know.*

He reads it once, cries a little, folds it up and puts it back in his Filofax.

265

You want pallbearers?

Bryant Gumbel is one still.

POSTSCRIPT: *Bryant Gumbel was said to be both "devastated" and "furious" over this piece. It was the first of a number of negative pieces about his aloof personality. But when Roy Firestone asked his brother, Greg, on ESPN's* Up Close *what he thought of the piece, Greg replied, "Pretty accurate."*

———◆———

What Would No. 62 Be Worth to You?

SEPTEMBER 7, 1998—Your mouth is bloody. A couple of your fingers are bent in three directions. Your watch is gone. But you came out with *it*.

Mark McGwire's 62nd.

Now people are pulling on you as if you're saltwater taffy. The security goons want you to come with them—*right now*. Some guy in an Italian double-breasted is offering you $500,000 for it, cash, *right now*. Three TV hairsprays are trying to interview you, your wife may or may not have fainted, and two unshavens have just bum-rushed you, trying to swipe the ball.

Panicked, you throw an elbow, spin 180 degrees and jailbreak it up the aisle, out the exit and into the parking lot, where you lock yourself in somebody's Winnebago. You need a second to think. The Winnebago owner is threatening you with a grilled kielbasa, and a very angry parade is right behind him. You're staring blankly at the dashboard, onto which the owner has Super Glued two five-inch action figures. One is Ty Cobb. The other is Babe Ruth.

Suddenly they start to glow. And move. And speak!

"You gotta give the ball to McGwire, kid," says the little Ruth. "It's the right thing to do."

You clean out your ears, rub your eyes and shake your head. That was a nasty bump you took.

"Don't be a sucker!" pipes the little Cobb, hopping up and down. "McGwire's not gonna give you any money for it! He said, and I quote, 'If somebody's going to hold this ball hostage for a dollar sign, you can take it home with you.' Easy for him to say, huh? Makin' almost $10 million a year. I mean, if some fool paid $500,000 for Eddie Murray's 500th, you'll get millions for this baby!"

"This ain't about money!" roars Ruth, poking Cobb in his tiny chest. "It's about morals! If McGwire hadn't hit it, that ball's just a chunk of cowhide. He oughta have it. He'd give you all the signed junk you want. Plus, you'd be his pal for life."

"Listen!" yells Cobb, pointing at you. "Whaddya pull down a year, $25,000 tops? You got a car that still runs on leaded. Your wife ain't had a new dress since the Nixon Administration. Your kids' teeth look like Stonehenge. You can't afford somebody else's morals!"

The tiny Ruth throws Cobb against the air freshener.

"You don't want that ball sittin' in some greasy billionaire's den forever!" shouts Ruth. "Look, a Florida man caught Barry Bonds's 400th home run last week and gave it straight to Bonds, even though a guy in the stands offered him $5,000. Orel Hershiser was so impressed, he gave the guy the five grand anyway!"

"Right," says Cobb. "Like Ron Gant is gonna rip you a check for a million. Hey! What about the kid who caught Roger Maris's 61st? Sal Durante? He went out and got what he could for it."

"And what has Sal Durante been doing the last 30 years?" asks Ruth.

"Driving a bus."

"See!" Ruth yells, really mad now. "Why's this gotta be about greed?"

"Because baseball is about greed!" Cobb bites back. He turns to you and says, "McGwire was one of the players who went on strike when the *average* salary was, what, more than $1 million? Free agents sell out teammates and fans every year for greed. Why do you think that ball you're holding is marked with a stamp that can only be seen in ultraviolet light? Because nobody else is thinking about money? If you give it back, you'll be the only guy in this *without* greed."

"O.K., so give it to the Hall of Fame," says Ruth.

"Nah. If you're too stupid to sell it, why not open up a store at the Mall of America and charge people $5 to hold it? You could sell stuff, too. McGwire T-shirts, McGwire sweat bands, Andro-6. You'd make a killin'!"

"Why, I oughta—"

The two tiny figures start to wrestle.

You think hard. Suddenly you snatch them up and zip them into your waist pouch. You unlock the Winnebago door and walk out, flipping the ball to the man with the kielbasa as the crowd gasps. From your waist pouch, you can hear the muffled Cobb and Ruth yelling, "What'd you do that for?"

A very large smile is on your face.

"Screw the ball," you say. "Do you have any clue how much I'm gonna make with *you* two?"

Finest Man I Ever Knew

AUGUST 24, 1998—I once asked Jim Murray if he kept a few extra columns in the bank for days when he had the flu or a tee time or an incurably blank computer screen. "Of course not!" he yowled. "What if I die one ahead?"

On Sunday, Jim Murray, the greatest sportswriter who ever lived, kissed his gorgeous wife, started to put on his pajamas, said, "Linda, something's wrong," and collapsed. The doctor was there in five minutes, but it was too late. Jim had died of a heart attack. He was 78.

He got his wish, though. He didn't have any columns saved up. Too bad. We could use a few laughs right now.

Murray on huge Boog Powell: "They're going to make an umbrella stand out of his foot."

On how they ought to begin the Indianapolis 500: "Gentlemen, start your coffins."

On baseball:"Willie Mays's glove is where triples go to die."

On Roger Staubach:"Square as a piece of fudge."

On Elgin Baylor:"Unstoppable as a woman's tears."

Murray could write anything; sports just happened to get lucky. He was TIME's Hollywood correspondent in the 1950s, and the stars loved him. He drank with Bogey, played cards with the Duke, dined with Marilyn. He carried a solid-gold money clip given to him by Jack Benny. Murray could've made millions in the studios. He used to moonlight doctoring dialogue for Jack Webb. *I'll pulverize ya!* the script would say. Murray would change it to, *Say, how'd you like to end up as six feet of lumps?*

He wrote the nation's best sports column for 37 delicious years at the *Los Angeles Times*, but, come to think of it, the column was about sports sort of the way *Citizen Kane* was about sleds.

Murray on an unfinished highway to a stadium in Cincinnati:"It must be Kentucky's turn to use the cement mixer."

On New Jersey:"Its principal export is soot."

On Philadelphia:"A place to park the truck and change your socks."

Murray's Banned-McNally became so famous that Spokane begged to be done."The trouble with Spokane," the compliant Murray wrote, "is that there's nothing to do after 10 o'clock. In the morning."

Murray never went on *The Sports Reporters*, never had his own radio show, never even liked his picture to be in the paper. But he had more impact than any sportswriter since Grantland Rice. The 10-shot cut rule in golf was Murray's idea. It was Murray who shamed the Masters into finally allowing Lee Elder to play, in 1975. ("Wouldn't it be nice to have a black American at Augusta in something other than a coverall?" Murray wrote.)

One time, at a U.S. Open, Arnold Palmer found himself in a ditch. He was trying to figure out what shot to play when he looked up and saw Murray."What would your hero Hogan do in a situation like this?" Palmer asked. Murray looked down and said, "Hogan wouldn't *be* in a situation like that."

It wasn't all laughs, yet through heartache, illness and sorrow, Murray wrote on. His son Ricky died of a drug overdose, and Jim blamed himself in part. The love of his youth—his first wife, Gerry—died of cancer 14 years ago, and I thought Jim would never turn the lights up in his house again, until Linda came along. His eyes had this annoying habit of going out on him. He dictated the column blind for six months and was still better than anybody in the country.

America tried to tell him. He won a Pulitzer. He's in the Baseball Hall of Fame. He was named National Sportswriter of the Year for 12 straight years, 14 in all. There was a little dinner honoring him a few years back. Nothing special. Kirk Douglas showed up. Dinah Shore. Barron Hilton. Some couple came in to hand Murray the Richstone Man of the Year community service award: President and Mrs. Reagan. Yet Murray was so humble that when you left him—even if you were the third-string volleyball writer in Modesto—you couldn't remember which of you was the legend.

Finest man I ever knew.

Lately, I was waiting for Jim to retire and hoping like hell he wouldn't. "Writing a column is like riding a tiger," he used to say. "You'd like to get off, but you have no idea how."

Rotten luck. He finally found a way.

POSTSCRIPT: *Jim Murray was my hero, mentor and friend. I read him as a child, studied him as a young man, and cherished him to the end. But who didn't? Murray carried his money in a gold money clip given to him by Jack Benny. John Wayne used to ask him over for poker. When Humphrey Bogart was dying, he was allowed only one drink. He'd save it until 6, when he could have it with Murray. I know the feeling. I'd give most anything to have one with him now.*

———•———

'Twas the Fight before Christmas

DECEMBER 27, 1999—You can take all your Tiny Tims and your Grinches and your Miracles on Whatever Street and stuff them in your stocking. The best Christmas story is about a boxer.